THE BORDERLINE PERSONALITY
V I S I O N   A N D   H E A L I N G

THE BORDERLINE PERSONALITY
V I S I O N   A N D   H E A L I N G

NATHAN SCHWARTZ-SALANT

CHIRON PUBLICATIONS
Wilmette, Illinois

Portions of this work have been previously published. The author has drawn upon material first published in *Chiron* (1984, 1986, 1988). Some of the material of Chapter One first appeared in "The Dead Self in the Borderline Personality" (*Pathologies of the Modern Self*, David Levin, editor, New York University Press, 1987). The material on projective identification found in Chapter Four was published in part in the *Journal of Analytical Psychology* and in the Proceedings of the Ninth International Conference of Analytical Psychology (M. Matoon, ed.).

Library of Congress Catalog Card Number: 88-25079

Printed in the United States of America.
Edited by Florence Falk and Jeannine Bradley.
Book design by Thomas A. Brown.

Library of Congress Cataloging-in-Publication Data:
Schwartz-Salant, Nathan, 1938-
    The borderline personality : vision and healing / Nathan Schwartz-Salant.
        p. cm.
    Bibliography: p.
    Includes index.
    ISBN 0-933029-30-6 ISBN 0-933029-31-4 (pbk.)
    1. Borderline personality disorder — Patients — Religious life — Case
studies. I. Title.
    RC569.5.B67S39 1988
    616.89 — dc19   88-25079
                                                               CIP

ISBN 978-0-933029-30-9 (Cloth)
ISBN 978-0-933029-31-6 (Paper)

Cover: The use of the "double head" by Jackson Pollock was graciously allowed by Jane Smith. Photograph by Thomas A. Brown.

For
Irvin Swartzberg (1906–1984)
with gratitude

CONTENTS

ACKNOWLEDGMENTS

In the process of developing my view of psychology's "difficult patient" I have found contributions by many people to be invaluable. It is a pleasure to be able to acknowledge some of them for their help, care and knowledge.

The work of C. G. Jung has been a steady source of ideas and inspiration. For all that may be said about the Jungian approach to the psyche, nothing will make sense without an appreciation of the *attitude* that Jung espoused: the psyche is not merely a personal affair. Jung's genius lay in his awareness of archetypal patterning amid seemingly mundane events. To be able to discover the spirit in matter is essential in dealing with the borderline person.

It is a pleasure to acknowledge the influence and work of my friend Michael Eigen. His insights into madness and the self, and his studies of Bion and Winnicott have been very important to me. There are others who have been most helpful. The works of Melanie Klein are indispensable to anyone attempting to comprehend the borderline person. Among those who have helped me to understand the subtleties of Klein's concept of the depressive position I would like to note a special debt to my friend, the late Henry Elkin. To this rather odd man, always an outsider and a maverick, I am grateful for discussions that were compelling and nourishing.

Within the context of understanding early childhood, I wish to acknowledge the works of Michael Fordham and conversations with him at the 1984 Ghost Ranch Conference. Other analysts of the London School of Analytical Psychology have also been a source of reflection and inspiration for my own work. I would like to mention the importance of the work of Rosemary Gordon and Judith Hubback, and especially acknowledge the work and friendship of Andrew Samuels who has always been gracious in the giving of his time and knowledge.

An important and ongoing source of input and reflection for me have been the annual Ghost Ranch Conferences at Abiqui, New Mexico. At these conferences I have presented several papers, all of which have been published in the Chiron Clinical Series, which contains the proceedings of the conferences. These papers were improved through the discussions at these conferences, and I wish to thank the participants for valuable input. All of the papers were enhanced through discussions with Murray Stein, my friend and co-editor of the Chiron Clinical Series. My years of work with him have been an inspiration and have greatly affected this book. I also want to thank Lena Ross for her help with Apuleius's *The Golden Ass*, and especially with the Cupid and Psyche tale.

I have paid particular attention to the editing of this book in order to make my thoughts clear and communicable. To this end I have enlisted the help of two editors. To Florence Falk I am extremely grateful for her interest in my work and for her considerable efforts in getting me to clarify the confusion that existed in my unedited text. The book then went through what I thought would be a copy editing, but proved to be a full, second editing, this time at the hand of Jeannine Bradley. Her editorial skill, insight and knowledge of my work have been extremely important to me.

This book has been five years in the making. My wife Lydia has helped in numerous ways, contributing through feeling and ideas. I am deeply grateful for her loving support.

I am indebted to Jane Smith, who graciously allowed the use of the Jackson Pollock painting for the cover of this book. Pollock's painting captures the split self in all of us, but especially the structural splitting that undermines the borderline person. I also wish to express my gratitude to Doug Ohlson for introducing me to Jane Smith, and for suggesting the use of the "double head" for the cover of this book.

My final acknowledgment is the most important: This book would have been impossible to write without the help of many patients. By "help" I mean not only the use of their material, but far more important, what I have learned from working with them. They have taught me what I know about the borderline patient, and I hope that this book is a testament to my respect for the mystery and depth of their suffering.

Ignorance is certainly never a recommendation, but often the best knowledge is not enough either. Therefore I say to the psychotherapist: let no day pass without humbly remembering that everything has still to be learned.

C. G. Jung, 1946, par. 464

INTRODUCTION

Neurosis is intimately bound up with the problem of our time and really represents an unsuccessful attempt on the part of the individual to solve the general problem in his own person (C. G. Jung, 1942a, par. 18).

The term *borderline* describes a particular psychological syndrome. Adolph Stern's 1938 paper, "Psychoanalytic Investigation of and Therapy in the Borderline Group of Neuroses," is generally recognized as marking the introduction of the term borderline into psychoanalytic literature. In it he described a group of patients with marked resistance to psychoanalytic treatment whom he experienced as highly narcissistic. They suffered, he said, from "psychic bleeding." Moreover, psychic trauma had caused emotional paralysis, for these patients manifested a rigidity in mind and body, were deeply insecure, often masochistic, and suffered from deep-rooted feelings of inferiority. Stern's work set forth the notion of a borderline syndrome that is neither neurotic nor psychotic but instead inclines towards the features of both. As the quest for understanding in a scientific rationale continued, other terms were suggested for these "difficult patients," among them "ambulatory schizophrenia" (G. Zilboorg, 1941), "latent psychosis" (Bychowski, 1953), and "pseudoneurotic schizophrenia" (Hoch and Cattell, 1959).

The psychology literature (especially during the last thirty years) is replete with descriptions of patients whose symptoms and behavior appear to veer from obsessional or hysterical states to psychotic anxieties and defenses but also include variable periods of rational, "normal" behavior as well. Indeed, these patients seem to manifest these states in so fluid a way that the concept of borderline has been endangered by its easy designatory availability for any person not readily classifiable into the established psychiatric categories of neuroses or psychoses. This lax use of terminology led Robert Knight (1953) to criticize the designation borderline as a "wastebasket diagnosis." Even now, the diagnosis of borderline is often the negative determination after other possibilities have been exhausted. Nevertheless, these difficulties do not do away with

1

the fact that such a category exists; patients with a borderline personality disorder do manifest particular symptoms and behavior, the latter related especially to the ways in which the patient strongly affects the psyche of the therapist. By now, the term borderline has become well accepted in psychoanalytic literature.

Most borderline patients live their lives in such a manner as to avoid the intense psychic pain of abandonment, and to this end they employ psychotic mechanisms such as defensive idealization, splitting, denial and obsessive–compulsive behaviors of *doing*, or the opposite, inertia. These psychic mechanisms exist in lieu of a well-functioning self that is the basic organizer of psychic life.

The self is the psyche's central regulating agency, and harmonizes opposites such as order/disorder, fusion/separation, progression/ regression, love/hate, mind/body. Jung writes:

> The unconscious does indeed put forth a bewildering profusion of semblances for that obscure thing we call the . . . 'self.' It almost seems as if we were to go on dreaming in the unconscious the age-old dream of alchemy, and to continue to pile new synonyms on top of the old, only to know as much or as little about it in the end as the ancients themselves. I will not enlarge upon what the *lapis* meant to our forefathers, and what the mandala still means to the Lamaist and Tantrist, Aztec and Pueblo Indian, the 'golden pill' to the Taoist, and the 'golden seed' to the Hindu. We know the texts that give us a vivid idea of all this. But what does it mean when the unconscious stubbornly persists in presenting such abstruse symbolism to a cultured European?
>
> It seems to me, everything that can be grouped together under the general concept [self] expresses the essence of a certain kind of *attitude*. The known attitudes of the conscious mind have definable aims and purposes. But a man's attitude towards the self is the only one that has no definable aims and purposes. It is easy enough to say 'self,' but exactly what have we said? That remains shrouded in "metaphysical" darkness. I may define 'self' as the totality of the conscious and unconscious psyche, but this totally transcends our vision; it is a veritable *lapis invisibilitatis*. In so far as the unconscious exists it is not definable; its existence is a mere postulate and nothing whatever can be predicted as to its possible contents. The totality can only be experienced in its parts and then only in so far as these are contents of consciousness. . . . True, [the self] is a concept that grows steadily clearer with experience—as our dreams show— without, however, losing anything of its transcendence. Since we cannot possibly know the boundaries of something unknown to us, it follows that we are not in a position to set any bounds to the self. . . . The empirical manifestations of unconscious contents bear all the marks of something illimitable, something not determined by time and space. This quality is numinous and therefore alarming, above all to a cautious mind that knows the value of precisely limited concepts.
>
> All that can be ascertained at present about the symbolism [of the self] is that it portrays an autonomous psychic fact, characterized by a phenomenology which is always repeating itself and is everywhere the same. It seems to be a sort

2

of atomic nucleus about which innermost structure and ultimate meaning we
know nothing (1953a, pars. 247-249).

Obviously the self cannot be dead or totally absent, but in the borderline
personality it appears to be. There are ways in which we can discern the
self's deeply unconscious functioning: for example, it manifests through
dreams that depict the borderline patient's plight and also avenues of
healing. But in its immanence, that is, its existence within space–time life
of the ego, the ordering power of the self appears to be overwhelmed by
power drives and compulsive states, the darker aspects of existence.

The immanent self in the borderline person is encapsulated in a
psychotic process. *Hence, it is essential that this person suffer deep-
seated abandonment fears rather than find material or spiritual ways to
avoid them.* For this reason the therapist must look for and confront the
patient's psychotic, reality-distorting fantasies and behavior patterns.

The link between the self as a positive force and the psyche's dark,
destructive qualities poses an important question. For if the self is encapsulated within or possessed by dark aspects of existence, are we to regard
these darker aspects as parts of the self? The answer is that it is important
to do so (Jung, 1953a, par. 25), for the therapist's *attitude toward* the self
is crucial for its potential regeneration in positive form. If we undervalue
the borderline patient's psychotic mechanisms and treat them as something to be suppressed or changed, rather than encountered and actively
explored in the face of a multitude of defenses that deny pain, we will
lose the self and at best gain an ego with an enhanced capacity for
repression. A religious issue is involved: the will of the self, itself apparent through dreams and fantasies, is too weak to incarnate into
space–time functioning. An act of faith on the part of the therapist is
necessary if the person is to embrace his or her madness rather than flee
from it, for the borderline person can imagine only the perils of change,
not the rewards, and experiences surrender as a descent into emptiness or
madness from which there will be no return.

Numerous observable characteristics accrue from the borderline
person's lack of a functioning self, and the psychotic process in which the
self is encapsulated. For example, the clinician L. Grinberg writes:

> Among the salient characteristics of borderline patients, as described in the
> psychoanalytic literature . . . I have personally observed the following: a pre-
> dominance of the 'psychotic part of the personality'; intolerance of frustration;
> preponderance of aggressive impulses; utilization of pathological splitting, nar-
> cissistic identifications, fantasies of omnipotence and omniscience, and idealiza-
> tion as central defense processes; identity disturbances; states of diffuse anxiety;

> defective contact with reality, though without complete loss of touch with it; temporary loss of control over impulses, with a tendency towards acting out; predominance of primitive object relations; depression and extreme, infantile dependence on objects; prevalence of pregenital strivings and liability to develop a transference psychosis, with a possibility of transient psychotic breakdowns (1977, p. 123).

While I, too, have observed these characteristics, I choose to emphasize another factor that is crucial for the incarnation of the self but usually disregarded in the psychoanalytic literature: the borderline person has split off and denied imaginal perceptions — the imagination becomes either unavailable or persecutory. The many clinical illustrations in this work reveal various manifestations of the borderline patient's *sight*, which is split off from his or her normal consciousness; this sight scans the therapist during a therapy session and patients suffer from its absence. Such sight is rooted in the power of the imagination to perceive unconscious processes accurately, and its recovery is an essential element in restoring the self to a functional significance. As well, the therapist's capacity to *see* the patient through an imaginal lens — for example, to perceive the split-off and frightened child scanning the environment from behind the ego's defenses — proves to be a containing vessel for psychotic material that might otherwise lead to an unmanageable delusional transference.

The imaginal process through which accurate perceptions of affective states and attitudes in other people may be discovered is a constituent part of every human being and probably functional at birth. It partakes of both psychic and physical life and draws upon kinesthetic experiences, feelings, and mentation. This mode of perception involves the thrusting forth of one's own images into outer forms (Corbin, 1969, pp. 218ff.) and offers discovery of what one would normally choose not to know. Moreover, clinical evidence indisputably reveals the patient's potential for unconscious perception of the therapist's conscious and unconscious attitudes. It is widely recognized, for example, that a patient's dreams can accurately portray aspects of the therapist's behavior and even aspects of the therapist's unconscious fantasies about the patient.

One patient recalled such perceptions from his early childhood: "I saw my mother as she was standing and thinking, but I also saw another kind of presence within her, a withdrawn person filled with hatred. Once I saw this, I realized how the mother I knew was like a machine acting a part that she was totally disconnected from. I *saw* this, and I was frightened because I knew I wasn't supposed to." The imaginal world of the child is a universe of vision. It is a world of seeing that was highly developed in traditional societies and shamanic practices and is alive in childhood as a result of the child's closeness to the archetypal world. But the child often relinquishes this expanded way of seeing rather than accept the awareness of how he or she is hated for any individuation efforts. At such times, the gift of seeing will mutate into a demonic form of perception that will attack positive aspects of the person and those with whom he or she interacts.

The therapist embarked upon the venture of recapturing the patient's imaginal sight cannot afford to overlook the reality distortions that afflict the borderline person. (To this end, and for a general understanding of the borderline patient, the psychoanalytic literature is invaluable; for example, Frosch, 1964; Giovacchini, 1979; Green, 1975, 1977; Grinberg, 1977; Grotstein, 1979; Kernberg, 1975, 1984; Masterson, 1976, 1981; Meissner, 1984; Rinsley, 1982; Winnicott, 1971.) Unless we deal with the way the world is split for the borderline patient (for example, into delusional "good" and "bad" objects) our attempts at reconnecting the patient with an imaginal reality will only cause a secret inflation and reinforce a delusional approach to reality.

Psychoanalytic literature describes the borderline patient in terms of psychotic and neurotic mechanisms. This way of thinking is useful in that it alerts us to the need to pay attention to the helpless part of the person — no matter how competent obsessional mechanisms make him or her appear — which is enmeshed in psychotic processes. In this work, however, I argue that attempts to understand the phenomenology of the borderline personality solely in terms of psychotic and/or neurotic mechanisms are insufficient to a full apprehension of the disorder. The French psychoanalyst André Green has suggested that the "borderline" category should be accorded an identity of its own (1977, p. 17) and that it may require a model that is not based upon psychosis or neurosis. I firmly agree with this point of view.

Borderline conditions exist within a spatial or interactional field whose unique qualities can easily be overlooked. This field bears similarities to the notion of *liminality*, a term used by the anthropologist Victor Turner (1974) to describe the ritual process. In these processes the neophyte progresses from the normal space–time world across a threshold (*limen*) into a realm of experience normally repressed and inaccessible to everyday consciousness. He or she then returns to temporality (and normalcy) with the experiences gained through access to this *a*temporal realm. Liminal experiences are those that host extremely powerful archetypal forces. And liminal rites revolve around prime symbols and symbolic actions "that are intended to arouse a gross quantum of affect — even of illicit affect — only to attach this quantum of affect divested of moral qualities in a later phase of a great ritual to licit and legitimate goals and values" (Turner, 1974, p. 257).

We might describe the borderline person who is suspended in a liminal transition, a condition Turner describes as *liminoid*, with the result that a "gross quantum of affect" is released but without its having a renewing quality — it does not lead to the creation of "legitimate goals and values." The renewing qualities of the liminal ritual derive from the fact that they have an archetypal source. But in borderline conditions, archetypal qualities of renewal combine with personally acquired psychic structures in a most confusing way. This fusion occurs because the patient's ego oscillates between different parts of his or her psychic material: 1) split-off complexes of extremely negative affect; 2) introjects of unconscious parental qualities; and 3) feeling states of absence related to failures in passage from one developmental stage to the next. This oscillation creates a situation in which feelings of omnipotence alternate with intense feelings of inferiority. The goal of therapy with borderline patients is not to repress these psychic states but to find an approach that will partake of the renewing potential of the archetypes underlying the general condition.

The character of the interactional field that we meet in treatment of the borderline person must be stressed if the therapist is to achieve the goal of embracing the renewing potential within borderline conditions. This endeavor will take us into the territory of alchemical thought resurrected by the remarkable research of C. G. Jung, and specifically into the "Psychology of the Transference" (1946), published as part of the studies that culminated in his magnum opus, *Mysterium Coniunctionis* (1955). The symbolic basis of alchemy provides us with a means by which we can begin to understand the meaning and purpose of borderline experiences. Jung's approach to alchemical symbolism can be focused upon the interactional field. This fertile area, invisible except to the eye of the imagination, is constellated in the transference–countertransference process, and envisioning it is an essential part of my approach.

A crucial issue is the *locus* of these elusive energy fields; the inability to locate them within our normal space–time perception leads to the recovery of the ancient concept of the *subtle body*. This concept is a mainstay of alchemical thinking and refers to experiences that can be called neither physical nor mental but partake of both realms. Moreover, the subtle body concept is inseparably linked to the alchemical notion of the imagination (in Latin, *imaginatio*), which was viewed as having both a psychic and material nature. We experience the effectiveness of the imagination through projective identification, that process whereby the unconscious parts of one person are felt to be entering into and affecting another person. The subtle body is a realm through which projections pass and transform; while its processes can be perceived by the imagination, they are not usually available for discovery by the rational mode.

The subtle-body concept has important correspondences to Winnicott's idea of transitional or potential space, but is more comprehensive in that it designates a field occupied with its own processes—one that is imaginally available when the transference–countertransference process is fully engaged. In a sense this process discloses the existence of a complex that has been governing the unconscious of both therapist and patient. The discovery of unconscious, interactional factors is the focus of my approach to transforming the structures and energies encountered within borderline states of mind.

Because these psychic energies can be so disturbing, it is not surprising that many therapists working with borderline patients sometimes choose to retreat into a conceptual framework that promises the safety of their being able to gain control over their affects. The therapist attempts to buttress himself or herself against intense affects of hate, rage, hunger and envy, rather than voluntarily suffer them. Furthermore, he or she will often flee from the experience of chaos and from the pain of an absence of emotional contact with the patient. A clinician's diagnosis of a patient as "borderline" is often a kind of word magic, an apotropaic device to depotentiate and subdue this "difficult patient."

Over the last three decades especially, the vast proliferation of literature on the borderline patient offers various models of internal structure and causal factors that explain this personality disorder. Although approaches to the borderline patient vary widely (Meissner, 1984), there has been a tendency among therapists to adhere to a "scientific attitude" that attempts to create order out of the phenomenology we call borderline. This "scientific attitude" provides a rational-discursive approach that conceives the borderline personality to be the sum of neurotic and psychotic mechanisms that accrue from an arrested individ-

7

uation process in early childhood. For example, many clinicians favor Margaret Mahler's concept of individuation in infancy and regard the borderline condition as the result of a failure to transit the Separation-Rapprochement Subphase of Individuation, which occurs at approximately 15–22 months of age (Mahler, 1980). Kleinian-oriented therapists view the borderline condition as emanating from a failure to enter and evolve through the depressive position; they believe the person suffering from this condition consequently remains subject to the persecutory affects of the paranoid-schizoid position (Segal, 1980). Otto Kernberg (1975, 1984) combines Kleinian and developmental approaches and has also integrated Edith Jacobsen's (1964) approach to ego psychology. William Meissner, alert to the limitations of any single existing model of the borderline personality, combines Mahlerian concepts with other considerations, such as familial patterns, genetic factors, and bonding wounds that occur prior to the second and third years of life (Meissner, 1984). A thorough familiarity with the effects of early bonding deficits to which these clinicians have called attention is crucial to an understanding of the borderline condition; indeed, one must seriously consider events transpiring in the first months of life. Although the approaches mentioned above should be valued and employed, they are limited in scope. Another, complementary approach is essential—the phenomenology so well articulated in the rational-discursive mode must be placed within an archetypal understanding that embraces the symbolic meaning of the term "borderline" itself.

"The symbol," says Jung, "expresses the best formulation of a relatively unknown thing" (1920, par. 815):

> Whether a thing is a symbol or not depends chiefly on the *attitude* of the observing consciousness; for instance, on whether it regards a given fact not merely as such but also as an expression for something unknown. Hence, it is quite possible for a man to establish a fact which does not appear in the least symbolic to himself, but is profoundly so to another consciousness. The converse is also true (1920, par. 818).

When therapists speak of the borderline condition, the term is often implicitly employed as a symbol for certain irrational states of being that cannot be fully appreciated in terms of what is consciously known. Rational understanding of the powerful transferential experiences clinicians often have with borderline patients does not sufficiently encompass the true nature of these experiences. Transference and countertransference dynamics cannot be apprehended without a clear understanding of how the subtle body may be experienced in the interactive field. The therapist must be able to recognize subtle states of mind. These states cannot be differentiated into mental or physical states of being, but quite palpably combine both; these subtle-body experiences are at the core of the borderline process. Within the interactive fields constellated in psychotherapy, different qualities of the subtle body can be specified. These qualities, which especially illuminate the borderline condition, are clarified by Jung's works on alchemical symbolism.

The symbolic aspect of the term "borderline" derives from the fact that treatment of the borderline personality involves states of mind that move within and around a border between personal and archetypal, so that aspects of each are interwoven in an often bewildering way. Thus, treatment situations oblige the therapist to deal with irrational elements that exist not only in the patient but also in himself or herself. These states of mind may seem explicable in terms of the patient's or therapist's complexes, but the fact remains that the interactive field can induce states of fusion, or of soulless distance, that preclude empathic understanding. Alternatively, states of union that transcend fusion/separation polarities may be encountered. None of these psychic states can necessarily be reduced to the therapist's or patient's personal issues.

This movement between personal and archetypal levels is critical: the borderline condition may be partially understood in terms of constructs from developmental theories and concepts of internal structure from object relations approaches. The truth, however, is that the experience of the states undergone through participation in the interactive field can never be fully contained by the therapist's use of such approaches. Instead, the therapist has entered a realm that is best apprehended by a symbolic attitude. The borderline person's psyche induces entry into domains not easily recognized and usually shunned, a sphere of chaos without which there is no renewal for any human being.

The "border" has existed in the myths of many cultures. It is the area in the psyche where the ego's orientation begins to fail and where powerful forces, over which one may have little control, constellate. Ancient maps sometimes portray the known world surrounded by chaotic regions of mists and sea serpents. These symbolic images are simultaneously expressions of fear and awe of humankind confronting the unknown and attempts to circumscribe and define the known. In ancient Egypt, Ethiopia was regarded as border territory, a domain inhabited by people who were in control of dangerous forces and who were adept at black magic. The Egyptians were conscious of the importance of the demonic qualities that raged at the "borders" and created fear and confusion. In fact, they initiated processes at the "border" for the renewal of Osiris, even though these "borderline" processes were the very ones that destroyed this principle of life and order. As in liminal ritual where the most disordering and dangerous forces are encountered for the purpose of renewal, the Egyptians attempted to incorporate such forces into the fabric of their mythology, thus avowing that the demonic was not to be separated from everyday life.

In Egyptian mythology, the central quaternity of gods comprises the positive Mother Goddess Isis, her consort the benevolent king Osiris, her sister Nephthys (who was associated with the Ethiopian queen Aso), and her consort, the devil and antagonist of Osiris, Set. Egyptian mythology can easily appear as a model of borderline states; its paranoid-like Eye roams the universe; the positive Great Mother Isis becomes the partner of the arch-demon Set in battle against her own son Horus; the battles between Horus and Set provoke Set to tear out Horus's eye and Horus to claim Set's testicles. We can say that this battle symbolically mirrors what often occurs in treatment situations with the borderline patient when, through an interactive field dominated by projective identification, the capacity of the therapist for imaginal sight and empathy diminishes; the result is an attack on the patient, a castration of him or her for "being so negative."

Egypt's most sublime creation, Osiris, is a dead god; that is, he is not a god of the dead. He lies helpless and inert in the Underworld, awaiting redemption (Rundle Clark, 1959). Osiris seems protected in his masochistic retreat; he lies motionless in the coils of a serpent who attacks him when he dares arise. This image reflects the experience of the borderline patient, whose very being is attacked for any individuation efforts. The intense energies of ancient Egypt's ritual of redemption for Osiris, a nine-day-long passion, mirror the enormous energy expended by the therapist in treating the borderline patient.

But the Egyptians did not create one of the most durable and remarkable civilizations ever known because they were a nation of borderline personalities. Instead, they had the genius to incorporate such border states of mind into their cultural awareness. They were able to recognize the paradoxically renewing nature of what appear to be the most destructive states of mind. In the treatment of the borderline personality we gain most of our therapeutic leverage from countertransference reactions—reactions that thrust one over the border into previously unactivated chaotic regions. But the prerequisite of treatment is to be able to see these conditions within a larger context, not as symptoms of failed individuation efforts, but rather as fragments of psychic and mythical structure whose fullness has not been realized.[1]

Jung said that the neurotic personality suffers the general problem of the prevailing time (1942a, par. 18). It is possible that the union of two people and the processes that attend union—in alchemical language the *coniunctio*—may be reflections of a new archetypal form that is emerging in the collective unconscious. Borderline patients are people who suffer from an anguishing inability to incarnate this principle of union. The borderline person's suffering can be understood in terms of archetypal processes that have been fragmented; the patient will experience the dark, disordering aspects of the *coniunctio* to the exclusion of its ordering and life-giving qualities.

In the Egyptian Sed festival the powers of order and disorder, represented by Set and Horus, did battle, after which followed the *hieros gamos*, the sacred marriage celebrated by the pharaoh and his queen, which symbolized the marriage of Isis and Osiris. Similarly, a new kind of order is latent beneath seemingly destructive borderline states of mind; this order arises from chaos and takes the form of the *coniunctio*. The *coniunctio* can be experienced within the imaginal realm of the subtle body. While the dark, disordering aspects that attend the *coniunctio* dominate the borderline condition and its treatment, a therapeutic awareness that a larger archetypal pattern is involved is crucial in the treatment of the borderline patient. Disordering affects of anxiety, rage or panic and associated states of mindlessness may be quelled by the therapist's taking a heroic stance. This stance is at times necessary, but the heroic mode precludes discovery of the purpose and meaning of the borderline patient's suffering. An approach to understanding borderline conditions that values body, imagination and states of union as having value equal to or greater than rational-discursive approaches, can transmute this suffering into a meaningful pattern.

In using the term "borderline" throughout this work, I gratefully

---

[1]One need not know Egyptian mythology to understand borderline states of mind, though I have made preferential use of it, as was also true of Jung. Certainly, other mythologies, as well as abundant literary sources, can be marshalled to reveal the borderline personality in an archetypal context. Earlier, I noted the importance of alchemical symbolism. The significance of the border in Shakespeare's *Othello* might also be mentioned, and in Apuleius's novel *The Golden Ass*, Lucius, the central figure, bears many features of a borderline personality (see Chapter Seven).

accept previous psychoanalytic contributions and draw from their models. But the symbolic understanding of the term borderline is also indispensable; this approach extends into regions that can never be fully grasped by rational means. Consequently, in this work, the borderline concept should be understood as a hybrid of symbolic and rational-discursive approaches.

Archetypal contents are characterized by a quality that Jung, following Rudolph Otto, called numinous. The *numinosum*, in both its positive and negative forms, poses exceptional difficulties for the borderline patient. It is the root of all religious experience. It is characterized by both sublime and demonic qualities and refers to a dynamic that is beyond conscious control of the will. The *numinosum* seizes one, and though we might rely on all sorts of rational devices to weaken its effect upon us, the fact remains that it is situated at the core of humankind's most central experiences. The function of religious systems, as G. Scholem (1946) has explained, is to separate humankind from the *numinosum*, whose energies are often considered too dangerous to endure. The psychoanalytic concept of primary process fails to recognize the true nature of the *numinosum*, which frequently manifests through emotional flooding and archaic imagery. Nor does the concept of primary process recognize the transforming power of the *numinosum*. Jung, however, said that his entire approach toward healing was based upon the *numinosum* (Letter, 8 August, 1945). By this he meant that the energies and structures of the archetypes have a powerful renewing potential and that to imaginatively engage these "gods" and "goddesses" opens up healing paths that would otherwise rarely become traveled. The role of the *numinosum* in both positive and negative forms is discussed throughout this work. The borderline person is beset by fear of the *numinosum* and is exceedingly vulnerable to its overwhelming power.

When Freud referred to "the Oceanic experience" he was using that term to reflect upon very early mother–infant fusion states (Eigen, 1987, p. 8, n. 10). The borderline person suffers from an absence of the nurture and support of this "Ocean." But he or she has often known a mystical realm, wherein the Ocean is not the personal mother but the *numinosum*. In the borderline person especially, the *numinosum* combines with the mundane. Treatment of the borderline person often thrusts the therapist into a region that lies "betwixt and between" ordinary consciousness and that unique, mysterious realm hitherto allocated to mysticism.

The affects of the borderline patient that are communicated in treatment are difficult to describe because they are not exclusively personal, and hence do not inspire the ready empathy that would normally accrue from the therapist's own early experiences. For the borderline patient is enmeshed in psychic levels of extreme intensity that bear intimate relation to many of the great archetypal themes in history—battles between god and the devil and life and death; the soul's rebirth; and especially the great drama of union that finds expression in the archetype of the *coniunctio*.

Chapter One discusses experiences commonly found in treating the borderline patient. Chapter Two differentiates the borderline patient from the narcissistic character, and Chapter Three considers the borderline patient's reality distortions. Chapter Four addresses the central significance of projective identification in treatment, and Chapter Five extends this issue into subtle body dynamics. Furthermore, these latter two chapters develop the idea that an unconscious dyad structures the interactive field between therapist and patient. Chapter Six explores the borderline patient's splitting into normal/neurotic and psychotic parts. This duality is reflected in terms of the *numinosum* and is further related to the peculiar logic of the borderline patient so deftly formulated by André Green. Chapter Seven employs the tale of *The Golden Ass* of Apuleius as a medium for further reflections—the healing of borderline conditions through an imaginal awareness and body consciousness, which can lead to the *coniunctio*.

CHAPTER ONE
EXPERIENCING THE BORDERLINE PERSONALITY

[There are] . . . experiences [that] come upon man from inside as well as from outside, and it is useless to try to interpret them rationalistically and thus weaken them by apotropaic means. It is far better to admit the affect and submit to its violence than try to escape it by all sorts of intellectual tricks or by emotional value judgments (C. G. Jung, 1952, par. 562).

Introduction

The term *borderline* has become a buzzword in clinical practice. In consultations with each other therapists acknowledge how "difficult they are" — that is, borderline patients — and are inclined to commiserate with one another. Describing a patient as "borderline" can be a device to absolve the therapist of any serious errors. Nevertheless, the borderline personality disorder exists and does in fact create exceptional problems in psychotherapy, not the least of which are intense negative reactions in the therapist.

At especially difficult times during treatment the therapist may dread the arrival of a borderline patient and experience anticipatory anxieties or become somewhat phobic toward the patient. It is not uncommon to wonder "How bad will it be this time?" or, "What will he say about my foul-up last time?" Most upsetting is the expectation of being attacked, not by the patient's words but by an underlying, hateful energy that seems prompted by nothing less than the wish for the therapist's complete dissolution.

In a strange way, the patient carries truth for the therapist. But it is a truth that lives in a destructive form. There is an Egyptian myth about the Eye Goddess — a symbol of the Great Mother archetype in the initial stages of creation — who roamed the world and destroyed everything it saw. We can say that the Eye represents imaginal sight in its destructive form and is analogous to the borderline patient's "truth." This sight is split off and unconscious in the borderline patient. It is primarily encountered in therapy as an unstated demand, an emanation that puts the therapist on guard; it induces guilt, uncomfortable bodily tensions and breathing constrictions, and furthers mind–body splitting. The sense of being scanned by the patient's unconscious sight is a common experience.

Under the pressure of the borderline patient's split-off sight, conversations often have pauses that are filled with a meaning that is known only to the patient; the patient appears to be waiting, as if certain inner processes are being held in abeyance until some revelation has occurred for the therapist. Such moments are perplexing because the weight of the pauses does not seem to correspond to the banality of the spoken phrase. Thus, whole conversations acquire a kind of syncopated rhythm in which the therapist feels foolish about missing some crucial subtext to a fairly casual conversation. Actually, a part of the patient is watching the therapist in desperate hope of being seen but with readiness to unleash an attack of rage if he or she is ignored.

Throughout the treatment of the borderline patient, the therapist is watched and judged by the patient's unconscious eye. This eye vigilantly measures the therapist's commitment in the battle between the baser demands of human nature and the higher demands of the soul. Thus, the therapist must constantly ask if sight of the soul is being retained during the struggle through the emotional roadblocks that have been erected. Indeed, when deluged by the trivia of daily living that become concretized into problems to be solved, one must especially bear in mind the patient's soul. For these "trivia" are the medium through which this soul must be discovered and met in a genuine "I-Thou" connection. Any tacit agreement that a connection exists between therapist and patient — when the therapist is essentially using words to repress an uncomfortable tension in the interaction — can be catastrophic for treatment. In this drama, unconscious sight plays the fierce role of protector of a severely wounded soul that has been nearly defeated by a lifelong trauma of hatred and lies. Yet this soul possesses the central most important meaning and treasure in the person's life.

With some borderline patients, unconscious sight is almost palpable as a separate presence that intrudes upon the patient–therapist interaction and produces an apprehension that tends to induce both persons to split off from the experience of their encounter. Even though it is so frequently denied, this sight, when engaged, will alert the subject to a life-and-death battle between truth and falsehood — a battle generally focused upon the authenticity of the patient–therapist connection. With other borderline patients, unconscious sight seems to be completely absent. In the course of treatment, however, the therapist's initial perception proves to be inaccurate. Instead, this organ of unconscious perception begins to emerge from a passive, inert state. These latter patients tend to be compliant and often manifest masochistic and hysterical character traits. But in all cases, as the arduous process of helping these patients connect to intense negative affects proceeds, a concurrent awareness of their unconscious scanning processes emerges.

In therapeutic work with any borderline patient, one major task is to discover, contain, and transform this imaginal sight, which often means seeing this sight and experiencing its wrath without withdrawing and without attacking it for the pain its truth conveys. Whether through a persecutory energy field or a benign one, the patient will communicate the imaginal perception of the unconscious, for as Jung says, "The unconscious mind of man *sees* correctly even when conscious reason is blind and impotent" (Jung 1952, par. 608).

The borderline patient has suppressed the ability to see emotional truth far more than most people, for in the early, formative years, this kind of sight was perceived by him or her to be extremely dangerous. Commonly, the patient unconsciously colluded with a parent in order not to see that parent's hatred and psychotic qualities. The tacit "agreement" to act as if everything were normal created an inner "fifth column," a dark shadow of hatred and rage fused with a requirement to be blind to both one's own destructive qualities and those of others. Hence, the therapist's failure to engage the kind of imaginal vision that sees what others would prefer to remain unseen (often including the therapist's own errors), becomes a reenactment of the patient's history of betraying his or her own sight.

From a psychological point of view, object-constancy is gained as a result of the act of recovering imaginal sight. In Egyptian myth, Horus overcomes the Eye's searing and destructive affects. The transformed Eye becomes a protector of the Sun, a symbol of rational consciousness, and assures its continued existence through its nightly descent toward the Apopis demon of chaos. But this potentially transformative process is often mishandled in therapeutic work, since the story that often unfolds is the sad one of the therapist's flight through ingenious deceptions from the patient's conscious or unconscious wrath, or of the attempt to kill the patient's sight through repression, splitting, and denial of his or her own errors.

The therapist may think: "If only he doesn't show up today . . . But then he will surely have some insight that shows how my way of approaching cancellations is wrong! I'll charge him for the hour . . . I have to. . . . Well, maybe not, perhaps I'll just do nothing and trust him to pay. No, I hope he will come. I'll just remain calm, centered, prepared to deal with whatever he brings." While it is somewhat caricatured, I think this soliloquy is familiar to many therapists treating borderline patients. The therapist has now become borderline! The patient is hated and treated without any sense of concern. The therapist becomes tricky about wanting to be paid. The patient is also defensively idealized as the therapist's hatred toward him or her is further split off through the ruse of deciding to be "open, calm, and centered." Throughout, the therapist's self-hatred builds as a reaction to feeling so impotent and cowardly.

Such feelings experienced by the therapist give a hint of what the borderline person feels: a deep self-hatred and contempt for the impotence experienced when trying to exert some positive effect upon his or her life. The borderline patient will dispense energy in "cowardly" fashion in order to avoid the inner feelings of hating and being hated. This flight only furthers self-disgust and despair. But that is not all, for the therapist's own reaction of withdrawal, even flight from the patient's affects, also confirms the patient's belief that there is no one truly present. The therapist's tendency to withdraw alerts the patient to the anticipated abandonment.

Actually, the borderline patient is often abandoned, at least in fantasy, and he or she is often excruciatingly aware of this fact. The borderline patient expects the void, expects that the so-called "good object" will not exist. In fact, both patient and therapist need to experience this condition of *absence* if any shred of the patient's authenticity is to emerge. This genuine bit of *being* is often found to be enmeshed in the bitter mood that becomes habitual when someone has been locked up for a very long time. But to the despairing patient it seems that the only hope is to be "good," to comply by acting as if he or she and the therapist were genuinely relating. The therapist will tend to assume a posture of "being open and ready" for the patient. This charade will tend to continue, for the patient often will be "good," and the therapist will appreciate it, all the while hoping that a "pleasant, agreeable mood" will be retained throughout the session. The therapist will often conspire to this end by sidestepping the patient's discreet references to "bad feelings."

The affects so apt to unbalance the therapist naturally create havoc in the borderline patient's inner world. As a result, the patient is terribly vulnerable to what may seem to be the therapist's slight errors in empathy. A typical scenario: the patient arrives with thoughts of hatred and revenge. As the session proceeds, the therapist may become somewhat bored and withdrawn and feel like an outsider rather than an empathic Other. If the therapist were to reflect, rather than act out this withdrawal, a sense of falseness might become palpable, perhaps a feeling that what the patient is saying should not be taken seriously. Upon further reflection, the possibility might come to mind that the patient's anger is actually aimed at the therapist. But the affects from which the borderline person suffers and constellates in those around him or her can be so intense that the therapist quickly fails to be reflective and to use the imagination that alone could process the interaction at hand. However, such a failure often secretly attests to the therapist's unconscious hostility to the patient.

As a patient described an argument with a friend, his self-righteousness and envy became oppressive. I temporarily lost my reflective stance and asked him about *his* role in the argument. In the next session he said: "All I needed was a little feeling from you, just caring for me for once in my life." With this remark, an energy field manifested that was shocking in its capacity to induce guilt. This energy destroyed my capacity to reflect and my ability to use my imagination. I felt as though nothing less than my total humiliation and defeat were desired. This interplay became manifest in the following sessions when the patient behaved as if I had never existed: continuity and history were annihilated and we felt each other to be strangers. All our previous work seemed to have been dissolved. It took several weeks for us to recover any sense of connection, and during this interval it was especially difficult for me to remember that this patient was being persecuted and attacked by the very affects he had induced me to feel.

The following example from a thirty-year-old woman who came to me for referral purposes illustrates the vicissitudes of imaginal sight occurring in work with the borderline patient. After sitting down she began speaking:

> I hate myself. I am overweight, I don't finish anything. I have a lot of talent but don't use it. At least that's what people tell me. I'm like putty, I have no identity.

19

Tell me something and I'll believe it, change it and I'll believe that. Why am I unable to be normal? I'm getting old. That scares me. I think of suicide, but I know that's only a cop-out. I really won't do it, at least for now. My father was depressed, unavailable to me. I'm sure that's a problem for me. My mother could never cope, she was always very anxious. That didn't help either. I'm always anxious. I've always been, and I've always tried to deal with it myself. I never bother anyone. I cope. I hide it. I had cancer five years ago. They tell me I'm okay now. I'm not working. My mother is supporting me. She doesn't know I'm not working, that would only make her more anxious and harder for me to get a job. Lately I've been trying macrobiotics. I've tried all kinds of nutritional approaches. Nothing seems to help much. I don't even know if I want to be a singer. They all say I've got talent. I know I'm a mess. I know I'm all over the map. I'm sorry if I'm swamping you. But this is how I am. One thing that really bothers me, though, is that I can't stop stealing. If I were caught I know I'd kill myself. But I can't stop myself. Everyone tries to help me, all of my friends are worried. I just have no identity. I have no sense of myself at all.

As she spoke I could find no way to reach her. I looked at her and she made marginal eye contact. I was slowly becoming swamped and it felt as if the air was getting damper; my grounding became more and more amorphous. Then I recalled a humorous sign I once saw: *It's hard to remember to drain the swamp when you're up to your ass in alligators.* I wanted to say something, but the only thoughts that came to mind were platitudes like, "I think there may be a way through this." Or, "perhaps your dreams will help." Fortunately I restrained myself. At a later moment when I felt under less internal pressure, I asked the woman if she had dreamed lately. She answered that she'd had dreams but had forgotten their content.

I was sitting with someone who was drowning and absolutely helpless to pull herself out. Yet I had no way of helping her. Nothing useful came to me, and I felt despairing. Then somehow I remembered to look at her and attempted to imaginally see her. In this state, having enjoined myself not to know but just to be and see, I also settled more into my body. A sense of *being in it* gradually developed. I felt free of omnipotent drives to interpret — in fact, only then did I become aware of how present these had been. I began to experience my imagination at play. It was like having dream images while in a waking state. I *saw* (and I use this term as an act of the imagination) as if I were in a dream world governed by dream images. Someone was talking to me from behind a dense barrier, and I *saw* her as being extremely furtive, and indeed, filled with panic.

With my eyes I had seen an extremely intelligent person describing her helpless situation. But by seeing through my eyes something else flared up, a vision of pathetic flight and terror. I *believed* I *saw* this figure glance at me and, with only the barest attempt, *see* me. But I focused on this probability and asked if she had a sense of being able to see into people. "Oh sure," she answered, "all the time." And in a very guarded way she told me that she was psychic. I asked her if she used this power for herself, that is, if she could believe what she saw and trust that what she perceived in this way had some truth to it. Her response was:

> I only use it for other people. But I don't trust it for myself. Sometimes I get overtaken by it. I thought of a number the other day, 114, and I knew it had a special meaning. Then I saw it was the number of a restaurant. I went inside and saw a man with a girl. I became obsessed with finding out who he was. You'd be amazed at how I tracked him down. Finally I found him. We had a brief affair, but as usual with men, he tried to attack me physically. All the men I meet are like that. I can get overtaken by a psychic sense and become totally possessed by it. That's why I avoid it for myself. But for others it works remarkably well.

During this recital she became more present and we had a brief moment of emotional contact—fleeting, but unmistakable. Otherwise, she remained completely inaccessible to me; there was no sense of contact and certainly no emotional meeting. The only time a sense of self was present was when I saw her and she saw me. Otherwise, she was cut off from her connection to her sight and, instead, completely involved in the struggle not to be overtaken by her unconscious. I had the sense, however, that her sight, which functioned so bizarrely, could potentially turn positive. My own listless, drowning sense of self was enlivened by the return of my sight, and I knew that the only way for me to connect to her was to experience my own helplessness; that is, to detach from an omnipotent stance, to risk not knowing and to become embodied.

Borderline Affects and Jung's "Answer to Job"

The archetypal energy storms that so afflict borderline individuals and through them, others, have traditionally been represented by myth and religion as the negative side of God. It is not far afield to interpret these harrowing experiences as being influenced by the gods, for their scale is monumental, always far larger than the ego. In Egyptian myth the devil Set, who is the enemy of the forces of order, represents overwhelming affects, including terrifying abandonment depression and dismemberment. Much Egyptian ritual revolves around the creation of a stable counterposition in imagery of principles of order, such as those represented by Horus, Osiris, or Isis. Negative manifestations of the Great

Mother are legion in the history of every race, prime examples being the fearsome witch who brings on terrors of death and abandonment, and her other aspect, the alluring, seductive witch who fosters splitting and delusional creations of reality.[1] In our Western contemporary culture the most evident dark manifestation of the unconscious is found in the Biblical account of the negative attributes of the Old Testament Yahweh. Jung analyzed this aspect of our Western Judaeo-Christian God in numerous writings,[2] but most decisively in his *Answer to Job*. This work is a mine of information about the overwhelming affects suffered by the borderline patient and contains a thorough examination of emotional flooding and persecutory anxiety. Jung's reflections upon the psychological significance of Yahweh, His affects and behavior, are a veritable description of what is known today as the borderline personality.

The *Book of Job* shows the patriarchal god-image in its most negative form. The phenomenon of Yahweh in this late Old Testament entry was particularly gripping for Jung, and his *Answer to Job* was the only work that he found truly satisfying as an outpouring of his soul's wisdom. "If there is anything like the spirit seizing one by the scruff of the neck, it is the way this book came into being" (Jung 1975, p. 20). While there is little explicitly about clinical practice in this study, *Answer to Job* has a good deal to say about psychotherapy with the borderline patient who lives in a psyche that can, at any time, be devastated by what feels like a natural catastrophe. These "Yahweh-like" affects can be far beyond conscious control. Healing can only begin when this terrifying phenomenon is somehow tamed:

> The Book of Job serves as a paradigm for a certain experience of God which has a special significance for us today. These experiences come upon man from inside as well as from outside, and it is useless to interpret them rationalistically and thus weaken them by apotropaic means. It is far better to admit the affect and submit to its violence than try to escape it by all sorts of intellectual tricks or by emotional value-judgments. Although, by giving way to the affect, one imitates all the bad qualities of the outrageous act that provoked it and thus makes oneself guilty of the same fault, that is precisely the point of the whole proceeding: the violence is meant to penetrate to a man's vitals, and he to succumb to its action. He must be affected by it, otherwise its full effect will not reach him. But

---

[1] In object-relational approaches to the borderline personality these aspects of the Negative Mother Archetype are cast in terms of split, internal structures. A good example is found in the Masterson-Rinsley model (Masterson, 1976), which includes a Withholding Object Relations Unit (WORU) and a Rewarding Object Relations Unit (RORU), analogous, respectively, to the attacking and seductive qualities of the witch.

[2] See Chapter Six for a further discussion of Yahweh and borderline affects.

he should know, or learn to know, what has affected him, for in this way he transforms the blindness of the violence on the one hand and of the affect on the other into knowledge (1952, par. 562).

These affects are part of the numinous, archetypal contents that afflict the borderline patient. Jung appears to counsel a kind of acting out of the transference, "giving way to the affect and [imitating] all the bad qualities of the outrageous act that provoked it . . . thus mak[ing] oneself guilty of the same fault." Jung insists that only in this way, by being affected by the affects, can one come to know and transform them. Could there be a fuller prescription than the above for "wild analysis" in which technique and a sense of process are abandoned in favor of focusing upon whatever strong affects and intuitions emerge within the therapeutic encounter?

If only things were so simple, so easily dismissed! The borderline person is ravished by Yahweh-like affects *but also fails to learn from the experience*. These affects devastate the person's soul and force it to live on the brink of the nothingness and within a constant fog of despair. Concurrently, this person is capable of the most blatant forms of denial and splitting from inner affective states so that they are not sufficiently experienced. The borderline patient is thus sometimes called the "as-if" patient. And the therapist is often left in the position of experiencing and reflecting upon Yahweh-like affects *for* the patient. One may not want to act them out, but to a degree this will always happen. Even if one carefully contains these devastating affect-fields, the patient will at least *unconsciously see* that they exist as part of the therapist's inner attitude. Failing to consciously register this, the patient will split from the experience of being attacked by intense negative feelings. In this the patient colludes with the therapist, for no one wants to experience these levels, whether they stem from induction or from one's own borderline sectors.

If the patient is helped to recover and consciously engage a once unconscious sight, what is often seen is that the therapist has acted badly by identifying with an inner, persecutory violence. One often succumbs to acting out or splitting from these affects, but does one also learn from the experience? That is the crucial issue Jung raises. What is often surprising about the borderline patient is that no matter how ruthless the person may be, he or she can often value an imaginal awareness. A borderline person can be relentless in focusing upon the therapist's errors in empathy or attitude, which may surface, for example, through inappropriate interventions and emotions. Such tenacity may be dismissed by the therapist as an illustration of persistent ruthlessness rather than recognized as an unconscious strategy for attaining profound attunement. It requires great courage to dare to be so persistent with a therapist who is defensive and usually misses the point.

To recognize the value of Jung's study for clinical practice one can imagine the Job-Yahweh encounter as a dyad that structures the unconscious aspect of the transference. When the dyad constellates, the therapist and the patient tend to unconsciously enact the roles of Job and Yahweh. Often these roles alternate with uncomfortable rapidity.

Yahweh-like affects can be withering as they sweep through the patient. They also affect the therapist through projective identification, known in Jung's works as preeminently as "participation mystique," "induction," etc. Jung's phraseology emphasizes that these affects exist in contact with a Oneness of existence. Through projective identification they are capable of spanning space–time laws and structures to affect one psyche or another. These affects, which ravish the soul, pose a severe moral problem. Are they evil, or is this only a value judgment of the object that experiences their power?

What can our moral stance be in all of this? And is a moral stance sufficient? We must first recognize the nature of the attack experienced. It is a mixture of Yahweh-like affects and of a kind of vision that allows the patient to see the therapist in ways that can be very painful. One is always somewhat liable to the penetration of the patient's *imaginal sight*, for however destructive the affect fields, they always contain some truth regarding moral deficiency. This deficiency can appear either in the form of a Job-like righteousness when the therapist is afflicted by what seem to be the patient's Yahweh-like affects ("Who, me? What have I done wrong?") or in the form of an unconscious identification with the tyrannical Yahweh aspect of the unconscious dyad that conceals a covert disregard for the patient. The borderline person can see this happening through a kind of vengeful Eye.

This kind of vision illuminates not only gross injustices but also details that have a significance to the patient alone. For example, the patient fixes upon unconscious mood shifts in the therapist that might be expressed by an inept turn of phrase or a careless action. A nonborderline patient can easily allow such events to pass, with the result that the therapist will then return to being related. But the borderline patient feels these moments with the therapist to be extremely dangerous. If the patient splits from this vision, he or she becomes inwardly persecuted by what has been seen, albeit seen in a severely dramatized and often distorted manner. In this way, the patient attacks with this vision, and is oblivious to the harsh effects that accompany this sight.

The therapist's soul is vulnerable and cannot withstand with equanimity the annihilating energy that accompanies the borderline patient's imaginal *penetration*. We may submit masochistically, just to get the patient to stop attacking us, or we may resort to narcissistic power-defenses through which we can match the patient's knowledge with our own. But almost invariably the patient sees through this meager defense. We may, however, find concern for ourselves and stop the battle with a thought like: "No matter how bad I am, no matter what I have done to this person in my unconsciousness, no matter how right he is, my soul is being attacked and I cannot allow that to happen."

In experiences with the borderline patient, attack and counterattack tend to be played out endlessly. What is often forgotten — and this is difficult to remember under strained circumstances — is the act of leaving the circle of battle to tend the wounded. We must apprehend the fact that a young part of ourselves feels terrified and unprotected. Seeing this inner state may permit us to become its ally and feel empathic toward its sense of abandonment. Through this imaginal act the therapist stands for his or her soul and the patient ceases to be the enemy. No longer is the patient seen as a Yahweh ranting with unbearable rage; instead, the patient is recognized to be a person possessed by the archetype. The patient's own soul, ravished by negative affects, is terrified that the therapist will be oblivious to this suffering and become angry rather than see.

Job represents an attitude that is soul-centered. He is concerned with his state of inner being, no matter how powerful and right the afflicting outer forces may be. Here a moral position of standing for the soul is emergent — it is a protective morality that judges ruthlessness as unacceptable even if it comes from a wise and powerful source; even if it is also "correct," as was Yahweh's knowledge of Job's shadow quality of self-righteousness (Raine 1982, p. 274).

We learn to recognize from clinical experience that our feelings of being overwhelmed are often an inductive effect of the patient's own interior process. This experience helps the therapist to empathize with the patient's own helplessness, which can be easily overlooked in view of Yahweh-like states that make the patient appear powerful. Jung's stance is to remain aware of the archetypal nature of the soul-killing affliction — and especially aware of one's powerlessness in the face of it — without flight into illusions of strength through identifications with the same tyranny! In the Middle Ages people held up the Cross to defeat the Devil; this meant that Satan could be overcome only through the profound vulnerability experienced when one appealed with an open heart to the Eros of Christ. In the pitched battle the ego stands aside while two archetypal powers fight.

In this conflicted state the therapist recognizes and adds a third thing, an imaginal awareness of an afflicting Job-Yahweh dyad and a deeply felt caring for the soul. In Jung's analysis the spacious attitude that Job represents makes him a precursor of Christ. But the awareness of the soul-killing quality of the Yahweh-like affects cannot come into existence as long as we identify ourselves or the patient with these contents. It will only emerge upon recognition that these archetypal affects are persecuting both patient and therapist, for such recognition opens us to the love of the soul. Clearly, an act of faith is involved, for there can never be any assurance that the third thing — namely, Eros — will enter. Rather, we need to proceed with a steadfast awareness that without Eros the soul is lost and the person reduced to power drives that possess the ego and create the illusion of control.

In this work we can never be certain that we will survive with an intact self the withering demonic vision stemming from the Yahweh-Job dyad. In his study of faith in the works of Winnicott, Bion, and Lacan, Michael Eigen writes that "It is [the] intersection of profound vulnerability and saving indestructibility that brings the paradox of faith to a new level" (1981, p. 416). He then quotes what he calls Winnicott's "most memorable expression of faith":

> The subject says to the object: 'I destroyed you,' and the object is there to receive the communication. From now on the subject says: 'Hello object!' 'I destroyed you.' 'I love you.' 'You have value for me because of your survival of my destruction of you.' 'While I am loving you I am all the time destroying you in [unconscious] *fantasy*' (Winnicott, 1971, p. 90).

The 'object' survives the attacks of the 'subject' just as Job survives Yahweh's attack. According to Jung, one is not only in a position of surviving another person's destructiveness, but one must also survive the destructiveness of negative, numinous archetypal energies. These can be dealt with apotropaically by reducing them to the frustrations of a developmental stage in which the patient once suffered maternal abandonment. But this approach, while important to keep as an essential perspective, would by itself repress and diminish the *numinosum* involved. "Yahweh is a phenomenon and, as Job says, 'not a man'" (Jung 1952, par. 600).

Job's unconscious has *seen* "Yahweh's dual nature" (Jung 1952, par. 600). But it is difficult to consciously stand for this kind of perception, for it is often dimmed or overruled by other forces, for example, Job's "comforters," those inner voices that would have us focus upon our own shortcomings. The scapegoat shadow-quality of a patriarchal god-image is: "I must have done something wrong, otherwise, how could my plight be so bad?"

Jung demeans Job's vision: "Shrewdly," Jung says, "Job takes up Yahweh's aggressive words and prostrates himself at his feet as if he were indeed the defeated antagonist" (1952, par. 599). And he adds, "The therapeutic measure of unresisting acceptance had proved its value yet again" (1952, par. 601). For Jung, Job's moral victory over the immoral affect fields represented by Yahweh is the decisive transformative factor leading to the psychological incarnation of acquiring an inner self structure. The value of Job's regained conscious, imaginal vision is not recognized.

In contrast to Jung, Kathleen Raine's study of William Blake's Job illuminates Blake's emphasis on Job's active engagement of the imaginal world. He is released only when he *sees* God (Raine 1982, p. 289).

> I knew you then only by hearsay;
> but now, having seen you with my own eyes,
> I retract all I have said,
> and in dust and ashes I repent (Job: 42).

Only after Job has experienced the transcendent energies of his God can he recognize the falseness of his previous "empty-headed words" (Job: 42). He grows aware of his narcissism and understands that he has been compelled to deny a falseness he apprehended all along. From a late-twentieth-century psychological perspective, it might appear that Job has gone into a masochistic regression fed by painful humility: "In dust and ashes I repent." But this interpretation does not account for Job's humbled feelings against the background of joy for having seen God. Job's vision earns him the right to question Yahweh: "Now it is my turn to ask questions and yours to inform me." This is hardly a regression.

Many borderline patients have transcendent visions. These can

27

occur in the form of religious experiences, or an out-of-the-body or deathbed vision, or they can be experienced simply because of the propensity to experience the *numinosum*, which results from a highly creative unconscious in combination with weak ego boundaries. Borderline patients often know, as well, the level of the Transcendent Self. What is not known is its immanence, for it has never incarnated.[3] The therapist's ability to see and comment upon this light in the patient (through active imagination in the therapy session) can have an important outcome. When the patient's own long-abandoned vision of the *numinosum* can be regained, it often has the same kind of restorative effect as did Job's vision of Yahweh. As with Job, this vision is also a main factor in incarnation of the *numinosum*. It is a path toward the nexus of the self and the Self, which is a crucial healing dimension for the borderline patient (Beebe, 1988).

We need to be aware that many people know this level and have split off from it. Our task, then, is to help the borderline patient regain conscious sight. That is, imaginal sight must be released from its compulsive activity of scanning other people, or in the case of some borderline patients, aroused from its condition of absence and inertia.

Fragmentation, "As-If" Behavior, Confusion, Splitting

Borderline states of mind are often characterized by psychic fragmentation. The therapist is dealing here with the splitting of the ego and object into all-good and all-bad states. But these separate states are really a multitude of psychic centers; each seems to encompass the patient's plight until his or her sudden shift to another center yields a completely different picture. Any therapist interacting with the borderline personality knows this experience: in Harold Searles's words, "I feel not simply intimidated or overwhelmed by this overbearing patient but, curiously and more specifically, *outnumbered*" (1977, p. 448).

This multiplicity of centers in the patient is a structural reaction to overwhelming affects and serves to dull pain. But it also has other purposes. For example, fragmentation may dominate a session in which, for example, the therapist does not experience the severity of the borderline patient's plight. The fragmentation that ensues prevents the therapist

---

[3]See Chapter Three for a further elaboration of this theme.

from becoming overly optimistic. Or, at the end of a session the therapist may feel too definite about an understanding, and merely skim certain details or feeling-states that do not fit into his or her interpretation of the patient's situation. The fragmentation that might suddenly appear has the effect of dissolving not only what was previously grasped, but also the therapist's own complacency.

The following example describes how things went with a male patient in an "off session" during which I was unable to recover my imagination and instead attended only to his spoken complaints. He began telling me how bad his life was and added that his hair was falling out and that he was losing his looks. I responded to an inner demand to say something. "Yes," I agreed, "you are losing some hair, though your looks seem the same to me. But generally I think you must recognize that you are having a very difficult time coming to terms with aging. You are forty years old, no longer a teenager. In fact, you are greatly admired by other people for your many areas of knowledge and experience." I then spoke of the pattern of the *puer aeternus*, and with "mythical authority" described the dangers attendant upon his psyche; death and even suicide that might prevail unless he came to terms with his adolescence. At the end of this discourse I felt quite pleased with myself. But the patient merely paused and went on to complain about not having any money. Stunned by his lack of response to my cleverness and erudition I felt hatred toward him but repressed it and instead, went on a merry chase. "You have more money than ever. Your feeling of having no money is a symbolic expression of the abandonment depression you are suffering." Once again there was a lull and then another seemingly disjointed problem appeared: "I don't know what I should do on vacation," the patient said. "Should I see my ex-wife?" And so it went. The message that emerged was unmistakable: "Don't you dare try to find meaning or make sense of this. There is no meaning and there will be none." This is another way of phrasing the motif of despair: "My life is bad: Don't you dare see it any other way."

Another patient said: "I don't trust the positive. I hate you when you mention it. You're a phony. You really don't see me when you do that. You don't see how awful I feel, how distrustful I am, and how real these feelings are for me. I'm terrified of anything positive. If I give in to it I'll be killed. It's very important that you stay with the negative. I don't trust any move to anything positive." I had tried to present this patient with the positive sides of his life. When this didn't work, I determined to stay with how bad things were and empathically felt into his pain. His response was: "So what should I do, kill myself? If there is no hope, what is the point of going on?" I then pointed out how he rejected anything positive, any hope. To this the patient (rightly) said he felt attacked and more hopeless than ever. I ended up feeling that nothing I had done was right.

My "empathy" here was false empathy because it was defensive. Only later did it become clear that my interventions were attempts to check the patient's attacks on me for his tormented feelings about his own life. I was grasping at straws to stop the pain of the process in which I was engaged. While errors such as these occur more frequently with therapists unfamiliar with treating the borderline syndrome, such tendencies to err are present in all therapists. One can never become altogether free from behaving in such outrageous ways, and the patient will feel the therapist's falseness as dangerous and persecutory.

Helene Deutsch's descriptive phrase, the "as-if" patient, often characterizes the borderline patient. But entire therapy sessions can easily take on an as-if quality as the therapist defends against experiencing borderline affects and their power to unhinge his or her thinking and imaginal processes. A patient, referring to an argument with a friend, said: "I have withdrawn, I will not come out to her, I am *too* angry and *too* disappointed." The word "too" was stated with the authority of absolute truth, as if this person's existence as a viable being hung upon the correctness of her assessment. I was emotionally paralyzed and could say nothing. I was outside a self-contained and closed system. If I said, "Yes, your friend has hurt you terribly, and I understand how you feel," I would be lying. If I said nothing, I would be sadistically abandoning the patient to her misery. I felt completely excluded from what was ostensibly an interchange between us. Yet I was not excluded by a schizoid withdrawal, or a narcissistic insistence that I "shut up and listen." Instead, I was excluded in a way that made me feel helpless to do anything, for I was shut out by a belief that the world and all its inhabitants were horrible. Yet this belief had something shallow and self-serving about it, "as if" the patient believed it.

But something more was going on. Embedded within this false assessment of the world, a truth acted like a lure to pull me in, challenging me to understand yet not try to change anything. At times, the work seemed a hopeless endeavor, and it felt impossible to make any headway out of, or into, the intensely harbored belief that everything about the world was wrong. I realized that on those occasions I had withdrawn under the stress of so negative an experience, but especially under a pervading sense of falseness, which led me to wonder why I bothered to put such great amounts of energy into something not truly authentic. Dealing with an as-if personality who apparently had as-if beliefs, I had become an as-if therapist — even to the point that I once nearly suggested that the patient consult her (real) therapist about some issue!

Who was the "real" therapist? I certainly was not at that moment. I think I only became the real therapist when I managed to overcome the as-if affect and began to *see* this patient. First, I had to be able to experience her without withdrawing, which meant to be embodied in the present. I was obliged to experience my bewilderment, despair, and anger at being excluded and rendered impotent over the potential for improvement. I also had to recognize my own sadistic and masochistic tendencies, both of which had been expressed through withdrawal.

Though I often found myself in a state of confusion, I gradually recognized that these sensations belonged to a stage that could become the ground of a gestalt out of which vision could emerge. It was only when I could *see* the patient's process that I could be real. With the help of imagination, it was possible to recognize a young child part of the patient that was in terrible pain, *and it deeply felt the despair the patient could speak of with an as-if quality.* What first appeared to be as-if behavior became entirely real to the eye of imagination.

An important phenomenon must be mentioned: when my patient said "I am *too* angry," the word "too" carried great authority. Patients may say something like "I will *not* take that job." The word "not" can ring out with remarkable authority, even though it may refer to some quite banal issue, such as a job there is no actual pressure to take. A simple word can thrust the therapist into the anguish of experiencing a bewildering play of archetypal forces. The patient's existence seems to hinge upon one's complete agreement with him or her, and any departure from this stance raises the threat of shattering the patient's world. And yet, if the therapist should ask why absolute certainty seems so crucial, the likely response will be denial that this is so. We then try to justify our responses (as, for example, by stressing the subtle affective tones and style of the patient's delivery), but these attempts are usually experienced by the patient as an attack. Our next response is to wonder if we have blundered; we may tend to reevaluate the patient's statement more positively, and to denigrate our initial reaction. Yet, if we recall the feeling that gave rise to our initial response, it will become clear that the patient has been communicating in ways that have completely eluded us, and that we have mismanaged the situation by reacting on the manifest level. We may question why the patient requires such absolute allegiance to his or her point of view. We then realize that at times such as these that we should have done nothing but allow ourselves to experience the uncomfortable feelings that exist between ourselves and the patient. But by now the communication will have been lost, for the patient will no longer be in his or her previous state of life-and-death urgency but may instead be capable of careful, unimpassioned differentiation. To explain away our responses instead of accepting them isolates therapist from patient and creates a power-based attitude resistant to any true understanding of the nature of the archetypal background that informs the patient's words and gestures.

In this instance, the patient's emphasis on being *too* hurt could indeed (as I saw through later experiences in therapy) be understood as a life-and-death matter with me. If the patient could have been true to her perceptions, she would have maintained that there was absolutely no contact between us. But I behaved *as if* there was an ongoing basis for our relating to one another. Such lies are extremely dangerous to the borderline patient. He or she can be thrust by them into an archetypal drama of a battle between truth and falsehood like those depicted by so many mythologems.

Often, the fact that archetypal and mundane levels coexist within the same phrase or sentence leads one to a certain reticence to speak plainly to a patient. Often the therapist will search for deep meanings where none may exist, or give a verbose response when a simple yes or no will do. When, during an initial interview, a patient asked whether I charge for cancellations, I became filled with anxiety. It took me about ten minutes of exploring to determine whether or not something very profound was going on. Meanwhile, the patient became more and more exasperated and anxious. When I felt more myself, and was finally able to state that I do charge for cancellations, both the patient's anxiety and my own vanished immediately. In this case the patient's obsessive mechanisms, idealization, and narcissistic defences dominated the next three years of treatment; during that time I experienced none of the anxiety of the initial session. Eventually, as an alliance built up between us, the patient's persecutory anxieties, linked with abandonment feelings, could be acknowledged and worked with in the transference.

The Borderline Person's Relationship to the *Numinosum*

Inspired by Otto's study, *The Idea of the Holy*, Jung described the *numinosum* as

> a dynamic agency or effect not caused by an arbitrary act of will. On the contrary, it seizes and controls the human subject, who is always its victim more than its creator . . . The numinosum is either a quality belonging to a visible object or the influence of an invisible presence that causes a peculiar alteration of consciousness (1937, par. 6).

Jung's personal and clinical examples of the overpowering, awe-inspiring, sacred or demonic quality of the *numinosum* are based upon his conviction of its centrality in all religious belief (1937, par. 9). He wrote:

> [T]he main interest of my work is not concerned with the treatment of neuroses but rather with the approach to the numinous. But the fact is that the approach to the numinous is the real therapy and inasmuch as you attain to the numinous experience you are released from the curse of pathology. Even the very disease takes on a numinous character (Letter, 8 August, 1945).

The borderline patient is both besieged by the negative *numinosum* and terrified of engaging its positive forms. The following material examines this fear of the positive *numinosum*.

A patient recalled an experience that had dominated her life. When she was three years old she had imagined a ball of light that gradually became larger. For some time this experience of light was extremely pleasurable, and she remembered being encompassed by its energy. But sometimes the ball would grow larger and larger, and she feared that she would be swept into it. On these occasions she waited in desperation for someone to save her but no one was ever there. This experience recurred throughout childhood. The patient could manage to repress the image, yet it always loomed dangerously in the background as something both extremely important and dangerous.

In her adult life the ball of light also played a major role, though she was careful to hide her secret. When she looked at a small light, as, for example, on a radio, the light would gain intensity and size until she would feel, once again, the threat of becoming lost and engulfed in it. She would then shut if off by turning away or opening her eyes widely. As a child, she had not been able to turn the light off so easily, and even as an adult she escaped it with difficulty. At times the energy field would come upon her when she was alone, even without the impetus of a light she could shut off. When this happened she would be driven to smoke a cigarette, which often helped to diminish the effect of the light.

In my work with the above-mentioned patient this energy field arose in the transference. Moreover, the same fears of engulfment erupted as she felt the energy field between us increase. Her only way of grounding it seemed to be through her sexuality, for, as she explained, she was able to turn the energy downward toward her genitals, thus sexualizing the encounter and controlling the experience. Unless she displaced her energies in this way, they expanded horizontally, becoming ever fuller until they reached toward the frightening experience of the *numinosum*.

This fear of the *numinosum* is characteristic of many borderline patients who anticipate that it will overwhelm both themselves and others. Furthermore, there is a tenacious belief that if the positive *numinosum* were consciously owned for one's individual needs, appropriation would be at the cost of taking the *numinosum* away from another person. For instance, my patient could recall wanting to do anything possible to create harmony between her parents. She believed that by allowing herself connection to the *numinosum for herself*, she was betraying them. It was as if there were a finite amount of energy to go around and that taking it for herself — for instance, in some creative work — would deplete the available supply.

That this patient was possessed by unconscious aspects of her parents (in this instance their envy), was revealed in her belief that whatever she took for herself was at their cost. The experience of envy is a dreadful feeling. To escape it, the child or the borderline adult will continually sacrifice the link to the *numinosum* in the hope that positive feeling will take its place. The concept of possession by destructive complexes helps to clarify an understanding of borderline states of mind. One does not know that one is possessed; instead, undermining thoughts and behavior, which deny the *numinosum*, are ego-syntonic. Also, the emergent experience of the power of the *numinosum* is felt by borderline patients as an assured route to abandonment: they believe that the divine and demonic energies within them will drive everyone away.

Creation, Disorder, and Borderline States of Mind
The borderline patient's experiences often contain a motif that is widespread in creation myths: when the hero takes the sacred substance of the

gods, they attack him. The hero, however, manages to preserve a portion of his theft, such as fire or grain, and bring it to humankind. Generally, the creative act of bringing unconscious perceptions into space–time life meets with disorder, which is experienced by the ego as anxiety. Hence, in addition to developmental deficits, the therapist is also dealing with transpersonal energies and archetypal patterns. The Separation-Rapprochement Subphase of Individuation (Mahler, 1980) is itself a creative act, a version of the heroic task of discovering the numinous and bringing it back to space–time life. Indeed, the toddler's separation-rapprochement efforts are rooted in an archetypal process, and the proper function of the mother figure is to help with the disorder the process engenders. What makes the hero a hero lies in his or her being able to withstand the counterattack of the unconscious, which is the inevitable result of taking its precious energies for human designs. The young ego cannot withstand the disorder and needs help. Thus the maternal figure has the powerful role of mediator in an archetypal process, and can use her capacities either to further the child's individuation or severely undermine it.

In adult life, the content of a creative act may vary; it may be a new artistic form, an embrace of a changing life-situation, a structural synthesis of ideas, or an expression of love. But the borderline person quickly recoils from whatever form this creation takes, and this abrupt rejection of the creative act can be severely destabilizing.

The following dreams illustrate how a patient was inwardly attacked when she attempted to grasp her own creative energy. She related the real-life situation preceding the first dream as follows: "I had chosen a present for my mother and had especially warm feelings about it, having spent some time thinking about what she might need. The day before my friend and I were thinking about particular books my mother might like, and afterward I felt somehow dissatisfied. Upon thinking about this later, I realized that I wanted more closeness, more personal sharing." That night she had the following dream:

> My mother has given me a large bouquet of various kinds of flowers. I began to snip off the bottoms of the stems before putting them into water, and my mother became very upset. She had no reason other than to say it would "ruin everything" if I continue. I persist, however, explaining to her that the flowers will last longer this way. But she is beside herself, terribly upset over this.

The next evening the patient had a second dream:

> I am doing something with my mother. I experience how my feeling, as it comes from me, disturbs her greatly. She wants none of my feeling. As I experience this I am extremely upset and awake in a state of nightmarish anxiety.

The bouquet of flowers is available for the daughter *as long as she doesn't attempt to make it her own*; that is, as long as she obeys her mother's wishes and allows the bouquet to be part of her mother's domain. This patient was engaged in the process of gaining a fundamentally new attitude, one based upon a sense of relatedness that was deeply rooted in her feminine nature and in sharp contrast to a lifelong modality of being effective, efficient, extremely competent in the world; she was always *doing* and rarely *being.*

In the first dream the attack by the unconscious takes the form of her mother becoming anxious and extremely upset. In the past, when she had encountered these maternal affects in life situations, she would relinquish her own interests and needs. She felt it was her job to heal her mother by creating a secure environment that would buffer her mother from paranoia and abandonment fears. The maternal attack takes a deeper form in the second dream: *the mother wants none of the dreamer's own feelings.* The first dream concerns separation; the second, rapprochement, the return to the mother with one's own energies. But the patient felt attacked, and even terrorized, by her mother's refusal to accept her true nature. The mother in these dreams surely represents the patient's experience of her own mother, but the mother also represents the patient's experience of the unconscious, especially as it would constellate when she attempted any creative act. In general, the borderline patient suffers the results of a severe lack of a positive response from his or her personal mother, especially when daring to own and enact creative impulses. In this patient's dream, her creative side is represented by the flowers; the unconscious presents the patient with an image of the numinous manifesting through beauty, and leads her away from her earlier conscious image of a gift of books.

The *Coniunctio* and the Fusion-Distance Dilemma

Borderline states of mind are dominated by an interplay of fusion and distance. A borderline person can, for example, merge with a person or group to the extent that any sense of individual identity is lost. What the person thinks and feels is strongly dominated by clues picked up from other people, and quite commonly and painfully, he or she is forced to participate in a kind of guessing game. For instance, a young male patient who feared ostracism always wondered whether his friends would reject him. Not being ostracized seemed to depend upon chance, as if he were caught in a game whose rules he did not know. Everyone else seemed to know them, and he desperately sought a link with the boys in his group by trying to sense "where they were at." But this repeated attempt was always marred by his anxiety so that the empathic abilities he had assimilated were always undermined. In this endeavor, his painful attempt to fit in by merging with the individuals in the group was contradicted by the simultaneous sense of being completely different from them. Success on any one day was no assurance against ostracism on the next.

Thus, while one is in a state of fusing with another person's unconscious, a state of psychic distance simultaneously exists that disallows any connection at all. It appears that these unreconciled states are the borderline person's unconscious strategy to maintain separateness and symbiosis at once. In this condition, the borderline person often is an outsider and consequently suffers the fate of being the scapegoat.

Fusion and Union

It is necessary to discriminate between states of fusion and states of union in order to understand the borderline condition. The experience of union differs significantly from that of fusion. Union describes an interaction between two people in which both experience a particular change in the energy flow between them; this is specifically recognizable as a kinship quality (Jung, 1946, par. 445), or in Victor Turner's term, a sense of *communitas* (Turner, 1974, p. 286). This quality is also implicit in Buber's concept of the I-Thou relationship.

States of union vary in intensity and quality. Some union processes are mainly unconscious, with neither person aware at the time that anything significant has happened, except perhaps through insights gained from dreams. Some processes are, however, quite intense and may take the form of a shared imaginal vision.

The latin term for union — *coniunctio* — expresses its archetypal nature. The *coniunctio* is that pattern of energy in which there is a coming together of opposites, notably fusion and distance, in perfect harmony. While hidden and arcane, the *coniunctio* is, in a sense, a well-kept secret, yet only when it is seen with another person can one become aware of what one has always known.

Fusion is characterized by a nondifferentiation of processes occurring between two people. For example, psychic contents that belong to a patient can enter the therapist (the reverse is also true), and the therapist may behave as if the patient's psychic state was his or her own. In such instances, we may lose sight of the difference between our process and the patient's, and our identity may become hazy. Or we may become aware that a fusion state exists between our own and the patient's unconscious psyches. This awareness is crucial in order for fusion states to have a creative outcome.

The following example points to the subtlety of many fusion states. A patient entered the consulting room and complained about having stepped on some gum, which he had trouble cleaning off his shoe. During the ensuing hour I found myself thinking that I did not want to touch my own shoe. Now I usually do not touch my shoe, nor feel an urge to do so, but during this session, even though my shoe was far from my hand, I still felt strongly resistant to touching it. Only after some time had passed did it occur to me that the patient had been talking about his shoe and the gum. But even after this recognition, the preoccupation persisted. I then became aware of the fact that a fusion state was manifesting between us. The patient's psyche had entered me, and I had been quite captivated by it, especially in the moments before I became aware of the fusion-quality of our interaction.

The latent content of this interaction was the patient's preoccupation with masturbation. Several weeks after this fusion experience, the patient's masturbatory compulsions came to light for the first time and could be discussed, with the significant result that his compulsive masturbation ended. In the interaction described, it was as if he had entered me during his masturbatory act and that a creative mixing-up and mirroring between our psyches took place. I felt no coercion during this time, nor any demands that I do something—or do nothing. A lack of coercion when two people are in a fusion state often signifies a creative mix-up of boundaries. In this particular fusion experience, I had a sense of containing the patient.

Fusion states may be used by the borderline patient to control another person—especially to deny loss, separation, or persecutory affects. A patient may complain, for example, that ignorance of the therapist's personal life makes it impossible to be trusting. At this point the therapist may experience one of two common reactions to a fusion demand: either to withdraw or to share personal material. The therapist's awareness of the conflictual nature of this state helps him or her to avoid acting it out; he or she may then arrive at a position of understanding the patient's fusion demand, which may be seen as a defense against abandonment.

But fusion states *can* be coercive and far more complex, as is shown in the following example. After I had written an article, I was surprised to discover that a person with whom I had discussed several minor points was enraged with me. He insisted that I had stolen his ideas and that the article should reflect coauthorship. I felt bewildered and did not know if he was joking or serious. But when he began specifying the contributions he had made to the paper it soon became clear that he was quite serious. I then realized that I had used a turn of phrase from a writer admired by this person. I immediately became tense and defensive, fearful that he was right. I was a thief after all! But as this man continued speaking, his argument began to lose its power; he explained that he had long been interested in the topic but had never published his ideas. It became clear to me, though certainly not to him, that he was accusing me of stealing ideas he had never voiced. To him, I was merely a scribe who had added some clarity to his thoughts. But for a moment, he had penetrated me and filled me with the illusion that I was merely putting into words ideas that had originated with him!

This was a very uncomfortable encounter. I felt violated and my sense of self was temporarily lost. During this period of my own identity diffusion, it also seemed that this man's survival was completely in my hands, and that if I did not appease him in some way he would go to pieces. Even though moments of clarity broke through, the tendency to fuse remained. These moments of clarity faded in and out and were too elusive to grasp. It was all quite mad, but I gradually regained enough sanity to suggest we could talk later about the problem. I prepared myself for another agonizing battle in which I would attempt to gird myself and not yield. However, when I next met the man, he had completely forgotten about the incident. He behaved, in typical borderline fashion, as if some trivial disagreement had long since passed!

Another patient complained that I did not emotionally support her and that I failed to see her as she really was. No matter how much we worked on this issue, she would continue to be filled with rage and despair about my lack of connection to her. She complained, too, of feeling empty and added that no amount of food ever felt sufficient to fill her up. Since beginning therapy with me, she had gained twenty pounds and could not take it off. And she was gaining more. I recognized that I felt guilty whenever she spoke of her weight and harbored the fantasy that if I did something different (it was not clear what), she would not be so fat. The fantasy then took the form that if I loved her more, felt something *more*, she would not remain empty. I recognized that I unconsciously believed it was my fault that she was not emotionally full and therefore physically thin.

All along, this patient had referred to a former therapist whom she loved and who cared for her, even though she eventually decided to discontinue treatment with him. But *he* cared. I felt his *caring ghost* and my inadequacy. Finally we recognized the nature of the idealization that had been operative and the hatred it concealed for the way he had "vampirized" her, stolen her energy and depended upon it for their emotional contact. This patient had at least decided that I did not do that! It was only after the dissolution of her idealization that I became aware of how much I believed her weight gain was my fault. And I realized how much I had hated her for what I experienced as her demand that I do something about it. Eventually, I told her about this feeling, and she came to realize that in some way she could have been making that demand. Furthermore, she recognized that she held a deep-seated belief that whatever was wrong in the therapy (and life in general) was her fault. We had been wed; we were two masochists unconsciously fused, and in this state we tormented each other. There was little contact between our minds and our bodies were filled with a tension that was imageless.

Finally, a clarifying though emerged: *It was all my fault.* We were both unconsciously and eagerly grasping at the whole fault! No wonder we developed a hatred of one another. There had been a lack of union, and instead, an abundance of unconscious fusion and conscious distance. Our linkage could be depicted as a hermaphrodite with one body and two heads. And our bodies carried our unconscious fusion through the complex: "It's my fault." Thus we had an extremely sticky linkage and at the same time an immense distance between us. Fortunately, there was enough of an alliance between us to be able to work through this dilemma, and see how we were fused through the agency of the same complex.

As the following example demonstrates, the state of union, the *coniunctio*, is neither a condition of fusion nor soulless distance. I had been seeing "Charlotte" for four years, although several years passed before I was able to recognize her spiritual nature. This part of her had been largely a private matter between her ego and a schizoid sector of her personality. During sessions I spent much time splitting off; this activity was a reaction to her splitting process and my countertransference. I consistently noted this behavior to her, and gradually Charlotte and I began to be more fully present in the room.

In daily life Charlotte functioned well, but she complained of poor relationships and insufficient professional acclaim. Several months prior to the sessions I will describe, she could begin to express what she felt were very negative feelings and, she claimed, "without any concern for your feelings; I don't give a damn!" She had never said such a thing to anyone before. In the past, I had experienced her splitting and withdrawal as a torment, and my anger had often been aroused. I experienced her seeming attack with relief because now she was more present than she had been before.

Following are recollections from the session previous to the one in which the *coniunctio* was experienced. On that occasion, I felt a lack of interest in Charlotte, was rather bored, and tended to lose focus and to dissociate. When I relayed these experiences to her, she recognized that she, too, was splitting off.[4] She said that she could understand how my splitting fit her expectations, though she felt this was only a partial explanation. It was also my problem, she added, for she insisted that she had been quite present at the beginning of the hour when I had experienced the greatest difficulty in not splitting off. We tried to sort this out, though I felt resistant and so did she.

In the next session, Charlotte began by saying that she had been

---

[4]The description of these sessions raises many questions. It is easy to regard the patient's splitting as induced by my countertransference. It is also possible to take the transformation of a sadistic brother image (see p. 43) simply as a transference statement representing the patient's response to my not attacking her with interpretations of her splitting. It is also natural to ask about boundaries: is the dissociation simply a result of too loose boundaries on my part, a fear of intrusion in the patient? Or is it caused by a fear that I have poor boundaries and hence that the therapeutic container is unsafe? In working with this clinical material I was quite aware of such issues. The approach of W. Goodheart (1984) who has incorporated Robert Lang's method, could be focused upon my work with this patient with interesting results. However, we are dealing here with fundamental issues that speak directly to the subject of psychological healing and the role of the *numinosum* therein. A good deal of acumen can go into observing the clinical interaction, with special attention to the destructive effects of the therapist's splitting. But this approach, while important, can also have a negative effect: everything that transpires in the patient and between therapist and patient is seen as the result of some intervention, some interpretation, or some behavior on the part of the therapist. This orientation overlooks the healing force of archetypal factors. It focuses our attention in a manner that is not attuned to the symbolic and numinous products of the psyche. The latter, especially in the synchronistic occurrence of the *coniunctio*, are even more readily overlooked or blocked. Thus, while I can reflect upon my behavior in this case and recognize that the patient may have been adversely affected by me in ways of which I was unaware, I strongly favor the approach I took because it is attuned to the numinous and does not neglect this healing factor in favor of a microscopic analysis of the therapeutic interaction.

angry all week since our last session. She restated her view that she had not expected rejection and that my splitting off from her was due to my disinterest. In contrast to the last session, she was now unusually present.

Charlotte then spoke about her brother who, she said, "always put me down, always humiliated me." A new kind of clarity gradually emerged concerning ways in which her ego was split. A link existed between one part of her ego and the spirit; the two participated in a distant connection, far from here-and-now reality and known only in deep, introverted ways. There was another connection, also split off, between a part of her ego and her brother-image, which represented an inner persecutory force.[5] I made this interpretation, and she responded positively and went on to say that her brother found her "uninteresting, and I align with him and give up on anyone liking me. I also become uninterested in communicating with you, and tend to dismiss you." I mentioned that in the last session I had carried the introject of her brother, and that I had also reacted badly to her resistance to communicating with me by being withdrawn, thus countering what I experienced as her punishing withdrawal from me. As we discussed these projections she recalled that when she had been angry months ago, it had felt good not to have to care about my feelings. I responded that when she was angry I felt she was more present. "Last time," she said, "I experienced you as a Hades-like judge." Charlotte explained that when she inwardly began to feel young and experienced her inner child, I had been critical of this child, especially when she presented problems with her relationships. I thought that I understood the Hades metaphor, for I had frequently felt inner energies rising to penetrate her, to "shove an interpretation down her throat."

We continued in this way, trying to identify our mutual projections. Charlotte began speaking about her brother. She said she could feel a sexual response toward him, and that this was a new experience for her. She then mentioned a man whom she disliked and noted that there was no sexuality in him, just detached sadism. I took this comment as a special enjoinder not to withdraw.

---

[5]The inner world of the borderline patient is often split in the fashion of persecutory and delusionally created, "positive" structures yielding alliances with the ego (Fairbairn's "libidinal ego," Masterson and Rinsley's "Rewarding Part Object Unit"; see Chapter Three). But I believe that these inner alliances of the ego and other parts can also have a positive, archetypal component, as in Charlotte's link to the spirit archetype, which provided her with a peaceful and rich inner life, a transcendent connection that should not be reduced to notions of schizoid withdrawal.

As I became aware of the erotic link Charlotte had with her brother, I experienced the emergence of an erotic energy field. Charlotte, too, experienced it. As we participated in this energy, my consciousness became more embodied and I imaginally perceived a shimmering image, which partook of both of us, move upward from below. I told Charlotte what I saw. She answered, "Yes, I also see it, but I'm afraid of it." I continued to share what I saw and experienced. I saw the image between us as white; she spoke of it as a kind of fluid that swirled about a center, and added that she was afraid of the intensity that might arise if she descended deeply into her body. Fear began to overcome her and she said she felt herself to be slipping away. I responded that she needed only to trust in becoming more embodied and to see.

A feeling of timelessness pervaded; I didn't know if one minute or twenty had passed. Charlotte worried about the next time. What would she do if this experience was not there again? A sense of kinship, a brother-sister feeling was apparent to both of us. There was sexual excitement and a pull toward physical union, but this tendency had its own inhibition, *as if the energy field between us oscillated, separating and joining us in a kind of sine wave rhythm*. This state was clearest when we each allowed our imagination to see the other.

The hour came to a close, and the kinship feeling that was released by this union remained potent. Not only did it bring us closer, but it resulted in a remarkable transformation in Charlotte's inner life. In the next session, she told of a dream in which, for the first time, her brother appeared as a positive figure who helped her to learn a subject that had always given her difficulty. I have seen this kind of result many times: after the *coniunctio* experience, there is a transformation of inner sadistic anima or animus figures. The dearth of positive inner figures in the borderline personality underscores the importance of the *coniunctio* experience for the transformation of the dead, persecutory inner world into a place of loving support.

In the sessions that followed this experience, Charlotte was depressed. Depression often emerges after the *coniunctio*. But the depression, or *nigredo* state that occurs is not a regression to earlier stages of therapy. Instead, both patient and therapist begin to sense a purpose or *telos* to the process initiated by the *coniunctio*. Charlotte related an awful experience she'd had with an uncle. Previously, we would have had to analyze this experience or relate it to the transference. Now it was necessary only to *remember* what had transpired between us and to explore the archetypal nature of the process. We also lacked a sense of connection in this session; Jung describes this condition as "soul loss" (1946, par. 477). A kind of deadness overcame us that was in strong contrast to the *coniunctio* experience.

The therapist may wonder if the *coniunctio* experience might be a form of collusion or seduction that sidesteps the negative transference. In fact, intense negative transferences frequently emerge after this experience. It seems that the *coniunctio* and the sense of deep kinship which is released form an archetypal representation of the therapeutic alliance. Supported by great trust and containment that stem from the *coniunctio*, both patient and therapist can risk more openness. For example, states of intense hatred and rage can enter therapy and be worked through.

The conscious experience of the *coniunctio* is an unusual and remarkable event. It is by far the exception to what ordinarily occurs in a therapeutic process, yet it does exist. When it occurs, it can have a healing, integrative effect on very old wounds, such as those commonly found in the borderline person. Incest wounds especially need to be mentioned, as well as those excruciating psychic attacks — stemming from the parental unconscious — that a child may feel when his or her sexuality emerges. Such traumas feel like attacks by God.

The *coniunctio* can also be experienced without a direct, face-to-face encounter. Even during a telephone hour two people may experience a current flowing between them, a flow with more than erotic energy. In one such instance, a woman patient related a dream of an androgynous young man who reached an orgasm that sprayed a golden fluid over her; this fluid traveled in a circle that seemed to be self-renewing. While the dream was being recounted we could feel a *coniunctio* between us; we shared imaginal experiences "occurring in the space between," as in Charlotte's case. This *coniunctio* was a very different experience from the transference–countertransference bond that had dominated our work for months and that had found special focus in this patient's oedipal complex. Now there was a qualitative difference stemming from a hitherto unconstellated archetypal element. As usual, this *coniunctio* was followed in another session by a seemingly inexplicable fall into depression, which was composed of previously unintegrated personal complexes. In this case, these complexes comprised hostile qualities rooted in the patient's father's lack of response to her sexuality and her continuing belief that I would respond in a similar way. But reductive analysis was not required at this time. A process with its own goal had been strongly constellated, and recollection of the *coniunctio* experience and amplification of its process—that is, an explanation to the patient that depression usually follows the union experience as part of the *coniunctio's* embodiment—was sufficient to contain the depression and to regain a sense of connection between us. Within this process, the patient could readily accept the personal shadow material that was the content of her depression, and her depression subsequently lifted.

In a following telephone session a feeling of deadness prevailed. This state carried previously unintegrated, preoedipal elements of a narcissistic nature (whose manifest content was an intense concern with what clothing my patient should buy for a party). But reference to the processes occurring between us in a here-and-now sense was essential, and reductive analysis was not required. The therapist's role at this stage is largely one of remembering, a task often made difficult by depressive affects and projective identification. It should also be noted that at times it is the therapist's countertransference, not the patient's transference, which reflects the "soul loss" Jung speaks of. A patient will sometimes return after a *coniunctio* experience feeling very present and engaged, whereas the therapist will be withdrawn and not want to engage in the encounter. Such behavior can be extremely painful for the patient. As a result of the *coniunctio*, however, individuals often stand up for themselves and point out the therapist's problems with a newly-acquired confidence.

It is extremely important for the therapist to note the fleeting moments of true contact, for unless we concentrate upon them—and there is too much pain of loss and humiliation for the patient to do so—we will tend to pay too much attention to the destructive states of mind that so persecute the borderline patient. These demonic states must observed and mentioned, but not amplified through excessive interpretation, nor secretly enhanced through an avoidance of true contact.

In borderline patients, psychic structure is split between fusion states and extreme distancing, so that little or no real contact is possible. The experience of union, the *coniunctio*, is vital just because it *can* unify these opposites. Borderline persons have a critical problem dealing with fusion, separation, union and nonunion in various degrees of intensity. For example, while on the surface two people may seem to be in absolutely no contact at all, in the unconscious they may be deeply fused with each other. The extremities of these states of fusion and soulless distance dominate in the treatment of borderline personality disorders.

45

The process whereby the *coniunctio* is created and dissolved has a specific pattern and has been apprehended and represented by the medieval alchemists in numerous works, and especially in the *Rosarium Philosophorum* (1550). Jung used this text in his study of the transference (1946). The *Rosarium* sets forth a series of symbolic images, each of which represents a state that is part of the creation of the *coniunctio*. The basic pattern that appears is one in which a preliminary incestuous condition is followed by union (the *coniunctio*), which, in turn, is followed by annihilation of the union and progresses toward a condition of radical dissociation. This is itself followed by a more stable form of union. These sequential states are represented by the woodcuts of the *Rosarium*. The first ten (of the set of twenty illustrations) were part of the alchemical *albedo*, and were followed by the second ten, the *rubedo*, which incorporated the energies of union in more depth than the condition of the first ten could allow. Mircea Eliade's interview with Jung offers a concise summary of such alchemical concepts:

> In the language of the alchemists, matter suffers until the nigredo disappears, when the 'dawn' (*aurora*) will be announced by the peacock's tail (*cauda pavonis*) and a new day will break, the *leukosis* or *albedo*. But in this state of 'whiteness" one does not *live* in the true sense of the word, it is a sort of abstract, ideal state. In order to make it come alive it must have 'blood,' it must have what the alchemists called the *rubedo*, the 'redness' of life. Only the total experience of being can transform this ideal state of the *albedo* into a fully human mode of existence. Blood alone can reanimate a glorious state of consciousness in which the last trace of blackness is dissolved, in which the devil no longer has an autonomous existence but rejoins the profound unity of the psyche. Then the *opus magnum* is finished: the human soul is completely integrated (Eliade, 1977, p. 227).

Through the imagery of the *Rosarium* we gain the sense that the entire life of the archetype of the *coniunctio* is one of a dynamic process in which the coming together and separating of opposites alternates with the ultimate goal of creating a combined form that transcends the original objects. The *coniunctio* archetype carries within itself meaning and purpose, which embrace both mind and body.

The borderline patient suffers from a distortion of this archetypal process. For this person, the experience of union has degenerated into fusion and deadness; what remains is a soulless distance between people, as "I-it" dyad. It is a state in which the self as an inner male-female union, or as a "third thing" that can unite two people, is lifeless; this deadness leads to the borderline patient's chronic feeling of helplessness. In this condition the self is incapable of creating order, identity, or purpose. Yet, when this deadened state is properly understood as an arrest at one point of an entire process, it becomes possible to bring other aspects of the process into focus and to become alert to the potential experience of the central mystery, the *coniunctio*.

Despair

In alchemy, the deadened state following the *coniunctio* is called the *nigredo*. This condition is extremely pertinent to borderline states of mind. The *nigredo* is a painful process and is experienced as depression, loss, emptiness, or sadness. Jung interprets this stage as a consequence of incest (1946, par. 468). But I have found that a core issue of *despair* also lies within the *nigredo*. Despair is associated here with the loss or sensed absence of the *coniunctio*. Despair stems from the patient's need to possess the union experience, as well as from recollections of previous lost unions. The latter may possibly begin with a trauma of loss at birth, in adult life recalled as a loss of God, and is expressed in the age-old idea that a child is a "child of God." This initial trauma is the consequence of the first union and its loss, and the trauma continues to elaborate throughout developmental phases such as the Depressive Position as described by M. Klein (Segal, 1980, pp. 76–90), the Separation-Rapprochement Subphase of Individuation as described by M. Mahler (1980) and the Oedipal stage. But what is felt as a loss of God—the "death of God" in our nihilistic epoch—may be a key trauma for the borderline patient. The therapist discovers this through the patient's *rage at God*, and an often dominating despair over the loss of God. This rage is an affect that does not fit into the framework of reactions to personal loss; it is usually kept secret, for the patient is wary of being thought crazy for having such feelings.

There is perhaps no emotion more difficult for the therapist treating borderline patients than despair. Yet despair is the soul's calling card. The borderline patient will often scan every moment, including those prior to the beginning of the therapy hour, for the therapist's optimistic beliefs. The therapist's need to fill the therapeutic process with positive thoughts, usually interpretations or amplifications, or advice-giving, signals to the patient that the therapist is incapable of dealing with despair.

Furthermore, emotions such as fear and anxiety that a therapist may experience when confronted with the despair of the borderline patient are apt to be solely his or her subjective countertransference reactions. These can be a very poor indicator of the patient's own process: when the therapist feels anxious and even panicky, that often proves to be largely his or her own reaction, rather than a syntonic countertransference that may be used to infer the patient's split-off affects. In these instances the patient is often not panicky. The borderline person knows despair only too well. The therapist's anxiety-laded reactions only engender more despair in the patient as well as rageful defenses.

A borderline patient is usually an expert in despair and also an expert in avoiding it through a myriad of splitting defenses. Knowing the depths of despair much better than most therapists, the patient also despairs at having to be the therapist's teacher. The patient is in the position of being the guide for the therapist without ever having had a guide in that area for himself or herself. Such a setup is fertile ground for the patient's envy and can destroy the therapy endeavor.

Despair often seems to border on an objectless realm, on a void, a chaos. But this perception turns out to be deceptive. Despair also has a companion lurking in unseen regions. The primary "inner" object for a borderline patient in the despairing state is a vampire-like energy field. Consequently, a very strange object relationship is created. This is a dangerous aspect of the *coniunctio* process. Frequently, it feels as if a satanic force has been set loose to cleverly convince the patient that there is no hope, that faith is yet untenable, and that it is best either to give up and blandly settle for things as they are — for falseness — or to die. Both choices seem to satisfy this background influence.

"The *coniunctio* is a con-job," rages a patient, daring to wound my narcissism. "I don't believe in it," says another. Remarks like these are extremely common *after* the experience of the *coniunctio*. For then the greatest dangers evolve: abandonment by the therapist is now the greatest threat — there is an upsurge of despair that can be suicidal. We also frequently experience these levels with the borderline patient when *no* union has occurred, such is the intensity of fear that surrounds the memory of the *coniunctio*. The *coniunctio* is avoided because the patient does not want to experience the intense levels of despair resulting from traumas of early loss. Better not to try than to risk so much pain — that is an inner motto that dominates much of the life of the borderline person.

Probably no image in life portrays the demonic inner state of despair better than the vampire, which is a negative form of the spirit archetype. In some legends, when the vampire looks in a mirror there is no image. The vampire represents a psychic force that has absolutely no identity. It is, in a sense, the perfect shadow side of Narcissus; the psyche without a mirror. The spirit archetype in its positive aspect is an inner image that beckons the individual to follow his or her individual calling; to fulfill his or her particular gift or genius.

The image of the vampire being killed by the rays of the sun, that is, consciousness, is an apt image of how consciousness can be destructive to the patient who is fused with this dark force. We are actually out the kill the possessing background force with our theories, ideas and intuitions. But since the patient is inwardly fused with this force, he or she may become disoriented and confused. Furthermore, the therapist's attempts at *knowing* deny despair and hence abandon the patient to its possessing dynamism. The patient then becomes further identified with despair as the only truth. A false, compliant self is all that can be saved by one's attempt to kill with consciousness the possessing background force.

Knowledge is often destructive in the face of despair: if we insist to patients that their despair will end, or that it is only a partial truth, any possibility of their dealing with it vanishes. *For the essence of despair is that nothing works.* All attempts at explanation and understanding feel fraudulent and any focus upon interpretive attempts is liable to drive the patient into a fusion state with the vampire-like force, to live in a schizoid depression, while hidden from life by a false self.

A major reason therapists shy from despair is that entering this domain threatens a loss one's own identity. Mirrors don't work. (It should not go unmentioned, in this regard, that the distortions of mirroring are also avoided in despair, and perhaps this is one of its major positive functions.) Consequently, there is often an unconscious mad scramble for a vantage point. Yet, the essence of the despair is that there are no ideas, no thoughts that will release one from its grasp. We can act out in various ways, and temporarily escape despair, but thought, interpretation, and actions do not truly help. Despair is a chaotic void that destroys ideas, and when we approach it our capacity to think quickly diminishes. A patient will sometimes say that the therapist has to ask the right questions, and in the right way. And the patient is right. For if he or she is true to feeling the state of despair, the borderline person cannot lead us (for instance, through associations) without employing a competent, false self. If he or she were to do so, the healing endeavor would be destroyed.

There is no chance at maintaining a stable union if despair is sidestepped. A fruitful union that releases and engenders soul is impossible unless despair has been sufficiently plumbed. Otherwise, one is caught in a fusion state (comprising the vampire-force and the person's true self), that sucks the union dry. For despair is a haunting *nigredo* that will shred any union and thrust the person into the hands of his or her unconscious bride or bridegroom, its vampiric companion.

The Dead or Helpless Self

As a result of a severe deficiency in empathic responses from "significant others," the borderline person lacks an internal representation of a positive self. This deficit contrasts sharply with the inherent potential of the person to have a transcendent connection to archetypal processes and numinous energies, to a transcendent Self. But this potential rarely incarnates to create an immanent self—that is, the experience of an internal symbolic presence that gives confidence and support and also functions to order experiences that might otherwise overwhelm the ego. The immanent self brings coherence to the many part-selves (complexes) that comprise any personality. These part-selves each engender a particular sense of self: we are all different selves at different times. The immanent self is one of these selves, but is unique in that it also functions to provide an experience of wholeness uniting all the parts.

The immanent self is functionally dead for the borderline patient, for the *numinosum* experienced as part of everyday life usually manifests in a strongly negative form, while its positive nature fails to manifest. Instead, it remains in limbo between outer reality and an inner world largely known through tortuous identifications with archetypes. The result of this identification is, as always, a psychic dismemberment. The potential beauty of the sacred turns into its opposite and feelings of ugliness of body and soul abound.

The self of the borderline patient is in a deathlike state. In alchemical language it lies in a *nigredo*, a putrefaction that the patient will sometimes concretize through strange perversions, such as a penchant for not washing, or perhaps repulsive mannerisms. Alchemical imagery is informative in explaining how these behavioral choices form part of a larger, albeit unseen and unfelt, process. Healing depends upon connecting the dark, disordering aspect of the borderline process to its roots in the archetypal dynamics of the *coniunctio* process.

The borderline syndrome is characterized by denial, splitting and dissociation, whereby strands of previous union experiences engulfed in despair exist side-by-side with states of nonunion and deadness. These opposite states of mind (of union and nonunion) rarely touch. Generally, only the dark and disorienting condition of psychic deadness rules, a condition that the person desperately attempts to overcome. The alchemical imagery of the *Rosarium* shows the archetypal process in which the borderline patient is entangled. As always, when the conscious personality is involved in attempts to escape anxieties, the underlying archetypal process manifests itself in negative forms. The borderline person is helpless to turn the archetypal process into a positive, life-giving form and has aptly been called "the helpless patient" (Giovacchini, 1979, p. 139). He or she suffers deeply from these states of inner deadness and the absence of a psychic connection to any positive object. The self in this state is much like the pathetic Osiris of Egyptian myth, lying in the coils of the underworld serpent of Chaos, masochistically numb and inert, and attacked if he attempts to arise (Rundle Clark, 1959, p. 167). In a spell from a Coffin Text his worshipers plead with Osiris (Rundle Clark, 1959, p. 125):

> Ah Helpless One!
> Ah Helpless One Asleep!
> Osiris, let the Listless One arise!

As Osiris is constantly threatened by the devil Set, symbolic of persecutory anxieties, so, too, the self of the borderline personality is constantly under the threat of dismemberment. States like the *nigredo* and soulless conditions of nonunion can be a terrible yet safe territory; to leave it risks experiencing the pain of psychic dismemberment and complete annihilation. The borderline patient hopes to get by with a minimum of pain by complying with others and with environmental demands. But this choice is never satisfying and the idea of death through suicide often lurks nearby as the consummate relief. Unlike the schizoid person who uses withdrawal as a main defense against the intrusions of other people, and unlike the narcissistic person who has a cohesiveness through which the effect of other people is nullified, the borderline person is caught in a drama in which he or she must make ceaseless yet futile attempts to contact other people.

The borderline patient's inner, death-like world is rarely satisfying, and the person commonly attempts to waken it in a very noisy way.

A patient said: "I am finally able to be a 5, previously I was either a 0 or a 10. I had to have very strong feelings in order to feel alive. I had to feel very deeply about other people, to have very intense contempt or rage, or feel this about myself. Then I was alive. Now I am beginning to have more normal feelings, to hate my husband but also feel some care as well. Previously this was impossible. I had to start fights to feel alive. Anything that approached a 5 was too frightening. It meant I would feel dead." Many borderline patients engage in negative interactions with others, and are addicted to such stimuli as self-mutilation, stealing and other self-destructive behavior. They make use of these patterns in order to overcome the omnipresent feeling of inner deadness.

The borderline patient's nonfunctioning or helpless self is revealed by the following example. A patient frequently said that there was something she had forgotten to tell me in a previous or even more distant session. One time, she said: "There was something I didn't tell you three sessions ago," and then to my amazement, added, "Do you know what it was?" I certainly did not, and as was usually the case when I was with her, I felt perplexed, not intuiting the meaning of what she was saying. She then laughed at herself. But when she had initially asked me the question she had been very serious. She then went on to tell me that over the course of the following sessions she usually forgot to tell me things. She said that she remembered almost everything she wanted to tell me last time, but that she had forgotten something the time before that and was certain that she'd forgotten to tell me something important the time before that. Feeling particularly dull-witted at the moment, I responded, "So what's the big deal? It will come back if it's that important and we'll pick it up later. Why are you so worried?"

She was very compliant as always and willing to go on to the next item on her agenda. But this time I finally understood and began to wonder: her odd question about what had happened three sessions earlier and how urgent it was for her to tell me everything she had planned to tell me finally made sense. It then occurred to me, and I shared the thought with her, that unless I had all the pieces she wanted to tell me, she couldn't function well. I began to understand what she had meant in times past when she complained that "It doesn't work well inside." This had always been very difficult to grasp, for this woman was intelligent and performed well in her profession. So I could make little sense of comments like "It doesn't work well inside," or "The head doesn't work." Now it made sense that what she was communicating in such phrases was the absence of a functioning self that would synthesize her experiences by collecting and pulling together a multitude of events and perceptions. She did not have such an operative center, and consequently she felt empty and helpless. It was vital to her that I gather up *all* the pieces and understand how they all fit together. Indeed, it was even more important that I understand than that she did. It seemed that I was intended to function as the self she didn't have. On the magical, *pars pro toto* level, a single unprocessed item was dangerous, for it aroused the threat that I would not carry out the vital function of being her self.

Here is a clinical vignette of how another patient's inner deadness manifested in therapy. He said "I feel dull, heavy." He spoke of being afraid and of having lived in fear most of his life. Then he mentioned how remarkable it was to feel a moment of peace, a moment free of feeling attacked. "Last time," he said, "was the longest I was able to just be with you, make contact in a clean, open way." Making use of what I believed to be an induced reaction, I asked why he was so frightened now? He answered that, "it's always there. I was attacked all the time in childhood by my brothers, mother, and sisters, to say nothing of my father. It's just in me. I always feel attacked."

Why, I wondered to myself, was I feeling so leaden, heavy, blank, empty? I didn't feel attacked, and not even uncomfortable, just dense, heavy, and without a glimmer of imagination. Nor was I able to open my mouth. It seemed glued shut. Was I being withholding, acting out something sadistic? Perhaps I was feeling his depression. That made some sense, but it didn't do much for me. I still felt blank and heavy, as if I had suddenly gained ten pounds.

Until then, I had said nothing. My patient began to talk about his son, and the son's problems. I felt drawn in a bit. It was something to talk about, something real, tangible, a problem to work with, but I restrained myself, and continued to wonder why I felt so leaden. The patient seemed fine, gaining energy in some way while I became more and more inert. He was connecting not only to his fear and even terror but also to a sense of joy and he looked alive and happy. As he spoke of joy in life, he added that he also felt frightened, for this joy surely would bring on attack. I wondered if my heavy, leaden state was just a cover for fear. Was I covering fear? His? My own? If so, fear of what? This inner dialogue envlivened me a bit and a sense of lightness began to dawn.

Thirty minutes passed in this way; there were twenty left. Would anything come of this session? What if I just remained dull? I was not too bothered by this. The session would just be what it was to be. I went back to the reflection: what am I afraid of? Am I now holding him off? Am I abandoning him out of a fear of a too intense sticky merger? This reflection seemed to yield some feeling of lightness. Little bits of imagination began to flicker. I *saw* bits of fear and imagined a kind of random motion between us, which I likened to heated molecules. It was a dull, dim vision, but at least it was something. I could now talk about his fear as I vaguely *saw* it and not as a defense against my discomfort. And then he said: "You know, I never have to see my parents again. It is my choice. I can make it!" When he said this he surprised himself, and added, "That feels like a moment of freedom, something much more radical than it sounds like." He then spoke of his gratitude to me for not being like "them," that is, like his parents and others who attacked him by unconsciously demanding that he save their lives and renew their dead relationship through killing off his own joy.

The interaction I have described recalls Winnicott's description of the process (referred to earlier in this chapter) whereby a self can come into existence. This patient had known very little of such interactions. Like all borderline patients his inner fantasy would have been:

> "I killed you (with my rage and joy that you wanted for yourself but could never own) and you stayed dead, and as I continued to (unconsciously) kill you, you acted as if I really meant to do just that. I could never use you, I always had to be too concerned for your survival. In the process I haven't survived. I am pathetic, helpless, dead."

Transforming this state of deadness back into the archetypal process, in which it must be embedded as a felt reality, requires the recovery of the imagination, the capacity to play and most crucially, to see. The borderline patient is someone who was prematurely thrust out of magical, mythopoeic space. This person is forced to structure reality precociously and gets caught between mythic realities and those of a rational world too difficult to understand. The borderline person is in limbo between two ways of experiencing the world. Healing requires recapturing the earlier, mythopoeic state in its imaginal essence — a venture that requires dismantling the defensive structures of denial and distortion that have been created as a way of survival.

CHAPTER TWO
CONTRASTING THE NARCISSISTIC AND
BORDERLINE PERSONALITY

"I'll be killed if I really show myself."

Introduction

It would be useful to have a profile that would help to identify the borderline person's psychic structure, but to do so poses certain difficulties. In an earlier work I listed qualities of the narcissistic person (Schwartz-Salant, 1982, pp. 37ff.), including extreme self-absorption, lack of empathy, inability to accept criticism, and grandiose and exhibitionistic needs. Furthermore, the intense manner in which the psychic structures of the narcissistic patient affect the therapist through narcissistic transferences is notable and not difficult to recognize. The borderline personality is, however, more problematic to describe. On the one hand, the borderline patient appears in many forms (Charlton 1988); on the other, this person's symptoms and transferences are more changeable than those of the narcissistic or perhaps any other patient. By contrasting borderline and narcissistic structures, we can better describe the borderline personality and highlight significant differences between these two character disorders.

Idealization

It has been suggested that idealization plays a crucial role in the formation of the narcissistic person (Masterson 1981, p. 13). According to this theory, the child has been the target of lofty and grandiose parental ideals. Through largely unconscious communications from parental figures he or she has been given the "charge" to fulfill unlived ambitions, which actually are the archaic forms of parental failures of individuation. It is clear that if the child is treated as "special," difficulties will arise from so concentrated a form of attention, since the base requirement is to overachieve. But the matter is far worse. The narcissistic

55

person has simultaneously been given a completely opposite message — namely, the devastating message of envy. This message is transmitted as follows: "You are wonderful and I hate you for it. You have it all, and since I don't, I despise you for what I don't have." Here, having "it all" refers to more consciously idealized qualities espoused by the parents.

The narcissistic personality forms by using the received idealization, adapting to its values, *and* creating an inner and outer barrier against the attack of envy. This barrier, called the narcissistic defense, makes for an oddly impenetrable personality. Tragically, the positive function of idealization is largely channeled into defensive patterns, and unless it is recovered through an interpersonal relationship in which idealization transmutes into an inner structure of ideals (Kohut 1971), the potential of the narcissistic person is rarely achieved. When it does occur, this "solution" is the best of possible outcomes; more often, however, the narcissistic person surprises others by his or her *lack* of success and is inclined to age badly and to cling to a past that all too clearly reveals its shallowness. In effect, remorse for unrealized potential becomes a major form of self-victimization, for such persons often become the proverbial "Jack of all trades and master of none."

The borderline person does not possess the cohesiveness and defensive capacity of the narcissistic person. The borderline person's development is characterized by environmental enmeshment: the family system provided support for clinging and dependency and persecuted the child by withdrawal of love and concern for any attempts at separation-individuation. While the narcissistic person generally shares this same history, in the case of the borderline person, parental behavior patterns are often of a more severely overt and extreme nature and idealization is not usually employed to advantage. In the development of the narcissistic person, the mixture of envy and idealization combine to form a self fused with archetypal processes and scornful of eros and relatedness. It is difficult to know if this inner fusion state of the narcissist is a blessing or a curse, but in any event, the borderline person has little of its stability.

The borderline person employs idealization to hide what he or she believes to be extremely negative qualities of the self and others, though this is an unstable splitting defense. So the borderline person is more unstable than the narcissist who can employ idealization to exert control over others, for example, by idealizing people and demanding to be idealized. Instead, the borderline patient might idealize someone and yet soon after feel violent hatred and scorn for the same person. These shifts in consciousness can be quite rapid when the person is in an acute stage of distress.

The borderline person uses idealization defensively, and idealization dominates his or her internal world in a particular way. The therapist can gain a sense of the power of this idealization by paying attention to the uncomfortable feelings of inadequacy that accrue, which seem to debunk whatever he or she thinks or says. It is as if there is an ideal standard that one is measured against. If one fails to live up to this standard, an attack for laying bare one's defects is imminent. There is a tendency to deliver a set of beliefs to one's patient—of how things *should* be—while simultaneously experiencing and denying the defensive nature of this diatribe. As a result of this denial, there is a tendency to become paranoid in the vicinity of the borderline patient. One becomes ensnared in an inner world of *shoulds*. This condition can decisively inhibit the therapist's spontaneous and natural affirmation of what he or she thinks, believes, or wants.

Idealization does not function in the same way for the narcissistic person. Narcissistic idealization is frequently experienced by the therapist as a comfortable, "high" feeling. (Some therapists may find an idealizing patient's fusion drives uncomfortable.) In the domain where idealization and the grandiose-exhibitionistic self (Kohut 1971) are intertwined (a mixed transference), we approach similarities to the transferences met in treatment of the borderline patient. When the mixed transference is in operation, the therapist treating the narcissistic person may feel that he or she is targeted by an unstated yet controlling demand to be ideal. The response might be to yield to the feeling of omnipotence, for example, the feeling that one *knows* the meaning of a particular dream or fantasy. While this mixed state that includes idealization is also found in the borderline person, it functions here in a more free-floating manner, as if some "knowing" intrusive spirit exerts pressure upon the therapist to have a "right answer." In the mixed transference with the narcissistic person, the therapist can feel both a pressure to "know" and at the same time often discovers answers that are truly satisfying. This quality of the mixed transference with the borderline patient leads to the same pressure to "know" without the therapist having concomitant depth of knowing, and instead a vague persecutory pressure takes its place. In response to this phenomenon occurring with the borderline patient, the therapist tends to split off and withdraw, while the narcissistic patient's controlling cohesiveness works against such withdrawal. Also, when dealing with the borderline patient, the therapist is subject to a spirit of idealization that spoils or blocks his or her initiative. The therapist then experiences the threat of being unmasked by the patient — especially since all traces of superficiality, all degrees of falseness in the therapist are painfully amplified.

The borderline patient's unconscious structures of idealization may induce massive insecurity in the therapist. He or she may then become inflated as an unconscious maneuver *to get rid of the patient* and undo the induced sense of impotence. Prior to this experience with the patient, the therapist may have been duped by a seemingly positive relationship and may have entertained thoughts of the inadequacy of diagnostics. The therapist may have determined that the patient had qualities of spirit and courage transcending the scientific reductionism of psychiatry. But, under the pressure of massive feelings of insecurity, such optimism quickly gives way to the harsh terms of diagnosis and prognosis and to sober questioning of whether or not the patient is suitable for therapy.

Idealization is intrapsychically fused with rage in the borderline person. This rage is usually directed against parental figures who failed to be suitably ideal — that is, who did not possess sufficient consciousness and self-esteem to carry idealized projections that are so necessary for the growing child. These early perceptions of parental failure were too threatening for the child to endure, so the lie of denial took the place of true perception, and idealization was thus defensively maintained in order to sustain ideal images of parental figures. The defensively idealized structures that are fused with rage operate in an unintegrated, disembodied manner, in which the ego is uncontacted except through emotional flooding.

The therapist can perceive that the purpose of this idealized structure is not only sadistic and vengeful, but also utterly demanding; its injunction is quite simply to always be one's best. So grandiose a demand — thrust into the therapeutic process where it can be exceptionally trying and also imposed upon the world at large — is rarely successful. In spite of the fact that there may be deposits of wisdom in these grandiose endeavors, it should not be surprising that most people refuse to accept the potentially positive aspects of the borderline person's too corrosive idealizing process.

An ensnaring *vision* is part of the borderline person's mode of survival. Under its pressure the therapist wants to get away. *Everyone* wants to get away from the borderline person who functions in this negative state. If this imaginal mode were to be integrated into a relationship with the ego, the borderline patient would be able to *see* the parts of the object that actually mean to do harm, that is, the harm of not being present with the patient in an honest manner. When not persecuting others and feeling persecuted by split-off vision the borderline person, often charismatic and creative, can be a link to the *numinosum*, to the power of the gods, and especially to those gods long since displaced by normal collective awareness.

To be sure, the borderline person may seem unreal and even a bit inhuman when dispensing such positive energy and knowledge. My notes after seeing one borderline patient typify this experience:

> There is a strange, uncomfortable, somewhat inhuman feeling to her. It feels somewhat like having a dream with an archaic figure who speaks in a stilted language from a distant century, yet carries a strong affect. She speaks to me in plain English, has affects I clearly recognize, is suffering, yet also seems inhuman, of a different species. Her words each carry a fullness that feels like they each link to a greater whole, yet they are expressed in a strangely shallow manner. Alternatively, she has great depth and insight. But each moment is strained, too full and also too empty. She seems an outcast, living on the fringes of the world, cast into a dark shadow of inhuman, archetypal processes and speaking through them as if she were partaking of a human dialogue. She seems a princess, a witch, a clown, a trickster. We are in a fairy tale world of abstract characters which quickly turn back to flesh and blood reality. I am left feeling guilty for ever thinking of her as anything other than genuine.

The narcissistic person rarely reaches this level of depth and complexity. For example, the therapist can escape the censure of superficiality as long as he or she does not impose upon the patient's need to be the absolute center of attention. With the borderline person, instances of superficiality or foiled attention come back to haunt the therapist. Any form of falseness is usually interpreted as a persecutory act. A word or phrase can suddenly dominate a session and severely undermine the therapeutic alliance. The borderline person is often severely critical due to a sure knowledge that such false slips, if allowed to pass, will add more demons to the inner world. The borderline person's life can seem to hang on the balance of a word.

Exhibitionism and Fraudulence

Exhibitionism is the act whereby the self, under the agency of the ego, manifests in a fullness of expression symbolic of the whole person. Whether it takes the form of an infant's display of and satisfaction in his or her prowess, or an adult's coming forth in the creative fullness of what he or she believes, exhibitionism is a vital aspect of individuation. In their pathological forms, the archetypal energies of exhibitionism are fused with the ego, leading to both ego inflation and constriction of the self—an undermining of its unfolding through deintegration (Fordham 1976). In their healthy forms, exhibitionistic energies are experienced as separate from the ego. But even when this differentiation is noted, there is still some fusion with archetypal energies in healthy exhibitionism. The process of individuation is never free from such "polluted" states— refining and separating from the fusion with archetypal energies is an ongoing process. Consequently, there is no firm demarcation between healthy and pathological forms of exhibitionism, but its pathological formations are most evident in the borderline patient.

On the one hand, the quality of exhibitionism found in the borderline patient is a deep layer of that in the narcissistic person and usually only becomes manifest when the narcissistic character structure begins to transform (Schwartz-Salant 1982, p. 155ff.). On the other hand, the narcissistic personality structure, because of its greater cohesiveness, is able to contain a greater degree of exhibitionistic energies than is found in borderline individuals.

Some illustrations will be useful to help portray the pathology of exhibitionism in the borderline patient. A male borderline patient says: "I'll be killed if I really show myself. I will be too vulnerable to criticism." For this person, the simple desire of wanting to be *seen* fractures into polarities of complete fusion or total lack of contact. At one moment, the person feels safe in the fantasy of being absorbed into another person; at the next, this fusion state is terrifying, for it makes the patient feel too vulnerable to the danger of rejection or absorption and an ensuing loss of identity. In the process of therapy I commonly experience the feeling that the patient wants to merge with me, but these states are frequently exchanged for long stretches in which there is no linking of any kind.

Another borderline patient speaks of being terrorized by his sexual energies. For not only does he risk vulnerability by revealing these energies, but he might also expose his power and greed, especially the consuming wish to devour his partner.

A woman patient explains that an awful sense of shame overtakes her when she begins to *be* rather than do, for in *being* her worthlessness will become evident and she will not be taken seriously. Another woman patient begins to tell me about something wonderful that has happened to her, then immediately imagines that she is inside a glass jar. I respond by feeling as if I'm with a storyteller who "acts out" intense feelings; consequently, these feelings don't reach me since her affect is cut off. This patient fears that if she is simply herself, she can expect nothing but a dull, disinterested response from me, just as her father was uninterested in her. The borderline person's most haunting fears usually come true. In this instance, the glass "jar" assures my patient's continuing isolation. She can live comfortably inside her "jar," but to disclose her thoughts and experiences to another is terrifying; the energies involved are too intense to bear.

When a borderline patient states that his or her exhibitionistic energies will become too powerful, we need to understand that this statement of omnipotence often expresses the belief that if power and creativity are actually felt and expressed, no other person will be a match for these energies and abandonment will surely follow. The borderline patient's childhood experiences have contributed to the formation of this belief system, and in fact, abandonment is often experienced in later life when exhibitionistic energies are displayed. But this expectation will not *always* prove to be correct; it is omnipotent and must be challenged. These possibilities—abandonment or the experiences of being accepted— are intertwined in the borderline person; moreover, the borderline person tends to provoke difficulties, since he or she usually enters relationships that become disastrous self-fulfilling prophecies. If we are to understand the borderline person, we must recognize that conventional definitions of inflation or omnipotence are often poor indicators for the profound fears embedded in such statements as, "I'll be too powerful," or, "I'll be so filled with greed that I'll devour you." We must be aware that the borderline person is open to powerful archetypal energies that can be emotionally overwhelming and dismembering to the ego. For this reason, these energies erupt and overwhelm the person and frequently the object as well.

The narcissistic person is protected from the archetypal realm by a narcissistic defense. The borderline person's defense system is less cohesive; he or she must depend upon defenses that are archaic and fragment-ing. The narcissistic person may fall into an enfeebled state if his or her defense fails, but this person can easily recover with the help of the therapist's empathic responses. The borderline person tends to rebound far more slowly.

Because of the borderline person's extreme vulnerability to emo-tional flooding, exhibitionistic energies are considered to be dangerous; even small quotients of it lead to guilt, fear, panic, and shame. This is also true of the narcissistic person when his or her self-esteem is threat-ened by loss of control. But with the borderline person the threat of being overwhelmed frequently obscures far deeper issues. A level of mindlessness prevails, and there is a sense that nothing—that is, no authentic self—exists. Instead, there is only void and deception. One of the borderline person's deep-seated fears is the exposure of fraudulence. While fears of displaying one's energies, or counterphobic excesses of exhibitionism are important, they usually cover the deeper issue of a sense of absence of an authentic self. Exhibitionism and a sense of fraud-ulence combine in borderline states of mind; muddled and complex inter-actions often become clearer when the therapist is able to grasp this connection.

During a group therapy session a woman asked the leader: "If someone has come to your beginning workshops, do they have to pay if they come again?" The leader was confused, and so was everyone in the group. No one could understand what she was saying. She repeated it. They still did not understand. The source of this confusion lay in a split-off anger that was masked by her seemingly clear question. A more honest statement would have been: "*You* want me to come to your work-shops; *you* are imposing that requirement on me. If I continue to come to them, which I really don't want to do, why should I have to continue to pay?" The woman herself had no idea why she hadn't been understood. But her matter-of-fact statement, which was a splitting device encapsu-lating what she really felt, confused everyone; each person in the group had a different understanding of what she was actually saying. This woman's fear of exhibitionism—in this instance a fear of revealing her true feelings—was too powerful to tolerate. As a result, she split, couch-ing her true feelings and questions—specifically her aggression—in dilute form. A degree of sadism was evident in this choice of behavior: the confusion of the other people provided this woman with the rare and pleasurable sense of being in control. But the far deeper issue that emerged in this context was this woman's struggle to hide her feeling of mindlessness and inauthenticity. Commonly, such confused states are split off and constellated in another person through projective identification.

One of my patients began a session by telling me a story about something she had accomplished. As she spoke, I felt myself become dull and listless; I had difficulty finding anything to say and in being spontaneous. The only response I could muster was: "That's a good story." Actually there was a genuineness in saying this, for I felt she was telling me *a story of her own*, and that her narration was a result of a good deal of psychological work she had already done. But my response communicated very little of this perception, and my minimal reply upset her. She complained that my answer was impersonal and aloof.

Once she communicated these feelings I felt more energized and found it easier to speak. I could now tell her what I meant by a "good story" and found that the answer satisfied her. I could also tell her that what she had accomplished was impressive; that is, I could personally relate to the tale she had told and finally recognize that my remark "a good story" was a meager response to her accomplishment. The patient asked the inevitable question: "What caused you to say at first that it was a good story?" Only then did I realize that she had made contact with me when she had become upset with my response, and that when she first began speaking, the lack of contact had enervated me; my initial feeling was one of swimming against a current of dullness.

As I reflected on this interaction, I realized that my original response had been that this woman seemed *contrary*. What she had been seeking was a warm, genuine, and engaged response. Yet she had split off from me, treating me instead like a spectator who was familiar with the appropriate conventions. However, once she contacted me with her complaint, my constraints vanished, and I could easily give her the simple, direct, and empathic response she wanted. In fact, my attitude toward her changed from near-neutrality to concern for the truth of what was taking place between us.

But why was my own involvement so slack? What might be a clue to my earlier minimal response? I could, of course, simply understand my sadism as a response to not having been emotionally contacted by her. This kind of countertransference is usually pronounced in the therapist working with the narcissistic person and represents the therapist's hatred at being treated as if he or she is not a real person. Or, relative to the narcissistic person, a therapist's constrained, minimal response can be an induced reaction connected with the patient's resistance to an idealized transference. For this woman something else was involved; beneath the genuine sense of accomplishment were unbearable feelings of being fundamentally unlovable. She also experienced feelings of dullness and emptiness and was convinced that her mind was blank and that she had nothing to offer. My minimal response is explained by the fact that she had split off from these feelings, and that I had introjected them.

The narcissistic person fuses with the exhibitionistic aspect of the self; the borderline person splits from it. When the grandiose-exhibitionistic self is constellated in the narcissistic person, its controlling effect upon others indicates a fusion state between ego and self. In a sense, the narcissistic person can appear to be completely undeveloped, whether we view this state as a secondary refusion (Kernberg 1975), or as a stalled development (Kohut 1971) awaiting empathic responses for its unfolding. But exhibitionism (and the self) develop differently in the borderline person, whose healthy exhibitionistic displays were generally *misused* by parental figures. Patients speak of having revealed their authentic selves to their parents, only to discover that they were valued solely as performers, not as separate persons, and that their true feelings were ignored even as they were tricked into believing these feelings actually mattered. Often the borderline person will complain bitterly that his or her talents were encouraged, then rebuffed, according to parental whims. This dynamic of parental misuse often proves disastrous. For the person experiences it as a rape of the self and, for survival's sake, has no other recourse than to split off from exhibitionistic longings, or display them in a manner that would assure their rejection.

As a split-off system, these exhibitionistic drives then assume an autonomous identity largely molded by internalized rage against the self and against parental figures. Eventually, as traumatic experiences energize it, this "system" becomes an internal enemy. It is clear that any genuine revelation of the self will then goad this internal system into activity, thus awakening the pain and hatred associated with it. But the most distressing aspect of this process is that the authentic self, with its exhibitionistic component, splits off and retreats. For the borderline person, entering this interior realm will unmask the most distressing "truth" of all: an endless, penetrating emptiness. Splitting becomes a way of life, and contacting the split-off exhibitionistic energies proves to be an endeavor that few have the heroic quality to endure. But while disclosure of the self is equated with psychic death, concealment is identified with fraudulence. The borderline person lives between these worlds, partaking of both but belonging to neither; hence, splitting from the pain of nonalignment offers temporary relief.

As a result of early defective object relations, the borderline person is left with little of a genuine, functioning self. For some borderline persons the *doing* of intellectual work becomes an obsessive activity that is meant to substitute for the ordering quality of the self, but in the process, any remaining vestige of *being* is undermined. Another alternative to having a functioning, inner self is for the person to gain a transcendent link to the *numinosum*, but this is usually accomplished only by undervaluing the shadow side of life. While often partaking of a genuine connection to spiritual energies, these endeavors are usually employed as a splitting maneuver to deny painful inner states of abandonment and associated, negative affects such as rage and hatred. Yet, in spite of this splitting device one often finds in the borderline person a deeper connection to religious matters than is the case with the narcissistic person, who is generally more concerned with appearances and tends to be more superficial in his or her beliefs. The borderline person's link to religious systems may be misused for splitting purposes, but one often finds an experience of the *numinosum* that survives, with modifications, as the borderline disorder heals. By contrast, the narcissistic person's religious leanings tend to be easily depleted, and the connection to the sacred is less authentic. In the narcissistic person exalted images and shallow intuitions often substitute for authentic religious experience.

Borderline and narcissistic persons relate in different ways to history. For example, in his or her despairing inner state, the borderline person can experience empathic failures as ruthless acts of disregard and will become ruthless in kind. But this ruthlessness is most upsetting. For the borderline person can behave as if the Other has never existed; history and continuity are decisively eradicated and the successful working-through of all previous interactions is dismissed. In work with the narcissistic person, the therapist's awareness of his or her own empathic failures and communication of them to the patient will usually restore the therapy process to its historical context, which had been submerged by the patient's rage at such failures. But with the borderline person, one often finds oneself in a kind of no-man's land, a painful state in which the governing truth is that absolutely no connection exists at all between patient and therapist.

The narcissistic person has a rather dim sense of his or her personal history. The frequent repetition of stories is symptomatic of the lack of a solid sense of history and the need to feel effective (Schwartz-Salant 1982, p. 39). The borderline person may have a keen sense of history, but is prepared to shatter it completely and is seemingly able to create a psychic attack from its fragments. The rage and hatred that precipitate the attack and the ensuing guilt then become a grave threat to the borderline person's sense of identity. These affects often lead to deep regressions and into psychotic states that diffuse identity still further.

The narcissist is adaptable and slick in social interactions and knows how to be seductive and manipulative. By contrast, the borderline person is often an outsider. Life is like a continual game in which the ruling question is: how bad will it be this time? This negative expectation projects itself into the environment almost at random. Uncertainty will arise over a simple encounter with friends, a new job, an impending exam — nearly anything. For the borderline person, everyone else "knows the rules and fits in"; he or she alone must gamble against what feels like loaded stakes, hoping that awkward efforts will go unnoticed. Indeed, the borderline individual usually does not "fit in," since splitting processes have depleted inner resources and positive identifications.

We can say that the narcissistic person was called upon to realize his or her potential — what one could eventually be — far too early in life. Innate talents and what these could produce were more valued by parental figures than one's actual being. In infancy and childhood the narcissistic person suffered from a devastating hatred unleashed by envy. The life of the narcissistic person is an incessant drive toward *doing* punctuated by interludes of depression and regression (Kohut 1971, p. 97).

The borderline person's potential rarely takes coherent form; nor does this person find solace in the troublesome "specialness" that haunts the narcissistic person. Moreover, the affects that temporarily deflate the narcissistic person furiously attack the borderline person in his or her struggle toward individuation. It would appear that the borderline person lives so close to persecutory energy fields that he or she remains chronically open to psychic dismemberment.

While the narcissistic person uses people until needs are met, and discards them only when other offerings prove more enticing, the borderline person goes through a far more rapid interplay. One day the "Other" represents everything marvelous and is treated with exuberant appreciation; the next day, when the borderline person feels "bad," this (ostensibly same) Other appears to be poisonous. The atmosphere can feel tense, the Other may have difficulty in breathing and may feel insecure. This hitherto admirable Other may talk a lot, or, alternatively, feel that it is hard to say anything. It is relatively easy to decipher and respond to the experience of rejection incurred with the narcissistic person, for as soon as one recognizes the nature of the narcissistic transference it is often possible to settle down and respect its purpose. This is not the case with the borderline person. Here, one feels driven to *do something*, and if these feelings are carefully examined, it soon emerges that the therapist's unconscious intention is to survive with an intact sense of identity. There is a mounting tendency know everything, to have a complete grasp of the situation. This urge to omnipotence is amplified by sensations of feeling mechanical, verbose and disembodied.

There are times when the borderline person is "normal" in the best sense of the word, that is, concerned with soul and aware of and disturbed by the suffering of others. Indeed, the borderline person is often more genuine than the "normal" person. It is worth speculating that swings between "all good" and "all persecutory" states may be defenses summoned against this soul-centered state, for to be genuine often leads to the experience of unendurable pain.

There is little passionate humanity in the narcissistic person, who is generally so cut off from the inner world that the notion of "soul" is rendered meaningless. The borderline person has more than passing acquaintance with the realm of soul, but carefully stores such connection from view. Despair is the major mode of concealment. The narcissistic person does not suffer despair, since it is carefully denied by the cohesiveness and density of the narcissistic defense.

A Clinical Vignette

"Jim," a forty-year-old male patient, told me about a house he wanted to buy. I alerted him to what felt to me to be his compulsion to act, which was masking anxieties about purchasing the house. He recognized that he didn't want to focus on these anxieties, since they represented a threat to him. "My anxiety might tell me how wrong this purchase is," he said and then speculated that focusing upon these anxieties would dilute his passion to have his own house. In fact, his mother had already argued against buying the house. I encouraged Jim to heed his anxieties, and as he did so, I experienced the field of anxiety that existed between us. My imagination focused upon certain things he had mentioned about the house, particularly the anticipatory joy of ownership and the fears that had immediately surfaced and disturbed that joy. Then I felt as if Jim's age were changing; it was suddenly as if I were with a young child. My mounting anxiety and bodily rigidity also guided me to mention issues that were underlying his fears. For example, I spoke to him of his concern over the condition of a well that serviced the house. Several weeks earlier he had spoken favorably about an arrangement that allowed the tenants of several neighboring houses to share the same well. Not wanting to dampen his excitement, I had let my discomfort with his reaction pass. Now, however, I was able to probe his doubts without damaging his enthusiasm.

In the next session Jim discussed the house more fully. On this occasion he praised the building inspector who had so responsibly assessed the problem concerning the well. At this point I stopped him and asked for more details. He replied that "if the sellers insist upon my being responsible for the well, I won't do the deal." This response seemed odd to me, for he seemed to be capriciously abandoning his desire for the house. I began to explore this statement with him with some energy, and I suddenly felt and began to speak as if I knew a great deal about this well. Then I stopped as I became aware of Jim's awkward and pronounced idealization of me, which had undoubtedly given impetus to my sudden spurt of "knowledge." Jim continued with some emotion: "What's happening here is very important," he said, "because I have no idea what *I* think about this well. All I know is that I don't want you or anyone to think I'm immature. Somehow I have to know what your opinion is concerning the right procedure. I know nothing myself."

Jim then tried to neutralize this confession by using intellectual props. At this point I stopped him, noting the anxiety present in our interaction. Jim wondered why he felt anxious. As we experienced this anxiety field together I came to the realization that he was afraid, and I said so. His answer was, "Yes, but why?" I answered that his fear might stem from daring to own his own creative process, symbolized by his venture to buy the house. I added that he was in same the situation as any small child in the process of separating from his family and that he was terrified that any genuine, autonomous action would result in abandonment. I then explained that any thought or act he contemplated was

68

always modulated by what he assumed other people, and, particularly, what I would think.

At this juncture, I experienced the sensation that we were glued together like siamese twins. This feeling had not been present earlier, when I had been placed in the idealized position of "knowing everything." As the idealization dissipated and we began to confront Jim's underlying abandonment fear, our dynamic changed. There was now a feeling of being glued together in a fusion state. It seemed that whatever I thought, he would try to think, and whatever I felt, he would try to intuit and feel. Soon it grew painfully clear to Jim that "mimicry," however much he disliked it, was a survival mechanism. I became the target, alternatively, of two typical narcissistic configurations, an idealized transference and a twinship, mirroring transference. Yet in this case it was evident that neither transference could offer the cohesiveness that would be accessible to a person with a narcissistic character disorder. These kinds of transferences can sufficiently isolate the narcissistic person from experiencing the underlying terror of persecution that attends abandonment fears. But in Jim's case, these abandonment states easily leaked into consciousness.

Had Jim suffered from a narcissistic character disorder, I could not have proceeded as I did, for he would have been terrified by my interpretations and imaginal penetration and probably would have become narcissistically enraged. Jim's psyche, with its more fragmentary nature precluded the cohesive-defensive quality that idealizing and mirror transferences offer the narcissistic person to control the object. In this sense, cohesiveness is both an advantage and a disadvantage. The narcissistic person can "get by" in life rather easily, often with little suffering. The price one pays, however, is superficiality of personality, a trait that usually worsens with age. When narcissistic transferences faltered in Jim (who had a borderline personality with an "as-if" quality), obsessional control took over; once this control yielded, a pool of pain and despair was evident. These same affects certainly exist in the narcissistic person, but the narcissistic defense and specific transference modes mitigate against the person's deeply feeling them.

But I was able to go further with Jim, who had by now come into contact with his fear. It was of little help for us to know that he was fearful. The borderline person's ego and sense of self are severely limited and connections to the unconscious (as, for example, through the experience of fear) are tenuous and unlikely to be able to connect the person to his or her self—to a core identity. Linkage to the unconscious through the therapist's interpretation can leave the patient feeling more helpless than ever.

I asked Jim to concentrate full attention upon his fear. As he focused on his apprehension I began to *see* a young child in him. He, too, could imagine an inner four-year-old child who seemed to adapt to his childhood milieu but was in fact anxious, confused, and unsure of anything he felt, despite his masterly performance. Life was a game of survival for this four-year-old child. It was characterized by a terrifying moment-by-moment existence. Yet the child's awareness of this state was masked by a plastic persona, and the child inside Jim did not know how awful he felt.

I suggested that Jim try to feel physically close to the child. He answered that he felt resistance to this child, for the child seemed empty and totally cynical. Indeed, he hated this child and was deeply ashamed that is was a part of him. He perceived this child's deep-seated cynicism and distrust of everyone to be terribly dangerous. Yet Jim also sensed that the child could offer useful insights and might even be able to solve the well problem in the house he was going to buy.

I explained to Jim that his feelings of total inadequacy and his inclination to identify with the wants of others (even to the exclusion of what he might wish for himself) belonged to the child part of him. This child part was inducing these states in Jim as a means of communicating with him. But this statement was not much help to him, for Jim was essentially terrified of the child within. He then asked whether he should "let the child speak in meeting with real estate agents," and I told him that if he could imaginally keep the child close to him, he would then be closer to his own body. Largely because Jim's borderline condition was mild, he was able to carry with him an awareness of this. Later, he could feel it during business meetings, and he eventually surprised himself with a capacity for clarity and assertiveness. Clearly, Jim's child-part carried crucial aspects of the self that had been split off as a result of his early familial experiences.

It would be a precarious venture to proceed with more severely borderline persons as I did with Jim. For with severely borderline persons, splitting, denial, and the sense of helplessness are more volatile. Jim could partially carry his own process; others with a less-developed capacity to do so might easily feel overwhelmed by the burden of the inner child. Borderline patients often have an ambivalent relationship to the inner child, especially because the child that first appears is often neither nice nor loving. The split-off child part is often hated because its despair and rage invade the ego and because (as far as the collective is concerned) it does everything it "shouldn't" and with violent affects. Patient and therapist must imaginally care for the child and, as in certain shamanic practices, speak directly to it to successfully link this inner child to the ego. In this way, the therapist can directly engage the patient's unconscious rather than route interventions and interpretations through his or her more conscious personality. Often, we must imaginally perceive and engage the inner child and be its advocate against the patient's hatred and splitting defenses. Jim was able to maintain contact with the child for several weeks. Then, under the stress of a new situation, this connection was severed, and he resorted to habitual intellectual defenses. Then, I had to recover the child for him and act as its advocate. This kind of support is of course gently withdrawn as the patient requires it less and can retain the child more securely.

Admittedly, this therapeutic approach proceeds through an imaginal set in which the therapist actively engages the patient's psyche. Without this kind of interaction the patient will be unable to integrate his or her split-off parts. Moreover, the split-off child part is terrified of the adult part who wishes its destruction. Hence, the therapist must strive for the imaginal act, since interpretation alone falters badly and leaves the person feeling helpless.

If Jim had had a narcissistic character disorder with a capacity for more stable idealizing and mirroring transferences, I would not have imaginally entered into his inner world, but would have been empathic toward the obvious and controlling demands of idealization and mirroring. Yet, if this same approach is taken with the borderline patient, the therapist fortifies the relatively normal/neurotic functional part of the patient, yet rarely penetrates the far more important world of the patient's split-off child.

CHAPTER THREE
PEOPLE AS GODS: REALITY DISTORTION
AND THE SELF

Incarnation [on] the human level appears as individuation. (C. G. Jung 1942, p. 171)

Introduction

The borderline person commonly distorts reality. For example, after several years of treatment a woman began to experience her abandonment fears near the end of every session, and especially on Fridays. Her weekends were then lived in withdrawal, sadness, and the pain of having no memory of my image. "You're completely gone," she would say. After about six months of hysterical outbursts at the end of our sessions, and ensuing painful weekends, I noticed that she was managing the upcoming weekend break better and even seemed to be taking it in stride. Then, as one Friday session ended and she walked to the door, she caught herself thinking, "It's Wednesday, and I'll see him on Friday." She became conscious that she had been denying, throughout this six-month period, that her Friday session ended the week. Her weekend experience eventually changed to include a more realistic suffering of the absence of my image. In the weeks that followed, memories of my image began to become somewhat more accessible to her, and she also became less withdrawn.

The borderline person often distorts reality with extreme "good–bad" splitting. For example, a patient may say he or she hates someone, but may in the next hour praise the same person as the "most wonderful friend in the world." This oscillation can become very perplexing; the therapist may be tempted to mention it. But if he or she were to do so the patient would undoubtedly feel misunderstood and attacked, and the abandonment experience so feared would, in fact, occur. In psychotherapy one must find more discreet ways to heal such "good-–bad" splitting, for through it the borderline person manages to hold off extremely attacking affects. Generally, such splitting and idealization plays a large role in the borderline patient's distortions of reality. As the borderline person tells stories about the marvelous qualities of another person, the distorted nature of these tales is often evident. It is not a matter of lies, but rather of the patient trying to retain a good object, even at the expense of denying its extremely destructive behavior. The borderline patient often takes a quantum leap forward in individuation when it becomes possible to tolerate hatred, not only his or her own hatred, but also the experience of being the target of malice of another.

In dealing with the distortions of the borderline patient it is sometimes necessary to stay on the level of the person's explicitly stated concerns. For example, a patient was not being paid by the firm for which he freelanced, which usually was thirty days late in making its payment. The firm sent him a contract to sign that would have set aside a large sum of money per year for his future work and told him that such an agreement would facilitate future payments. "To teach them a lesson," he planned not to sign the contract, especially because he had found two clauses in it that were not in his interest. I explained that he was distorting the actual situation by maintaining an illusion that the company was an all-good object that should love and respect him and immediately meet his needs, and that he had reacted with anger when the object failed to comply with this illusion. This interpretation made him angry with me for "not understanding him" and for "undermining his need to confront people." (We had previously been working on his inability to be confrontative.) In the following session he appeared quite chagrined. He had reread the contract and found that he had earlier misread it. He had almost sent it back with an angry note to the effect that he wouldn't sign unless the two clauses were changed and he was immediately paid. As it turned out, the clauses were what he desired after all! If he had acted out his feelings, which my intervention appeared to block, he probably would have lost the account, something he could ill afford to have done.

If I had acted upon the notion that responding to him on a manifest level would ignore his real (latent) communication to me about our therapy process, I would have been risking creating a serious abandonment experience by refusing to take notice of his outer level needs at a time when he was not accurately perceiving reality. Had I acted in this fashion, I would have essentially allowed him to destroy his account with the company.

The reality distortions that occur in treatment of the borderline person often revolve around splitting a painful situation into an "all-good" and "all-bad" opposition and then denying the "bad" opposite of this pair. In the first example, my patient denied it was Friday; she had thus split off the abandonment threat of the weekend and replaced it with a positive image that I would see her on Wednesday. In the second example, an "all-good" or "all-bad" quality was alternately projected onto the firm for which the patient freelanced. In this way he attempted to gain mastery over an inner, persecuting state and in the process distorted reality. Generally, reality distortion follows upon the heels of splitting, for this process requires that the opposites be kept separate so that "the left hand doesn't know what the right hand is doing." Reality is distorted to achieve this aim. At times, the therapist will work with the borderline patient in ways that feel like a juggling act in order to join the opposing responses the patient denies. Having done so, the therapist may have the impression that some synthesis has been achieved. The patient might seem capable of facing another person's hatred and able to handle the fear and negative feelings engendered by such an awareness. But at the end of the session, he or she may make some remark that completely undoes everything that has transpired, indicating that the most blatant splitting and idealization have returned. The therapist has been foolishly acting as if moving the tip of an iceberg could change its course.

The act of splitting objects into "all-good" and "all-bad" opposites is not the only behavior that underlies reality distortion. Instead, the inner world of the borderline person may become extremely fragmented, with each different part having autonomy. For example, a woman inwardly denied the loss of her father by creating four inner "fathers," any one of which could determine her attitudes toward an abandonment threat in her life or the therapeutic process. These delusional constructs allowed her to deny her pain, but also resulted in severe distortions of outer reality. For example, one of her "fathers" was an idealized image that was projected onto her husband; consequently, she failed to notice that her husband was having affairs with other women, a distortion that eventually brought her a great deal of misery. This was but one of many ways through which she distorted reality. She was forced to deny numerous other perceptions to keep her splitting process intact. Generally, the splitting of the patient's ego into two or more opposing parts is the underlying factor in reality distortion, and the projective processes that accompany it can create considerable confusion.

An example of reality distortion that includes both splitting and projection is illustrated by the following story. A man had decided to work on a weekend and felt reticent to tell his wife about it, knowing how much she disliked his doing so. When he finally told her, she accused him of betraying her trust and going back on his word. He was shocked by this reaction, for even though he knew she would be displeased, he was unprepared for the intensity of her reaction. As they spoke, he began to feel confused, especially as she, with seeming precision, was able to recall that in their previous discussions he had promised to not work weekends. This time, however, he experienced this interaction with her to be familiar, and this was an important change for him, since it indicated a newfound capacity for reflection. He was able to refrain from his usual reactions of becoming hysterical and defensive, and simply asked her what she meant. His wife referred to their earlier conversation about his work schedule. As she spoke, he again found himself becoming confused, defensive, and guilty; thinking became very difficult. With great effort he was able to recall a conversation in which she had indeed asked that he not work on weekends. But he then remembered that he had never agreed to this, and instead had sidestepped the issue by saying he would try. In saying even that much at the time, in the face of his wife's assaults that he could barely withstand, he had felt quite heroic. But in fact, his cowardice came back to haunt him, for his failure to state firmly and clearly that he might have to work on some weekends led his wife to create a new version of the reality between them. Her image of a husband who did not work weekends (which to her meant that he did not abandon her) was projected onto him. When he did not separate himself from this projection but instead remained noncommittal, she introjected it *along with his implicit consent which was transmitted by his not taking a firm stand.* She then distorted their conversation to conclude that he had agreed to her proposition. It was no wonder that he felt some trepidation in telling her that he was going to work on the weekend.

This type of interaction is common with the borderline patient who manifests paranoid features. The patient projects psychic contents onto the therapist and then introjects the projection *along with contents that are generated by the therapist's unconscious process.* This may be a thought or feeling that the therapist has but does not mention, or, as in the last example, it may result from allowing a vacuum to form by not being explicit, a vacuum then filled by the patient's own projected needs, which are then reintrojected. When this content is later presented as something the therapist has actually said or done, it feels extremely confusing, since it is a mixture of the patient's projection *and* aspects of the therapist's unconscious process that the patient has introjected; this communication feels strangely correct but also grossly distorted. These experiences of reality distortion are made even more complicated by the kinds of issues already discussed concerning the borderline patient's accurate perceptions—namely, that the person's perceptions about the inner workings of the therapist can be very much on target. Consequently, it is easy to assign an unusual "knowledge" to the borderline patient. When the therapist operates with this mind-set, he or she is easily battered by the patient's statements, even when these are primarily fabricated through splitting, denial, and projective mechanisms. It is important that the therapist not sidestep negative affects in a quest for harmony.

I would like to focus upon a quality of reality distortion that manifests in splitting, idealization and denial but is very difficult to uncover and has a powerful influence upon the life of many borderline people. It is an archetypal projection onto a human being of an Old Testament-like god-image. One can find a good deal in Jung's writings about the psychological meaning of this image (1942, 1952).

Object Relations and Internal Structure
Jung often states that he was led to investigate the history and psychological origins of religion and alchemy as a result of his clinical work with patients who were in the depths of the individuation process. He believed he could understand his patients only by delving into ancient strata of the mind, beyond what could be solely attributed to structures acquired through introjection and identification processes of infancy or later development. Jung's writings on the Old Testament patriarchal god-image, Yahweh, help us to understand the ways in which this image can function in the borderline person. One often finds a projection operating in this patient that is extremely difficult to uncover and dismantle: the object is invested with the image of the father god, and because of the delusional nature of the projection it is extremely difficult to effect its withdrawal.

The psychological condition that Jung called the world of the Father is a state in which "Man, world, and God form a whole, a unity unclouded by criticism" (1942, par. 201). "The world of the Father typifies an age which is characterized by a pristine oneness with the whole of Nature, no matter whether this oneness be beautiful or ugly or awe inspiring" (ibid.). "It is a passive unreflecting condition, a mere awareness of what is given, without intellectual or moral judgment. This is true both individually and collectively" (1942, par. 270). "Yahweh is not split but is an *antinomy* totality of inner opposites. . . . " (1952, par. 567). Yahweh is thus a *complexio oppositorum,* a numinous whole, and not an "all-good" or "all-bad" part object.

This has radical implications, since it means that *Jung's starting point for the acquisition of inner structure is a whole object. This approach differs from the part-object psychology that most other approaches usually take as their point of departure.*[1] This is a crucial clinical issue, for it affects how we view the earliest days and months of life. One can argue that a child, in this view, is a "child of God" (Elkin 1972) born with an Object and not in an autistic or preobject state. The experiences the infant has in its earliest (perhaps prenatal) months of life leave a residue that haunts many borderline people. It is the residue of a joy that has been lost and of a link to the *numinosum* that seems forever severed. Yet, the desire for that dimly remembered state lingers, taking the form of an unconscious quest for the Father.

It should be noted that "God the Father" can be projected onto and carried by a male or female object, just as maternal archetypes can be projected onto and carried by a male figure. We are dealing with a particular archetypal constellation that exists a priori to the objects which may carry it through projection. In some mythologies, what Jung calls the "Father" may also incarnate in feminine form.[2] We are dealing with a pattern of a nonincarnate Spirit that is projected onto a real person. The Father is an aspect of the *spiritual Self,* but is only one of the forms that this Self takes, though a significant one to be sure. Most of us have been brought up within the reigning power of the Old Testament god-image.

The hallmark of a creative relationship with a patriarchal god-image is the ability to link with an outer Object that is felt to be numinous, whole and caring, richly complex and full of meaning and depth. The Object that is so endowed can also have negative characteristics. In

---

[1]An exception is found in R. Fairbairn, who postulated an original whole object (1952).

[2]For example, in aspects of the sky goddess Nut from Egyptian mythology, or in qualities of the Shinto sun goddess.

78

the borderline person, the premature loss of this relationship to the *numinosum* is a trauma that clouds future development. This person's individuation process is then fixated on a search for the sacred link and pathological attempts to recreate it. The pathology lies in the borderline person's unconscious and delusional identification of a human being with the numinous image. This person is likely to employ idealization, splitting and repression for the purpose of creating someone in the image of the archetype.

The nature of the patient's relationship to the archetypal god-image is not revealed if the therapist considers it to be merely a narcissistic, idealized transference. On the one hand, an unconscious process is occurring; the patient does not know of its existence and is unaware that his or her psychic energies are being devoted to the task of keeping the projected god-image alive, even at the cost of engaging life on one's own. On the other hand, when the therapist points out the faults of the object carrying the god-image, and even if these faults are very clearly seen by the borderline patient, the projection remains undisturbed. This is contrary to what happens when an idealization is shaken. The nature of the archetypal transference is deeper than that of a narcissistic transference. At times, working through an idealized transference is a precondition for uncovering a schizoid dynamic that hides archetypal, delusional material. This schizoid dynamic should in no way be considered to be a defense against an idealized transference.

The patriarchal god-image when projected onto a real person caricatures the borderline person's connection to the Godhead. No human object is suited to carry the god-projection. When a person is invested with this image, the vitality of the projection must be repeatedly energized. A man reported a repetitive childhood dream of riding on the back of superman while having anal intercourse with him. It seems that he had to do this in order to keep superman going! A woman maintained a father-god projection onto her lover by making him potent through the energy of her own sexuality. When she departed from this behavior, discontinued her seductive behavior, and waited for his sexuality to function without her, he became impotent. This was the beginning of her awareness of the nature of her projection. But the hope that the potency and transforming power of an object can change one's life and create a self can go on in the face of the most glaring contradictions between reality and the god-projection. Usually, this expectation only dissolves after years of therapeutic work. To complicate matters, the observer

79

usually does not know that a delusion has been working behind the scenes, for the patient who is possessed by the delusion often appears to be realistic about the actual characteristics of the person who carries the god-projection. The patient may complain about the hopelessness of the relationship and be painfully aware of the deficiencies of the object. Yet the relationship continues. This bond is loosened when the patient is able to experience and come to terms with abandonment fears. But defense against abandonment, in spite of its central importance, does not sufficiently explain the patient's resistance to change, which has to do with a delusion at work—one that incorporates the belief that the object *is* the patriarchal God so fervently desired.

Clinical Example

The following material illustrates the transformation of the delusional relationship to the patriarchal god-image. A woman reported the following dream:

> I am with my boyfriend. My father is small and on a shelf some distance away. A chicken lies next to me. I take my boyfriend's penis off his body. But it starts to become alive and move on its own, and I become frightened and insert it into the backside of the chicken. Then I worry the penis will now be poisoned. I hurry to put it into a refrigerator.

I first saw the chicken as a maternal image, and the act of taking the penis an envy-related theft. The woman's envy, in this line of thought, spoils her introject of the father's phallus, and she is left feeling persecuted and in need of strong splitting defenses. This interpretation, which refers to her deep-seated hatred of her father for his emotional absence, had little effect until a far more profound fantasy was uncovered.

Only when this woman came to the realization that she was living a delusional belief, that is, that the man in her dream was a person with whom she could have a harmonious relationship—one through which "God the Father" might be experienced—could change begin to occur. We could also begin to realize the dream's much deeper meaning. In this later, more satisfying, interpretation, the penis represents the patient's drive to reenergize her father, for the chicken is not primarily a mother symbol but represents her father's "chicken" anima. The woman had described her father as being agoraphobic and terrified of the world. In spite of his ardent spiritual values, which took the form of study and meditation, he was unable to actualize these values. He was, so to speak, "on the shelf." By taking the penis, the woman was attempting to energize him so that he could support her Father projection.

This imaginal act was fueled by incestuous fantasies. It was also contaminated by envy, which sprang from this patient's belief that she could never have the emotional sustenance that she really wanted. The incestuous element acted as a barrier to the incarnation of the patriarchal god-image as an inner self-experience within this woman. In the years prior to her therapy she had had numerous dreams of special objects (for example, spaceships or marvelous birds) descending from heaven but becoming poisonous upon approaching earth. Thus, the god-image, poisoned by incest, could not become part of an interior self.

A significant portion of the dream is that in which the penis frightens the dreamer by gaining its own life. The penis is a symbol of the dreamer's autonomous and archetypal phallic power. To take the penis for herself would mean this woman had relinquished the fantasy of healing her father. This is an aspect of a syndrome that may be described as follows: the energy of the *numinosum* is sacrificed and given to a parental figure in the hope of regenerating that figure. The patient's fear of the *numinosum* is based upon his or her daring to take its power. In the case of this patient, fear was also a significant aspect of the "poison" she faced as archetypal images approached her ego-consciousness.

Once the delusional nature of the quest for a patriarchal god-image is faced, a severe, even schizoid, depression can set in. This is the point at which one acutely feels the absence of an inner self; death itself becomes an ally. Life ceases to seem worth living. Yet if the loss of this god-image can be sustained, a new phase can be entered and the inner self can begin to grow. In this particular case, the woman's painful process of realizing that her quest for harmony had been distorted by delusions led to a dream in which she saw a beautiful copper mandala situated behind a tombstone. Copper is usually associated with the Goddess Venus, and the patient was aware of this. The death of the old God would thus reveal the feminine values she had rejected. This transformation imagery concurs with Jung's exploration of the kinds of images that arise after the death of the patriarchal god-image (1937, p. 82, 94; 1952, p. 397). According to Jung's findings, a feminine aspect of the Self, denied and split off by the patriarchal attitude of the Judaeo-Christian religion, is latent in the collective unconscious. This feminine aspect is capable of transforming patriarchal Self-images that emphasize mind, spirit and laws in opposition to body, relatedness, and psychic reality.

The death of the delusional god-projection is necessary for the creation of an internal self. Little progress can be made in this regard unless the delusion is destroyed. A life based upon a delusional quest for the "Father" considerably influences the way a person's internal structure develops. It would appear that the delusion serves to split off a preverbal, helpless self, and while it is often possible to dissolve the delusion, frequently *a split-off infant part of the self remains untransformed*. In the case described above, the more adult side of the woman began to function more soundly. When dissolution of the delusional system diminished the splitting that had previously kept this infant part hidden and separate from the ego, more difficult treatment issues manifested.

My patient became more centered and creative in her daily work after the death of her delusion, but I found myself unwilling to see her desperate state of helplessness and instead aligned myself with her newfound strength. Eventually, this behavior brought forth her extremely ambivalent feelings toward me. She (correctly) perceived that I was behaving toward her as her father had, demanding that she be strong while he was emotionally absent. Partly as a result of the therapeutic "error" that elicited these negative feelings about her father, we were able to work with her negative feelings toward me. I find this process of "working through" a frequent occurrence in my work with borderline patients. We need to affirm the fact that errors must inevitably occur within the course of therapy, and that treatment evolves through their repair.

It is important to underscore that one major source of error likely to occur in work with the borderline patient is to overestimate his or her strength. For example, another woman patient, who had retreated to her borderline sector, was feeling more and more unable to function in life. At a certain point in the treatment she began to have many dreams in which the motif of a circle appeared. She asked for source material so that she could read about the circle image, and I suggested several sources. When she found one reference but not the other, she interpreted this as her "failure"; a state of panic state ensued, energizing an already florid death drive. This patient needed me to actively and carefully show her the reference, rather than merely allude to its source.

The Fourfold Structure and Feminine Aspect of the Self

How does a person's internal world come into existence? Does it stem from some larger and originally whole Object that must, in part, incarnate? Is this Object a numinous and transcendent Self, as Jung described the patriarchal god-image? Or might this Object be a romantic hypothesis that is easily undone by observations of infant development? Is a more adequate hypothesis one which states that the inner world is erected up through accumulations of pleasurable and unpleasurable stimuli, modified by internal processes and the empathy of an external mothering figure? And does the pain and suffering of early individuation result from the child's intense abandonment anxieties, an absence of the "good-enough mother?" (Winnicott 1971, p. 10). Should such an interpretation provide the model for the vicissitudes of all later development? Or is this pain of childhood and adult individuation the prerequisite for the incarnation of a far greater wholeness whereby this transcendent level contributes to the formation of an interior self?

In Jung's approach to the psyche, the universe of introjects of interpersonal relations is not the primary source of internal structure. Jung was extremely wary of the way in which object relations could distort truth. He placed little positive value on the process of identification, whereas object-relational approaches emphasize the heavy dependence of inner structure upon outer objects.

Jung's research into the transformation of the patriarchal god-image led him to conceptualize the *numinosum* as that energy which can become an internal center for a person. This incarnating process, however, is never complete; Jung likened it to the continual incarnation of the Holy Ghost, which, "On the human level appears as individuation" (1942, par. 233; 1952, par. 742). In object-relational approaches, the creation of a stable and organized inner world is also a major goal. Perhaps expression is being given to the same core matter in different ways; one approach is based on myth, the other on science.

Consider the following quote from Jung:

> Although the birth of Christ is an event that occurred but once in history, it has always existed in eternity. For the layman in these matters, the identity of a nontemporal, eternal event with a unique historical occurrence is something that is extremely difficult to conceive. He must, however, accustom himself to the idea that 'time' is a relative concept and needs to be complemented by that of the 'simultaneous' existence . . . of all historical processes. What exists . . . as an eternal process appears in time as an aperiodic sequence, that is to say, it is

repeated many times in an irregular pattern. . . . *When these things occur in modern variants, therefore, they should not be regarded merely as personal episodes, moods, or chance idiosyncrasies in people, but as fragments of the pleromatic process itself, which, broken up into individual events occurring in time, is an essential component or aspect of the divine drama."* (1952, pp. 400–401, italics added)

Jung differentiates what he calls eternal processes from the fragments of this process that shape themselves into individual events in time. He also refers to these eternal, atemporal events as occurring in the *pleroma* or *Bardo* (ibid.). These are two of the terms he uses in his writings to differentiate the space–time realm from the eternal order; others are the *Unus Mundus* (1955, pp. 462f.), *Mercurius* (1955, p. 465), and the Collective Unconscious. It is precisely this differentiation of events in space–time (for example, the stages of an infant's development) from the larger process in the pleroma, that distinguishes Jungian approaches to clinical material from all others:

> The causalism that underlies our scientific view of the world breaks everything down into individual processes which it punctiliously tries to isolate from all other parallel processes. This tendency is absolutely necessary if we are to gain reliable knowledge of the world, but philosophically it has the disadvantage of breaking up, or obscuring the universal interrelationship of events so that a recognition of the greater relationship, that is, of the unity of the world, becomes more and more difficult. Everything that happens, however, happens in the same 'one world' and is a part of it. For this reason, events must possess an *a priori* aspect of unity. . . . (1955, p. 464)

Jung's approach and pleromatic model is precisely the same as David Bohm's concept of an *implicate order* in modern physics (1980). Both turn attention to that greater unity out of which fragments (the discrete events we witness in space–time) fall and to which they return. In affinity with this ancient Hermetic wisdom (Bamford 1981, pp. 5–25), Bohm writes:

> Physics has become almost totally committed to the notion that the order of the universe is basically mechanistic. The most common form of this notion is that the world is assumed to be constituted by a set of separately existent, indivisible and unchangeable 'elementary particles', which are the fundamental 'building blocks' of the entire universe. Originally, these were thought to be atoms . . . but then, these were in turn found to be subject to transformation into hundreds of different kinds of unstable particles, and now even smaller particles called 'quarks' and 'partons' have been postulated to explain these transformations. Though these have not yet been isolated there appears to be an unshakable faith among physicists that either such particles, or some other kind yet to be discovered, will eventually [explain] everything. (1980, p. 173)

Bohm's model of the universe includes a primary state of whole-ness. His implicate order corresponds to Jung's pleroma. But in the normal space–time world, characterized as the explicate order, events are discontinuous and discrete, and their underlying wholeness vanishes from view:

> In terms of the implicate order one may say that everything is enfolded into everything. This contrasts with the explicate order now dominant in physics in which things are unfolded in the sense that each thing lies only in its own particular region of space (and time) and outside the regions belonging to other things. . . . What distinguishes the explicate order [is] a set or recurrent and relatively stable elements that are outside of each other. . . . In the prevailing mechanistic approach . . . these elements are taken as constituting the basic reality. . . . When one works in terms of the implicate order, one begins with the undivided wholeness of the universe, and the task of science is to derive the parts through abstraction from the whole. . . . (Bohm 1980, pp. 178–179)

We can see how clinicians understand psychic reality in terms of internal objects, part objects, complexes, transference and countertransference, etc. These are all conceptualizations that reside within the confines of the explicate order. If we apply Jungian theory, the same conceptualizations may be seen as fragments of the larger pleromatic process — just as Bohm insists that quarks and partons are fragments of a far larger implicate order.

Thus, developmental issues, including Klein's paranoid-schizoid and depressive positions (Segal 1980, pp. 113–124), or Mahler's Separation-Individuation process (1980, p. 9), can be seen as processes in space–time that stem from the larger pleromatic processes. We easily forget the vast energy sea of the pleroma or the implicate order when we cast these events into a developmental framework.

These observations are not meant to criticize the indisputable theoretical advance that developmental models offer psychology. But if we are to fully partake of their value, we must not allow the archetypal source of developmental stages to drift into a remote metapsychological background.

For instance, the paranoid-schizoid position is a state in which all linking (Bion 1967, pp. 93–109) is attacked. Alchemists would refer to this assault as a loss of the *vinculum,* the connecting function of the soul (Jung 1946, par. 504). From the perspective of an ego entering space–time, this state often induces intense anxiety that must be suffi-ciently neutralized by "good enough mothering" (Winnicott 1971, p. 10f.). But, what is the function of this intense, persecutory anxiety? It is believed by object relations theorists to instigate the dissolution of omnipotence and is sometimes linked to abandonment anxiety. Furthermore, persecutory anxiety of the paranoid-schizoid position is linked by Klein to the "death instinct." In Freud's view the "death instinct" drives the ego toward an *eros* relationship with objects (Freud 1923, p. 56). But if we accept Bion's view that the paranoid-schizoid state can dissolve psychic structures so that new ones might develop (Eigen 1985, pp. 321–322), we move closer to the offerings of archetypal imagery. For example, picture seven of the alchemical work, the *Rosarium,* reflects the phenomenology of the paranoid-schizoid position and reveals that the purpose of this extreme disorientation is to transform personality structure in order to facilitate a new embodiment of union. Hence, this stage of "the ascent of the soul" — in which an intense persecutory energy field attacks all connections with oneself and others — is vitally relevant in that it prepares the psyche for the eventual incarnation of the Self.

There are vast implications if we can experience these "death dealing" affects from the viewpoint that they have a genuinely mysterious purpose. Winnicott's brilliant observation that the self is created through the continuous destruction of fantasy objects that survive (Winnicott 1971, p. 90; Eigen 1981, p. 418), offers scope for this more comprehensive perspective and enables us to experience these often devastating interactive fields with a faith in the basic oneness of which they partake. This is truly alchemical thinking and it accords with Bion's exemplary faith in "O" (Bion 1970, p. 32; Eigen 1981, p. 426). Intense persecutory anxiety is part of the process of the Self's incarnation.

In the depressive position the oppositional "good" and "bad" breasts combine into a whole object. Depression is thought to result from the child's awareness of the harm it may now *also* do to the "good breast." Klein suggested that in the depressive position, the omnipotence of the "good" or "bad" mother is lost, and with it, the child's sense of omnipotence. Henry Elkin's view, however, is that "It is not the question of impotence or omnipotence . . . that gets to the core of the depressive position, but rather *the infant's new capacity to distinguish physical omnipotence from mental omniscience*" (1972, pp. 404–405). But the depressive position can also be seen as a stage of mourning for a loss of union, depicted in the *Rosarium* as the *coniunctio.*

The Rapprochement Subphase of the Separation-Individuation process can also be seen as a space–time fragment of the *coniunctio* process. In this subphase, the child's separation and energy-laden return may, as in the case of the depressive position, represent the *coniunctio* process and its effects as they incarnate into space–time. In the depressive position, the opposites unite in the background of the child's psyche while the child is still in fusion with this sacred event. In the Rapprochement Subphase, the child is more of an actor in the drama of union. But it is a union attempt composed of two discrete parts, a separation and a return, polarities that attempt to harmonize but lack the "glue" of unity, as it can be known in the archetypal rhythmical quality of the *coniunctio*. The search for unity, which is the archetypal root of rapprochement, may explain why this phase is usually seen to be a lifelong endeavor.

The oedipal stage represents yet another pattern of the joining and separating of opposites. This process is contained in the imagery of the *coniunctio*. On the oedipal level the ego approaches the culmination of its sacrifice of fusion with the numinous energy of union; libido is now cast under the control of the incest taboo. From Layard (quoted in Jung 1946, par. 438) we learn that this sacrifice allows for the development of inner structure, especially in the sphere of a differentiated relationship to the feminine qualities of the psyche. The danger of fusion with the archetypal sphere requires the incest taboo and the oedipal transit.

Jung correctly emphasizes that healing depends upon a person's ability to link to the larger world of the pleroma. Consequently, we must be able to comprehend developmental processes not only within their space–time matrix, but also as aspects of a divine drama. The following example illustrates this with reference to the Rapprochement Subphase of Individuation described by Mahler.

A patient who had been seeing me for several years suffered from a severe rapprochement failure. Her initial dream, which contained repeated sequences of being with me, separating, then having great difficulty in finding me again, focused upon this core issue. This pattern did not immediately manifest in the transference, though eventually it became repetitive. For approximately eight months, our therapeutic connection was based upon a positive transference that allowed the patient to sustain an internal connection to me from one session to the next. But as soon as negative transference elements appeared, she quickly lost this object constancy, and I began to disappear from her memory between sessions. Each time she returned she had slight recall of the content of our past session. These memory lapses led to thoughts of termination because (as this patient reasoned) "after therapy ends we would have no relationship, so what's the point?"

After some time had passed, we could begin to reconstruct the early childhood traumas that undermined this patient's development. In particular, her mother's depression and withdrawal during the rapprochement subphase became clear from memories and dreams. This discovery was of great importance because her mother's behavior was replicated in my countertransference reactions, many of which seemed to be induced. Such discoveries, along with experiences of affective union in the therapeutic setting, were the working substance of at least two years of therapy in which union experiences would always give way to her rapprochement trauma. We would then analyze her splitting defenses, mind–body dissociations, and her painful states of feeling ugly. This pattern grew familiar: each time a harmonious contact was reestablished (sometimes taking several weeks to achieve), her trauma would reemerge, and there would be a sense that nothing of any structural significance had transpired.

The nature of the contact I am describing is akin to the *coniunctio,* but these union experiences were partial and only faintly felt and had much of the character of a fusion experience. They never led to an experience of a subtle-body field that had the character of a "third thing" between us. Had this field appeared there would have been a transcendence of fusion/distance polarities. Also, up to this point, our therapeutic work only marginally addressed the negative transference. During the fleeting moments of union, however, an experience of kinship emerged that was strong enough to allow her to suffer, over and over again, the pain of loss of union.

Thus, we could deal with her rapprochement failure in the manner of the alchemical motto of *solve et coagula* (dissolve and coagulate). But how could this central failure be seen as part of a divine drama? Up to this point in the therapeutic process I had viewed it in terms of developmental issues and their replay in the transference–countertransference process. The larger significance emerged after the patient experienced an "inner light" while meditating.

In the next session my patient's psyche seemed "layered," with her recent uplifting experience in the foreground and the previous rapprochement issues in the background. I felt the induction into me of depression and feelings of deadness, as well as the warmth of "Light." For some time, I noted the interplay of these states within me. I could begin to comment on what I was experiencing, though with an acute awareness that it was important not to tread on her experience. In this manner, she began to able to see her abandonment expectations, *but now they were set in relief by her daring to reveal her true power, a power derived from the numinosum entering into space-time life.*

Prior to this event the patient's life had been split into secular and religious components. Part of her life was devoted to meditation and healing practices; her careful understanding of issues of psychotherapy was kept quite separate. Now the two parts met, and it was possible for her to understand the pain and suffering of rapprochement as part of the larger drama of the incarnation of the *numinosum.* Before this transition occurred, the patient had had an awareness of the *numinosum* as an outer, transcendent reality; now the *numinosum* had an interior life in her. Accordingly, her feeling of inner emptiness and the absence of a self began to diminish.

This patient's tortuous history of abandonment might be seen as a replay of her second and third years of life. But it may also be seen as a fragment of a larger process of the incarnation of the *numinosum* into her psyche. This was expressed in her terror of abandonment if she dared allow this process to occur—if she dared own the effectiveness of the *numinosum.* This form of power cannot be usurped by the ego; it can be known only through opening one's heart to others and to the larger source that can gracefully enter one's being. The patient had been fearful: what if she was open and nobody was there for her? She now faced the aloneness endemic to the individuation process. In this interpretation, rapprochement indicates a link with the *numinosum,* and suffering is the torment of bringing the awareness and experience of that union back into space-time reality. Thus, this patient's rapprochement failures can be seen as fragmentary aspects of a divine process, manifest within the vicissitudes of early nurturing.

Many developmental approaches begin with a conception of oneness. Erich Neumann refers to this oneness in terms of both the maternal or matriarchal uroboros, followed by the paternal or patriarchal uroboros (1954, pp. 17-19; 1955, pp. 317-319). Ego development and the internal world are said to emerge from these stages. Neumann, like all developmental theorists, shifts the focus of his analysis from the realm of oneness to the *parts* of this foundation. However, in developmental theory, the initial state of oneness is usually not associated with any high order. Mahler sees it primarily as an autistic ("pre-symbiotic") state that precludes meaningful contact with a mothering figure. Fordham's starting point is a *nuclear self* that eventually must "deintegrate" (Fordham 1976, p. 16); parts of this unity manifest as new psychic structure. He grants an initial state of oneness that is not characterized by notions of symbiosis (Fordham 1986) or common boundaries between a mother and her infant. Instead, the child is considered to participate in a unique process that can be observed without reference to a mothering figure and without undervaluing the mother–infant interaction. Fairbairn posits an initial state that he calls the Original Ego. He believed that out of this state the internal structure develops into the central ego, the libidinal and anti-libidinal egos, and the superego. He also insists that this "Original Ego" is a whole rather than a part object and that it is subject to repression, an assertion that object relations theorists assume to be a developmental acquisition (Rinsley 1982, p. 85).

The tendency of developmental theorists has been to observe the evolution of *parts* of psychic structure. This is so with Neumann's notion of the maternal and paternal uroboros, Mahler's autistic stage of the first month of life, Fordham's nuclear self, or Fairbairn's original ego. And while among theorists there are widely differing approaches to the development of an individual self, most ignore the possibility and potential of a basic background order, almost as if there were a positive value in becoming heroically involved in the space–time matrix of daily life at the expense of a wider, more comprehensive orientation of wholeness. In most developmental approaches, the essential concentration is on the *parts* from which inner structures are formed; there is little regard for the living relationship of these parts to a background oneness.

The emphasis upon "oneness" can certainly appear to be a mystical, if not wish-fulfilling approach, to therapy. What, one might ask, does such a viewpoint have to do with ill patients? Aren't most people injured in the early years of childhood, and doesn't their cure depend upon "working through" developmental failures? Isn't a therapist who links a borderline patient's failure to negotiate rapprochement issues to incarnation of the *numinosum* into space–time existence aligning with the patient's delusional and primary process thinking? Certainly to avoid developmental issues and the way that they appear in the transference-countertransference relationship would be poor therapy, at best. Yet, the age-old wisdom of the Hermetic tradition (Bamford 1981, pp. 5–25) is that healing depends upon a return to origins. If we follow the spirit of this wisdom, we return not only to images and experiences of the personal mother, but also to experiences of the pleroma, the matrix of life — the *eternal return*: "Everything that happens . . . happens in the same 'one world' and is part of it. For this reason, events must possess an *a priori* aspect of unity" (Jung 1955, p. 414).

While developmental approaches provide important clinical insights and are definitely useful, they also contain a shadow element in that they reduce the self to a content of the ego and the archetypal feminine to the personal mother. For example, Mahler's theory of individuation has four stages. The fourth, Consolidation of Individuality and the Beginning of Emotional Object Constancy, differs from the other three in being "open-ended at the older end" (Mahler et al. 1975, p. 112); the fourth stage continues throughout life. A fourfold model that distinguishes the "fourth" from the other three components is found in P. Federn's distinction between active, passive, and reflective *ego feelings* and *medial ego feelings* (1953). Medial feelings signify those feelings that convey a basic awareness of one's existence. We have already noted Fairbairn's approach, in which an original whole object splits into a libidinal ego and an anti-libidinal ego and also into a central (or reality) ego. To these three ego parts, Fairbairn added a fourth, the superego, which may have not only harsh aspects, stemming from the sadistic, anti-libidinal ego, but also ideal aspects, stemming from the original whole object (1952). Fairbairn's schema was extended by H. Guntrip (1969, pp. 73–74), who suggested that a piece of the original pristine oneness splits from its fusion with the libidinal-ego, to form a fourth part, the so-called "regressed ego" or the "true self" (ibid., p. 77). The Masterson-Rinsley model of borderline structure, describing a rejecting part-object relational unit and a withholding one, incorporates Fairbairn's ego divisions, including his description of a reality ego that is severely depleted by its need to deny abandonment (Rinsley 1982, p. 41).

Underlying many developmental approaches is the concept of a fourfold inner structure, or a model of an individuation process that unfolds in four stages and in which the fourth stage is qualitatively different from the other three. But when we look at the qualities of these quaternity structures, we see that they bear only a superficial likeness to Jung's. Object-relational approaches derive from the strong determining influence that outer relationships impose upon inner structure; the Jungian view of the unfolding of inner structure is largely rooted in the concept of the autonomy of the archetypes (1952, pp. 469–470). Jungian theory conceives archetypes to be the psyche's ordering structures; they regulate fantasy and structure dream life. The simplest, most mundane dreams have an underlying archetypal form, even if the numinosity of the archetype is not evident as it is in so-called "big" or archetypal dreams. While the creative or destructive functioning of the archetype can be affected by conscious attitudes and behavior, the archetype also possesses an autonomy through which the evolving forms of the psyche manifest. Jung traces the autonomy of this evolution in many works (1937, 1952) and shows how the "fourth" element is always the necessary though problematic aspect of wholeness. This "fourth" represents what was discarded by previous cultural developments that stressed the value of consciousness within trinitarian models. Jungian theory commonly fills the place of the "fourth" with the archetypal feminine but also includes evil as a fourth element.

When we include a feminine perspective in our apprehension of psychic processes, the clarity of rational-discursive thought becomes less prominent though it retains its value. Exclusively "objective" approaches to the psyche become questionable, and an approach through the imagination and attitudes that value a "subjective-objectivity" (von Franz 1974, pp. 128–131) becomes the primary focus. When we employ Jung's approach to the archetypal feminine, a psychic interiority emerges that includes a concern for the body as a source of consciousness and psychic life.

As psychic interiority becomes meaningful, the importance of dreams and the imagination for exploration of this interior world becomes central. Theories by which psychic products may be ordered become less important. When the therapist includes a feminine perspective in his or her approach to the psyche, "being right" is less important than being related. The feminine mode also embraces the importance of the subtle body, which is an integral part of the interactive field between two people. I believe that the attitude Jung designates as "the feminine" is one in which *relations per se* is the main psychic unit of this field. The masculine domain is more concerned with *things related* and represents an attitude that clearly separates and observes in the attempt to objectively describe and causally relate one psychic state to another. Ultimately, both attitudes are necessary, and the alchemical image of the *coniunctio* of Sol and Luna represents their combination.

Jung's approach, which emphasizes the archetypal feminine, may be further contrasted to object-relational approaches. It should be noted that the latter emphasize the consolidation of the ego and the achievement of object constancy; the idea of a person's having a conscious relationship to his or her psychic reality is of far less importance.

The Jungian attitude also values outer adaptation, but stresses that this adaptation should not be at the cost of repressing the inner world and psychic reality. Object-relational approaches emphasize a "reality ego" and objectivity; the Jungian emphasis is upon a mythical or imaginal consciousness that can appreciate and be guided by symbolic manifestations of the psyche. It should be noted that the quality of consciousness and internal structure that enters with the integration of the "fourth" is not merely an extension of a third phase or structure. The "fourth" is a highly autonomous structure whose numinosity links the world of ego-consciousness to the oneness of existence (von Franz 1974, pp. 128–131).

The idea of innate destructiveness, conceptualized by Freud and Klein as the death instinct, has never become popular with object relations theorists. Destructive impulses are generally seen as results of frustration due mainly to a lack of "good enough" mothering. This view is a throwback to the doctrine of the *privatio boni* view of evil, in which evil is regarded as a mere absence of good. Jung discounted this view, emphasizing instead the substantial reality of the dark side of the psyche (1952, par. 600, n. 13). From a mythological perspective, this dark side is the Devil. Furthermore, Jung stressed that "the shadow and the opposing will is the necessary condition for all actualization" (1942, par. 290). Only with a conscious integration of the shadow can the positive *numinosum* actualize. This means that an individual lives with an acute awareness of his or her dark nature in which there is an alignment with a pull toward death. This dynamic includes psychopathic qualities that function without any moral sense. When the shadow and its destructive consequences are integrated, conscious alignment with the positive *numinosum* becomes an ethical issue, a matter of choice. One must side either with God or the Devil. Only by integrating the shadow does a person develop the ego-strength to actively relate to the *numinosum*. The shadow brings us closer to our ugliness, to aspects of our nature that may be beyond redemption, and enforces an awareness that we are embodied creatures with real limitations. The experience of our *embodied size* is essential for the *numinosum* to gain actuality; without this knowledge of our limitations, and hence, an awareness of our humanity, contact with the *numinosum* leads to an inflated state. When we become inflated, the numinous aspect of our nature, which had seemed so tangible, withdraws to an ephemeral, potential existence.

Jung emphasized the moral function of human reflection and

consciousness in the process wherein the patriarchal god-image is transformed and contributes to an inner self structure. Jung's model does not
omit an awareness of the shadow, expressed theologically by the doctrine
of the substantiality of evil (1942, pp. 134–136).

> One of the toughest roots of evil is unconsciousness . . . I could wish that the
> saying of Jesus, 'Man, if thou knowest what thou doest, thou art blessed, but if
> thou knowest not, thou art accursed, and a transgressor of the law,' were still in
> the gospels. . . . It might well be the motto for a new morality. (1942, par. 291)

Jung's approach to morality emphasizes the destructive quality of lies
propagated and maintained by unconsciousness. In treatment, the therapist's unconscious lies are often manifestations of the "evil" that the
therapy process inevitably includes. When the therapist can admit to his
or her own unconsciousness and shadow, then he or she can deal with the
patient's shadow. Only when the patient gains the courage to *see* the
therapist's darkness as well as light, can the process of incarnating the
numinosum begin. The ability to accept the reality of evil and to consciously own one's destructive nature is a necessary achievement if the
Self is to incarnate. An inner, functioning self — related to the Self — then
emerges.

The lie that must be uncovered when one is dealing with the
delusional projection of the patriarchal god-image is the patient's resistance to seeing the true qualities of the object. The patient may accurately see negative qualities in the object, and this is essential, but the fact
that a god-projection exists, that the object is really being treated as a
god and not as a person, is totally ignored. The capacity to *see* things as
they are has been hidden away in the schizoid layer that thrives upon the
delusional belief system; reclaiming it is always a shock.

An important difference between Jungian approaches and those
rooted in object relations and developmental models, is that the latter do
not recognize the psychic reality of the archetypal feminine. If this feminine force does appear, it is almost exclusively in the form of the outer
mother and in the processes through which the "breast-mother" becomes
internalized. The goal in object-relations theory is separation from the
mother and her internalization, so that in life further separations, as well
as the capacity for realistic object relations, can develop.

Since the archetypal feminine is the essence of the quaternity
structure, the implications are critical: relatedness, empathy, and *being*
(in distinction to *doing*) flourish, and an entirely different approach to
consciousness and the body emerges. The heart becomes more central

than the head. Moreover, the recovery of feminine modes of consciousness and behavior supports the realm of the *imaginal* and a continuing
enactment of *embodied seeing*.

CHAPTER FOUR
ARCHETYPAL FOUNDATIONS OF PROJECTIVE
IDENTIFICATION

Doctor and patient thus find themselves in a relationship founded on mutual unconsciousness. (C. G. Jung, 1946, par. 364)

Introduction

The borderline patient's inner world is highly charged with archetypal material. Projections of this material can create foreign yet captivating states of mind in the object. This dynamic of *projective identification* plays a significant role in the treatment of the borderline patient whose exceptional propensity for "getting under one's skin" is well known. In Chapter One, I gave a number of examples of experiences with borderline patients in which such inductive affects were dominant. In this chapter, I shall explore the concept of projective identification in its Kleinian form and also from the point of view implicit in Jung's "Psychology of the Transference" (1946).

In 1946, Melanie Klein published "Notes on Some Schizoid Mechanisms" in which she coined the term "projective identification." Klein's paper employs the mother–infant object relation and outlines a concept of part objects, whereby parts of one person are, as it were, put into and identified with another person. In the same year, Jung published the "Psychology of the Transference," wherein he used the arcane symbolism of alchemy to explore the same phenomenology. Klein's paper, as D. Meltzer has noted, had an "electrifying impact [upon] the analysts who were closely working with her" (1973, p. 20). Jung's did not have such an impact. For most therapists, including Jungians, Jung's alchemical model seems too abstract for direct application to clinical practice. Yet the "Psychology of the Transference," though couched in alchemical imagery, is centrally concerned with the phenomenology of projective identification. Inherent in this study is an approach to projective identification that not only richly elaborates the findings of Klein and other

97

psychotherapists, but also deepens our understanding and widens the possibilities for clinical usage. Jung's work also helps to delineate the limitations inherent in the concept of projective identification.

Let us return to Klein's description of this phenomenon as she applies it to the infant:

> The phantasized onslaughts on the mother follow two main lines: one is the predominantly oral impulse to suck dry, bite up, scoop out and rob the mother's body of its good contents. . . . The other line of attack derives from the anal and urethral impulses and implies expelling dangerous substances (excrements) out of the self and on to the mother or, as I would rather call it, *into* the mother. These excrements and bad parts of the self are meant not only to injure but also to control and to take possession of the object. In so far as the mother comes to contain the bad parts of the self, she is not felt to be a separate individual but is felt to be *the* bad self.
>
> Much of the hatred against parts of the self is now directed against the mother. This leads to a particular form of aggression which establishes the prototype of an aggressive object-relation. I suggest for this process the term 'projective identification.' (1946, p. 8)

Klein further describes how both good and bad parts of the self can be projected. When this is excessive, she says, the ego becomes weakened and impoverished (1946, p. 9), cannot assimilate internal objects, and feels ruled by them (1946, p. 11). In an elaboration of these Kleinian principles, J. Grotstein emphasizes that projective identification is imagination (1981, p. 124), a "mental mechanism whereby the self experiences the unconscious phantasy of translocating itself, or aspects of itself, into an object for exploratory or defensive purposes" (1982, p. 123).

R. Gordon has observed that Jung's usage of the terms unconscious identity, psychic infection, *participation mystique,* induction, and the process he called *"feeling-into,"* are synonyms for projective identification (1965, p. 128). Jung's definition of "feeling-into" highlights its imaginal nature. It is a kind of

> perception process. . . . It conveys, through the agency of feeling, an essential psychic content into the object, whereby the object is introjected. This content, by virtue of its intimate relation with the subject, assimilates the object to the subject, and so links it up with the subject that the latter senses himself . . . in the object. The subject . . . does not feel himself into the object, but the object felt into appears rather as though it were animated and expressing itself of its own accord. This peculiarity depends upon the fact that the projection transfers an unconscious content into the object, whence also the feeling-into process is termed *transference* in analytical psychology (Jung 1920, p. 359).

Jung's statement refers to positive aspects of projective identification that lead to an aesthetic awareness (Jung 1920, par. 486), empathy, and a deep, imaginal search for processes in the object. His statement that "The subject . . . does not feel himself into the object" refers to a subject who already has an ego-self differentiation. But in other instances of projective identification, the subject (or at least certain ego functions of the subject, as Klein emphasized) does project psychic material into the object, and this can lead to a state of confusion and to a weakening of consciousness that leads to emotional flooding by unconscious processes. In extreme instances, a relationship dominated by projective identification can trigger psychotic episodes. Through projective identification, the image of the self can hide in an object, with the consequence that the subject feels invisible (Grotstein 1981, p. 130). This feeling can become extreme, leading to a sense of a "loss of soul" and a terror that the self can never be found.

Negative aspects of projective identification, such as confusion, identity loss or panic often appear dominant. However, projective identification also has the power, as R. Gordon has explained (1965, p. 145), to break down inner psychic boundaries, as well as those between a person and the object world. This breakdown of structures is essential to any qualitative personality change.

Jung often stressed the negative features of projective identification. His therapeutic goal, stated in his commentary to the *Secret of the Golden Flower,* is the dissolution of such fusion states between subject and object. In this text, Jung refers to these states as *participation mystique* (1957, pars. 65-66). But this goal appears questionable when Jung explains that once the self becomes the center of the personality, *participation mystique* is abolished and "results in a personality that only suffers in the lower storeys, as it were, but in its upper storey is singularly detached from painful as well as from joyful happenings" (1957, par. 67). It would appear from this statement that one cannot totally abolish the process of projective identification except by banishing it to the body. This is hardly a desirable state and can only lead to mind–body splitting. In the above remarks Jung was centering upon what he called the "compulsion and impossible responsibility" (1957, par. 78) that can accompany interactions dominated by *participation mystique.* Thus he emphasized the role of the self in breaking the compulsive tie between subject and object, which is the negative form taken by projective identification. Jung struck a different tone in his study of the *Visions of Zosi-*

mos. Here, he conceived *participation mystique* to be "a special instance of the mode of thinking typified by the idea of the microcosm" (1954, par. 123). Generally, Jung was aware of both the creative and the destructive aspects of *participation mystique* and thus of the phenomenology of projective identification. That he was influenced by both possibilities is made clear in his analysis of the alchemical imagery from the *Rosarium Philosophorum.* The *Rosarium* was Jung's Ariadne thread that led him through the complexities of the transference (Jung 1946, par. 401). The dominant image in the *Rosarium* is the hermaphrodite, a male-female image that represents the soul or *vinculum,* the linking aspect between opposites. Both constellations of the hermaphrodite can be experienced in projective identification. When the opposites, such as conscious and unconscious or solar and lunar consciousness, are harmoniously linked, that process is symbolically represented by the positive form of the hermaphrodite (Jung 1951, pars. 292, 293, 297). When the opposites become conflicting "things" rather than complementary aspects of a process, chaotic states rule, as in the fusion and splitting typical of borderline states of mind. In that condition, processes are organized by the negative constellation of the hermaphrodite (see "Psychology of the Transference," 1946, par. 533).

In the "Psychology of the Transference" Jung addressed unconscious processes that "have an inductive effect on the unconscious of [the] doctor" (1946, par. 363), a theme that is repeated in variations throughout his study (1946, pars. 364, 365, 367). Jung stated that the phenomenology of projective identification activates the unconscious and the archetypal transference:

> The doctor becomes affected, and has as much difficulty in distinguishing between the patient and what has taken possession of him as has the patient himself. . . . The activated unconscious appears as a flurry of unleashed opposites [such as hate and love, and] calls forth an attempt to reconcile them, so that, in the words of the alchemists, the great panacea, the *medicina catholica,* may be born. (1946, par. 375)

Thus, a person may become aware of the self through apprehending projective identification. As a result one may uncover the prized states of the *nigredo* and *massa confusa* (1946, pars. 376, 383, 387).

I will be employing Jung's approach to the *Rosarium* to explicate projective identification and the transference. It should be emphasized that he used the accompanying set of woodcuts and associated commentaries in an extraordinary way. With few notable exceptions (the *Mutus Liber* is one), the alchemical tradition rarely specified two people working together; certainly there was little explicit concern for mutual processes. The alchemical tradition, like tantrism, with which the imagery of the *Rosarium* has important similitude, was primarily concerned with the union of opposites *within* the individual; interpersonal interactions would have been, at best, a tool along this path. Yet Jung envisioned the *Rosarium* woodcuts as a series of images representing the unconscious process between two people; this represented a great stroke of genius. We are thereby led to consider the implications of his model. In doing so we must recognize that alchemical speculations addressed processes in the subtle body. Jung's analogy to the subtle body was to the linking between the unconscious structures of anima and animus (rather than the conscious personalities of two people). Yet, one must focus upon the locus of such processes, since it is clear that they do not take place either inside or outside of individuals. As Susan Deri has emphasized in her critique of D. W. Winnicott's idea of transitional space (which is akin to the subtle body concept), transitional phenomena cannot be located either inside, outside or even between people (Deri 1978). These phenomena apply to another dimension of existence, a *third area* whose processes can only be perceived by the eye of the imagination. Notions of *location* are, in fact, inadequate.

Generally speaking, the alchemists' approach addressed processes in this third area. They called both this area and the process occurring therein *Mercurius,* whose transformation was a goal of the *opus. Projective identification has as its objective the transformation of the structure and dynamics of processes in this third area, and through this, one's perception of these processes.* For the sake of convenience, we may refer to this area as "between" two people, for it can be experienced as an interactive field structured by images that have a strong effect upon the conscious personalities. But the more deeply this field is entered, the more spatial considerations vanish. We are dealing here with an imaginal world, a *mundus imaginalis* that has its own processes. Individuals can partake of its processes. Indeed, as Jung says, as two parties become involved in the transformation of the third area—Mercurius—they themselves are transformed in the process (Jung 1946, par. 399). As a consequence, an individual's access to and faith in the psychic reality of the imaginal world is strengthened. As Jung explained in the *Zarathustra Seminars,* the subtle body is usually a hidden area through which projections pass (1934 #39, part 10, p. 144). Alchemical speculations address the reality of the subtle body and its transformation. The latter depends upon the apprehension of processes of projective identification.

Clinical Examples

Projective identification may be employed for exploratory or defensive purposes. "Employed defensively, projective identification rids the contents of one's mind or, when the experience is severe, the mind itself. An object, hitherto separate, becomes either the container for the negated contents, or confused with it through identification . . . " (Grotstein 1981, p. 124). Such workings of projective identification can be painful to the object who is the targeted "container" for contents projected into it by the subject.

A male patient began a conversation with me and paused midway. This pause happened suddenly, and in the context of our conversation, it would have been more natural for him to have continued with a remark or question. Yet he behaved as if nothing were wrong. Soon it became clear that each of us was waiting for the other to say something. As he looked at me, I began to feel awkward. The pause rapidly became more painful, and I felt called upon to bridge what was becoming an intolerable tension.

During this painful pause, projective identification was occurring. The patient was putting his blank mind into me, attempting to use me as a container for a sense of *absence* or *mental blankness* that overtook him midway through our conversation. He was easing this "absence," encased in a paranoid shell, into me, then watching me in hope that I would somehow return to him his (functioning) mind. Consequently, when I disengaged and ended the encounter, the patient grew angry. I was left with the guilty feeling that I had failed a test, and I felt coerced to reestablish emotional contact with him. The patient's mind did not return to him during the pause. But his anger jarred him out of his schizoid state and into more affective contact with me. This event passed without comment; its meaning remained unintegrated and a similar exchange would be certain to recur.

As important as it is for communication, projective identification plays an even more important role: it is goal-oriented and can both create and break down unconscious, imaginal structures between two people—structures as real as the phenomenon itself. Like dreams, these structures are normally invisible to waking or normal consciousness.

An image descriptive of the unconscious structure of the above-mentioned interactional field would be the alchemical hermaphrodite; a being with one body and two heads (Jung 1946; McLean 1980). This conjoined body-aspect would represent the fusion desires between the patient and me (which I felt in the form of a need to maintain contact with him); the two heads would represent the opposing tendency to split (which appeared in my desire to break contact with him and thereby avoid the pain of mental blankness).

Projective identification can initiate the process of gaining access to and transforming interactive relational fields. These fields are depicted by the couples in the *Rosarium*. The alchemical process is devoted to overcoming the dangers of fusion states, especially the ego's tendency to merge with and (inappropriately) identify with the archetypal energies of the interactive field.

In alchemy, the existence of what we call projective identification was crucial for the initiation of the alchemical *opus*. Apprehending it was synonymous with the *fixing* of Mercurius, and could result in finding the *prima materia* or the *massa confusa*, or in arriving at the stage called the *nigredo*. In clinical practice identifying projective identification is dependent upon the therapist's (or patient's) distancing himself or herself from extremely strong feelings that had previously seemed perfectly justified. Bion described this distance as stemming from a "temporary loss of insight" (1967, p. 149). Without this distance, the therapist will continue to enact the patient's fantasy and will fail to recognize that he or she is being manipulated to play that part. The therapist's means of gaining emotional distance varies greatly. The spectrum ranges from the therapist's splitting from the encounter, to the act of imagining the effect on the patient should the therapist speak or behave in ways that he or she might feel to be justified but which in fact are destructive. Such imaginal acts will often jar the therapist out of an arrogant complacency and into the awareness that a very complex and dangerous process has been at work.

During a session with a woman patient I began to feel that her right to have any thoughts at all had to be preceded by these thoughts *first* flowing through me. Then, and only then, could she have them! I was a dictatorial container. It felt right that she be contained in me, that her autonomy and thoughts be allowed to exist only if they were contained by me. And it felt as if this was for her own good! Until I jarred myself out of this state, it felt perfectly right. Projective identification also dominated the previous vignette, when during the long pause, I had a strong belief that my reactions were completely justified. Only later was I able to recognize that I was being manipulated to recover my patient's lost mind.

The following case demonstrates the kind of imagery that can evolve from two people imaginally reflecting upon projective identification dynamics. A female patient began the session by looking at me with great penetration. Then she said, "When I see that bored look on your face, that is, when I believe I see it, I just want to go away. I get anxious, and I withdraw."

I felt stung by her criticism. I had sometimes been bored in the past, but I did not feel that way today, and certainly not when she had spoken to me. Why did I feel so jarred by what she said? Where was she seeing clearly? I began to realize that if I retained contact with her while at the same time being connected to myself, she became very anxious and withdrew. When I said this, she agreed; after some reflection, she looked at me. At that moment I found myself looking away, though only for a second; it was clear that I was avoiding her. I acknowledged this, but she, too, had noticed my avoidance and had become very upset. This same behavior was repeated, she realized, not only with me, but in all her experiences with men, for as she expressed it: "They don't want to contact me, they run away. Why did you run away?"

I had no answer. In fact, I felt surprised by her question. By revealing that I had withdrawn, I thought I was offering an observation that would make her grateful. Instead, she was angry with me! Clearly, I had opened up for more than I had bargained. I thought about my response. Why had I run away? Did I want to avoid emotional contact with her? Then I realized that my act of briefly looking away was actually a chronic pattern in our interactions.

I felt myself growing angry; I was consumed by furious thoughts. This woman wouldn't let me have any of my own process, I couldn't be in myself at all, but had always to be linked to *her* and focused upon her and our interaction! After a moment, my anger passed and I came to my senses. I described the process I had just undergone, and while I wasn't sure of its source — me, her, or our interaction — in telling her about it I hoped to bring these destructive contents to consciousness. I did not ascribe my state to an induced process, but it did have the sense of foreignness to my ego that is common to projective identification. From this point on, I was open to the possibility that the fantasy was not merely a product of her psyche and mine, but that it also might be a spontaneous product of our interactive field.[1]

I communicated these feelings to my patient and noted both their foreignness and the fact that they were part of my own reactions. This led her to a flood of memories. She had often been treated as a greedy and controlling person who allowed no other person autonomy. Her considered and authentic response led me to wonder if my turning away from her had been prompted by her projective identification inducing in me a sadistic withdrawal. I wondered if my reflections on third areas and imaginal couples was a way of distancing myself from a more direct encounter. This would have been the shadow side of this approach to projective identification: using this approach (which orients toward third areas) can be a way of avoiding affective linking.

Our looking at projective identification as something of *hers* being acted out by me was useful, but it soon felt unsatisfying to both of us. After all, why did I act it out? What did this say about me and my feelings about her? I had the urge to protest that I actually had done a good job of not acting out—that I had only *barely* succumbed compared to the experience she'd had with other people. But small or slight withdrawals can be even more sinister than outright accusations that a patient is boring, for these withdrawals cloak themselves in the lie that there is only a slight lapse in a state of otherwise real contact.

So we returned to examining our interaction. It seemed clear that we were acting like a couple who did not want union. When this anxiety-provoking dynamic was active, I would withdraw when she contacted me. Conversely, when I contacted her, she would withdraw. We seemed to be ruled by an interactive couple whose roles we enacted. By approaching our interaction in this way we submitted to a third element that was having its way with us. Like the alchemical Mercurius described by Jung, it was an "elusive, deceptive, ever-changing content that possessed [us] like a demon who flitted about [between us] as the third party in our alliance, [and] continued its game, sometimes impish and teasing, sometimes really diabolical" (Jung 1946, par. 384). We were able to sense this presence through an imaginal act, a metaphorical way of viewing our

---

[1]The interactive field is, in H. Corbin's terms, *a mundus imaginalis* (Corbin 1972; Samuels 1985).

105

interaction; by doing so we could speak of this third presence as if we were constructing a dream that was filling in for our missing consciousness. Our interaction can best be conveyed by the image of two couples simultaneously present: the patient and I, and an unconscious dyad.

Through focusing upon this subtle body interaction, we established the presence of an imaginal couple that seemed to thrive on sadomasochistic dynamics. For example, if I followed the rhythms of this dyad and withdrew from my patient, she felt pain. In turn, she would flee from me and create a similar effect, a nonmirroring of my eros which was painful to me. The act of imaginatively *seeing* this couple freed us from its power. This is similar to what occurs when a person engages in the process of active imagination. As my patient and I worked together in this fashion, a new field of mutually shared union began to manifest: our imaginal *sight* began to transform the nature of the couple. We could feel ourselves working together in an interactive field that seemed to possess its own creative power; images and feelings appeared with a spontaneity we had rarely known in our work together.

I now found myself in the midst of a new fantasy: I began to *see,* in my mind's eye, and fleetingly in the space between us, a wild red-haired man, who looked much like the ancient representations of Ares, the wild man. He and I began to merge, and he-I was very angry with the patient. This rage had an imaginal presence: "Anything that goes wrong here is your fault! If you dare to split from me or in any way mess up now, you're in for it!" I was surprised by the power of this fantasy; when I related it to my patient, she recognized my fantasy as being her greatest fear. She became very upset, and she told me that she had always been held accountable for anything that went wrong in experiences of union.

What about the wild man? In a sense he represents a sadistic urge that I had acted upon by withdrawing. Now this urge was revealed in a more devastating, persecutory form. But the imaginal act of patient and therapist experiencing this imagery and affect together now led to something else. For my patient recognized the "wild man" to be *her* energy, her libido or Yang power, which she felt men hated and from which they always withdrew. Always at the moment when she would dare to feel this power, men would accuse her of being unrelated. Now, for the first time, she could experience her phallic power as potentially positive and not ruinous of union.

As long as I was dealing with the "parts put into me" by the patient, or "parts I put into her" in counterprojective identification, I was approaching our interaction through a Kleinian metaphor. That is, I was dealing with projected parts and attempting to understand them through a spatial model that had a clear inside and outside. But when my patient and I were able to perceive the interactive couple in mutable states of fusion, union, or radical nonunion, we began to enter a different kind of space, one composed of couples and their relationships rather than projected parts.

This space is a transitional area between the space–time world (where processes are characterized as an interaction of objects) and the collective unconscious — the *pleroma* (Jung 1952, par. 629). This area has a fundamentally different quality from the space–time world. In its pathological form, the pleroma invades the conscious personality as primary-process thinking. But in its creative form, it is the source of healing through one's experience of the *numinosum*.

Images have the capacity to lead a person into the mystery of the pleroma. Marilyn Ferguson explains how T. S. Eliot's poems refer to the pleroma: "The still point of the turning world," she noted, "is neither flesh nor fleshless, neither arrest nor movement. Eliot wrote: 'And do not call it fixity, where past and future are gathered. Except for the point, the still point/ There would be no dance, and there is only the dance' " (Ferguson 1982, pp. 24–25). Ferguson also records an ancient Buddhist sutra, which describes this level in which oneness, rather than discrete events, is the guiding thread:

> In the heaven of Indra there is said to be a network of pearls so arranged that if you look at one you see the others reflected in it. In the same way, each object in the world is not merely itself but involves every other object, and in fact *is* every other object. (1982, p. 25)

The physicist David Bohm (1982) refers to this dynamic phenomenon as the *implicate order* from which the *explicate order* of discrete space–time processes evolves. The physician and scientist, Alex Comfort (1984) has suggested that Bohm's implicate order can be understood as a space in which *relations* — not *things* related but *relations per se* — are the central feature. Images have the power to link a person to the implicate order, and the particular images that depict *relations* may have a special role in clinical practice. By discovering an unconscious couple through its fragments experienced by projective identification, one can undergo processes in a third area that can connect one to the pleromatic fullness of the implicate order. One thus follows the fragments known by projective identification back to their pleromatic roots. The couple in its *coniunctio* form then becomes an image with the power to engage both patient and therapist in a field that links them to the oneness of the implicate order.

The space in which one can experience a couple whose "ever-changing dance is the only reality," is the subtle body area that links ego consciousness with the world of the implicate order. A new level of awareness has been reached when one becomes conscious of the existence of this area. It is best not to identify the third area with either implicate or space–time orders, but to allow it to be a connecting domain that cannot be cast in spatial categories. The third area is neither inside, outside, *nor* "in between" people. It is neither material nor psychic, "neither flesh nor fleshless," but is a realm of ethers and of concepts that have been discarded but stand in need of our reconsideration.

Projective Identification in the Imagery of the *Rosarium*

How did the alchemist apprehend what we know to be projective identification processes and turn them into structure-creating, dissolving and transforming modes? How were those processes approached in which, as Jung says, the alchemist "no longer knew whether he was melting the mysterious amalgam in the crucible or whether he was the salamander glowing in the fire" (1946, par. 399). This process of "psychological induction," Jung continues, "inevitably causes the two parties to get involved in the transformation of the third [Mercurius] and to be themselves transformed in the process . . ." (1946, par. 399). The key to the transformation lies in the containing power of the archetypes, those primordial images that alone have a "spellbinding power over . . . *Mercurius* [and do not] allow that useful though dangerous enemy to escape" (1946, par. 396). Of all primordial images the one that best suits this task is the *coniunctio*.

The discovering of an unconscious couple and recognition that it is the creative source of an interaction beyond the powers of the conscious personality, is often a discovery accompanied by awe. This can be a numinous moment, an experience of the archetypal transference. The discovery by therapist and patient of their unconscious couple, through being affected by the inductive processes of the third area, can lead to its introjection as an internal self-structure (cf. Meltzer 1973, p. 85).

Jung's alchemical approach to the transference allows one to situate projective identification in a proper container for its Mercurius-like ambiguities. In the *Rosarium* woodcuts we may recognize the workings of projective identification as they are coupled with the evolution of processes in the third area of relations. Projective identification plays a major role in creating the illusions and arrogance by which the ego identifies with processes in the third area, but it also leads to the capacity to discover the unconscious couples who are the central images of the third area.

Projective Identification and Interpretation

By thinking in terms of the imagery of parts of one person put into another, one may discover an unconscious couple that is part of a domain larger than the ego, a couple whose energy and structure has been influencing the conscious personalities all along. Discovering the unconscious couple *in this way* has important advantages over intuiting its existence or even discovering it from dream material that reflects upon the transference and countertransference. For one then moves out of a sphere of omnipotence, in which the therapist knows more than the patient, and into a domain in which both people can discover how they have, so to speak, been acting out a mutual dream. At this point patient and therapist are *in the psyche* as much as it is inside of them. The usefulness of spatial metaphors declines, and one can experience the imaginal processes of the third area. This is the realm in which *relations per se,* rather than the things related (for example, complexes belonging to one or both people) are the main focus. Concern over which parts of the psyche belong to whom fades as both people become aware of a linking structure that has determined the nature of their interaction. They may then also recognize how previous attempts at understanding, through the metaphor of patient–therapist projections, were ultimately power positions.

What is one to do with the part objects known through projective identification? On the one hand, they provide important data for the interpretation of the patient's splitting off from greed, envy, hatred, joy, love, etc. On the other hand, sacrificing interpretations—by an act of noninterpretation—can enliven the interactive field in a way that allows both people to engage it. By focusing upon processes in this third area, experienced as an interactive field, *and not reducing them to pro-*

jections that must be withdrawn, two people can apprehend a variety of linking structures, notably fusion, distance, and union. If one approaches the part objects through an analysis based upon withdrawing projections, as Jung did in his study of the *Rosarium* (1946, pars. 503–505), one limits the creative potential of projective identification and of the alchemical process illuminating the third area in the transference–countertransference.

This motif of the sacrifice of solar consciousness, that quality of consciousness that would be engaged in analyzing and withdrawing projections, is found in the imagery of the *Rosarium.* These woodcuts depict changes in the interactive field, notably picture twelve, wherein Sol enters the well of Luna, and picture eighteen, wherein Sol is swallowed by the green lion (McLean 1980, pp. 74, 104, 128). Clearly one must first be able to employ this aspect of consciousness before it can be sacrificed—and this consciousness is afforded by the Kleinian style of processing projective identification.

The *Rosarium* depicts a process whereby the vitality and bonding capacity of the third area is eventually stabilized into linking structures, such as the hermaphrodite of picture ten. The *Rosarium* is a mixture of imagery that represents the overall teachings of alchemy's fundamental attitudes toward the soul and its development. Additionally, its imagery pertains to specific stages of the transformation of the unconscious dyad. Picture twenty shows the resurrected Christ, or the *corpus glorificatum* (McLean 1980, p. 115). In some renditions of these images—they are drawn and painted differently in various copies of the *Rosarium*—the eternal battle of Set and Osiris is shown in the background. This reminds one of the fact that no matter how exalted a transformation may be, issues of psychic dismemberment and abandonment are never entirely abolished. Indeed, we might say that they form a background against which life must be approached. This last woodcut, which represents the overcoming of death, suggests that one cannot truly live unless mindful of mortality. This woodcut also symbolically portrays the final but never-attainable goal of the complete integration of the archetypal sphere into the human being, in which the transcendent Self and the individual self are identical.[2]

---

[2]The *Rosarium* is the best known of alchemical texts and was quoted more frequently than any other by Jung. Since his study of the first ten woodcuts, (to which he also added the eleventh, which he took to be analogous to the fifth), there have been other attempts to analyze these pictures. Notable are the approaches to all twenty images found in the works of J. Fabricius (1976) and A. McLean (1980). Fabricius approaches the *Rosarium* from a developmental context, and in an

The First Ten Pictures of the *Rosarium**

Picture one of the *Rosarium, The Mercurial Fountain* is "an attempt to depict the mysterious basis of the *opus*" (Jung 1946, par. 402). The Fountain is filled by "lower waters" that circulate through the fountain's three pipes, which are different aspects of Mercurius. Fabricius describes this picture:

> In the woodcut, the mercurial fountain with its base of lion-claws overflows with the mercurial waters of the prima materia. These appear as the 'virgin's milk' *(lac virginis)*, the 'fountain's vinegar' *(acetum fontis)*, and the 'water of life' *(aqua vitae)*, all spouting from the mercurial fountain inscribed with the 'three names' *(triplex nomine)* of Mercurius philosophorum. These refer to his three manifestations in the fountain as 'mineral,' 'vegetable,' and 'animal,' matter. Yet the inscription on the rim of the basin admonishes that *unus est mercurius mineralis, mercurius vegetabilis, mercurius animalis*. These manifestations of the triune earth-god of alchemy reappear in the two-headed *serpens mercurialis* which is also *triplex nomine*, as its inscriptions *animalis, mineralis, vegetabilis* bear out. The mercurial serpent or dragon spews the poisonous fumes of the prima materia which contain the seven planets or metals in evil mixture and disorder. (Fabricius 1976, p. 19)

The libido that fills the fountain is twofold: it arises through the Mercurial fountain and also has a source in the two-headed serpent, the dyadic, "upper" form of Mercurius, which manifests differently from its "lower" form. The fountain is thus filled from above and from below. Mercurius, as he manifests from below, is the chthonic libido (Jung 1946, par. 403), counterpart to the Heavenly Trinity. This lower aspect of Mercurius represents "want, desire, instinct, aggression and determination" (ibid., par. 407); he is a creature of "venerable nature," the earthbound partner or complement to the Holy Ghost, analogous to the Primordial Man (ibid., par. 416), Hades, and "the pagan god of revelation" (ibid., par. 418). The "lower waters" exert the "unholy fascination" of incest (ibid., par. 419). This "fiery, chthonic Mercurius [is] the sexual libido which engulfs the pair" (ibid., par. 455). Combined with these "incestuous

---

ingenious manner views the series of woodcuts as depicting the stages of life, from its prenatal forms through individuation and into old age. He employs a variety of models taken from Klein, Mahler, and also from LSD experiences to buttress his thesis that these woodcuts actually portray the life cycle. At times his analysis is convincing, and at others it seems to be quite forced. McLean notes his debt to Jung, and recognizes the significance of the tantric imagery in the woodcuts. His analysis is extremely useful, especially in regard to his linking the first ten and the second ten woodcuts of the *Rosarium*; I shall also be referring to his valuable analysis of the tenth picture, the hermaphrodite. This woodcut has a special significance in terms of the way in which interactive fields encountered with borderline patients may transform.

I shall deal essentially with the first ten woodcuts, using them as models for exploring projective identification and the interactive fields encountered in borderline conditions. I have already referred to several images from the last ten woodcuts, noting that twelve and eighteen can be seen as referring to the sacrifice of solar consciousness. Generally, the imagery found in illustrations eleven through twenty elaborates the earlier process.

*The second ten pictures of the *Rosarium* are shown at the end of this chapter.

elements" are the fumes descending from the heads of the serpent. These heads face in opposite directions and "are the two vapours whose condensation initiates the process which leads to a multiple distillation for the purpose of purifying away the . . . clinging darkness of the beginning" (ibid., par. 403). Thus a libidinal stream that can foster dangerous fusion states mixes with an opposite stream, also of equally destructive potential, that fosters splitting; yet, as the inscriptions on the woodcut show, they are identical. The verse that accompanies the woodcut reads: "No fountain and no water has my like/ I make both rich and poor men whole or sick/ For deadly can I be and poisonous" (Fabricius 1976, p. 19).

The woodcut appears graphically and symbolically disjointed; the upper part contains the two-headed serpent, and the lower part, the Mercurial fountain. McLean has noted this split as an essential aspect of the picture and tells us that the soul is depicted with a split upper and lower form (1980, p. 120). Western civilization has been plagued by this split since Plato and before.

We are familiar with such states from our experience of borderline conditions in which radical distance and fusion exist simultaneously; this is the negative state of the hermaphrodite. In the case of the borderline patient, this pathology of the interactive field can possess the patient and therapist; the same phenomenology occurs—though with less destructive potential—in *anyone* encountering his or her mind–body split.

To summarize: in this picture we find a variety of ideas concerning the *opus*: primary is the imagery of the fumes of *Binarius* (the devil)—the dyadic form of Mercurius. The fumes are also known by the alchemists as the *massa confusa* or *prima materia*; they are hostile elements representing incompatible states ruled by splitting. These elements mix with the "lower waters" to create the confusing mixture of qualities of splitting and fusion states that we frequently meet in borderline conditions. The soul is represented here in a split "upper" and "lower" form, characterizing a mind–body, or spirit–matter split. If this woodcut were to represent a fully individuated psyche, the upper and lower parts of the woodcut would link at the apex of the Fountain (corresponding in tantric symbolism to the heart chakra). This woodcut depicts, instead, a different kind of connection: upper and lower spheres are related through the fumes.

The fumes of Binarius form a perfect analogy to projective iden-

tification. In working with them, the alchemist sublimated or distilled states of unconscious identity with processes in the third area, which were filled with split and hostile opposites. The fumes link above with below—mind with body and spirit with instinct. The awareness that projective identification can link above and below, instinctual and mental processes, is thus a clear part of the alchemical image of the mercurial fountain. This role of projective identification has been clarified by Bion, and Grotstein has followed his thought by portraying projective identification as a "conduit for the id into the ego, and from both into the superego" (1981, p. 161).

In the first woodcut these fumes are shown in their ambivalent form. They link above and below; yet, as commentaries on these fumes show (Jung 1946, par. 403 and n. 10), they also block the sun and the moon. Projective identification that obscures the light of consciousness and the imagination appears here—like the alchemical sulphur—as captor of the imagination and renders it dull and lifeless. Yet the sulphuric quality of the fumes can be refined into less and less compulsive forms when therapist and patient work imaginally with them (Jung 1946, par. 403). This alchemical process involves transforming the state that we call projective identification from a negative one into a positive one, but without undervaluing its dark and chaotic aspect. One solution, apparently, for the alchemist, lay in his valuing the fumes' obstruction of the sun and moon. Psychologically speaking, one must value the darkness of despair and the tormenting, soulless state of mindlessness; this is a lesson that must be repeatedly learned by both therapist and patient.

The alchemical model in the *Rosarium* employs the imagery of a couple that must be transformed during their passage through states of dangerous fusion and confusion. For example, projective identification dominates picture two, "the left-hand contact." The "perverse fascination" of incest (1946, par. 419) writes Jung, "like tentacles of an octopus twine themselves . . . round doctor and patient" (1946, par. 371). Jung saw this fusion state, partaking of the "lower waters" and the dynamism of projective identification, as a dangerous condition because identity could be lost through the interplay of psyches. Yet he also recognized the value of this state, for "the hidden meaning of the incest in picture two is revealed to be a repulsive symbol for the *unio mystica*" (1946, par. 419). Incest energies are thoroughly identified with projective identification, and link spiritual processes with the chthonic depths of sexuality (1946, pars. 418, 455). Picture two can thus be seen to represent the dangers of

Figure 1.   The Mercurial Fountain.

Figure 2.   King and Queen.

114

fusion states in the interactive field. While the erotic element is basic to union, when two people find themselves in this state of unconsciously driven contact it becomes more dangerous.

The fusion drives of incest are opposed by the descending dove, (which variously symbolizes the Holy Ghost, the energies of the *unio mystica,* or ecclesiastical wisdom). The dove is necessary to avoid the danger that the field might degenerate into either a false spiritualization or a concrete literalism.

Picture three, "Naked Truth," addresses other dangers encountered in the work of transforming the unconscious dyad. The commentary to picture three is almost a litany against narcissism, especially against the pride and arrogance that may cause one to lose sight of the greater-than-ego powers at work (Jung 1946, par. 450). The banners that attend the woodcut carry the following phrases: Sol says: "O Luna, let me be thy husband," and Luna says: "O Sol, I must submit to thee." (1946, par. 451). The injunctions of Sol and Luna, like the compensatory function of dreams, can be seen to counteract a field of quality of the couple's resistance to a true meeting. In clinical terms, this image addresses narcissistic transference and countertransference resistance.

In picture four, the focus is upon the erotic energies exposed through projective identification, but the admonition against narcissism has been given, and these energies can now be seen to have a positive, transformative quality. Erotic energies are constellated in the interactive field and serve primarily as a bath of transformation for the unconscious dyad whose processes determine so much of the behavior and fantasy life of the conscious couple. Psychoanalytic approaches to sexuality tend to focus upon the negative aspect of erotic energies within the therapeutic field. Emergent erotic energies between patient and therapist would commonly be seen as a defense against anxiety. The alchemical approach remains alert to pathological tendencies and also emphasizes the positive, transforming power of erotic energies.

This stage in the transformation of the interactive field leads to the *coniunctio,* picture five. Here alternating states of fusion and distance — opposites whose painful conflict is usually denied and falsified by the deceptions of projective identification — are transcended in harmony. In this woodcut, the descending dove, so prominent in the previous pictures, is absent; this is a sign that a spiritual attitude is now beginning to be integrated into the interactive field. Prior to the *coniunctio,* the field had been dominated by fusion or splitting. In the interactive

Figure 3.   The Naked Truth.

Figure 4.   Immersion in the Bath.

116

field portrayed by this woodcut, the tendency to act out — thus concretizing the processes in the third area — becomes less of a danger. Generally, working in the third area engages processes that are both literal and symbolic (Samuels 1987).

The *coniunctio* is an event that may be experienced in the present; its rhythmic quality and capacity to transcend opposites of fusion and distance may be directly experienced. As mentioned before, it is also an event that often occurs unconsciously (Jung 1946, par. 461). An important result of the *coniunctio,* whether it occurs as a conscious or unconscious event, is that it leads to the therapist's image being introjected by the patient, and the patient's image introjected by the therapist. As a result the patient can have the imaginal experience of being contained by the therapist both inside and outside of the session. Without such containment the patient will be hindered in experiencing the kind of kinship that furthers growth and encourages both patient and therapist to risk the exposure of vulnerable areas. In Winnicott's sense, the *coniunctio* leads to a "holding environment" (1971).

The *coniunctio* field has an atemporal aspect that is transmitted through the *unus mundus.*[3] This communicative experience may also be seen as a linking of two people through projective and counterprojective identification, a mutual "feeling-into" experience that bridges the limitations of space and time. The *coniunctio* is thus a highly prized state; the alchemist aimed at creating this field quality in a stable form. The woodcuts that follow the *coniunctio* in picture five deal with issues that paradoxically destroy this field yet are also necessary for creating its eventual stability.

Picture six shows a dead, hermaphroditic structure; this is a critical stage in the eventual embodiment of the self. This *nigredo* results from elements of the couple's incestuous intertwining through projective identification during the previous *coniunctio* and will uncover unresolved incest issues in both therapist and patient.

The deathlike state is often experienced by therapist and patient through feelings of depression and despair. Envy also becomes a dominant affect here, for as memories of early losses emerge, they do so along with envy-dominated beliefs that union can never again exist. A person

---

[3]This is a phenomenon linked in occult literature to communication on the astral plane.

Figure 5.   The Conjunction.

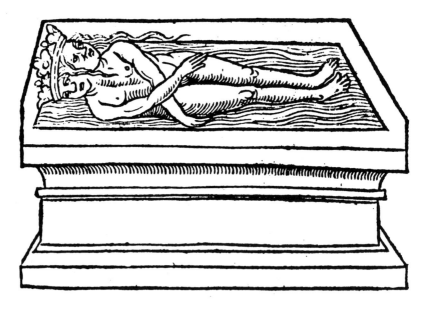

Figure 6.   Death.

in this state will often experience depression and envious attacks through projective identification.

The therapist may easily make use of interpretations rooted in developmental theory. For example, he or she may focus upon part objects stemming from the patient's failure to transit the depressive position. But instead, therapist and patient may reflect upon states of union, occurring in the period preceding the *nigredo,* rather than pursuing such a reductive analysis of affects. This perspective is important because the affects of the *nigredo* are strong enough to repress memories of what has previously occurred. The *Rosarium* sequence thus acts as a guide for dealing with mutations and transformations in the interactive field. If we interpret through the metaphor of projected parts, the patient's despair may be undercut and reduced to a personal level and will not be seen as part of the experience of the loss of sacred energies.

Picture seven, depicting the stage known as the "extraction of the soul," is likened by Jung to a schizophrenic dissociation (1946, par. 477). Up to this point in his analysis of the transference he had employed a model of the *coniunctio* to grasp the union of opposites; this *coniunctio* model was based upon the image of the *hieros gamos* or sacred marriage—a state that can reflect the unconscious relationship between two people. When Jung analyzed picture seven he moved toward another model of the *coniunctio,* namely the *unio mystica,* the *solitary* ascent of the soul to God. This change in model is significant: for while a couple engaged in the interactive field may experience extreme disorientation, more is happening than meets the eye. While therapist and patient may experience a severely soulless condition, the model of the *unio mystica* helps elucidate an unseen process between them. As Jung says, "The psychological interpretation of this process leads into regions of inner psychic experience which defy our powers of scientific description" (1946, par. 482). The soul—the linking quality between patient and therapist—is actually being renewed in an ascent to the transforming powers of the collective unconscious. Yet, the couple's conscious experience of the third area during this time is characterized by a complete absence of linking.

This soulless state is commonly experienced by both patient and therapist, who feel as if they are in parallel or alternate universes. This experience is often frightening and, for the therapist, can be humbling unless his or her narcissistic defenses are too strong. For the state of being out of touch with another human being is difficult to accept,

Figure 7.   The Ascent of the Soul.

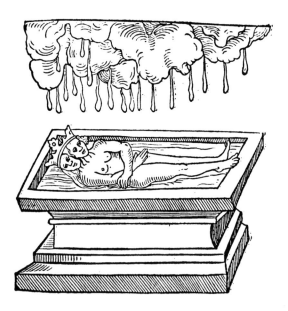

Figure 8.   Purification.

especially for the therapist, who usually feels adept at connecting to people and to psyche. At this juncture, it is possible to make interpretations based upon the theory of projective identification, but to do so would falsify this painful state of a complete absence of connection. For example, states of psychic deadness and impotence that the therapist may feel can readily be interpreted as induced affects. But this is off the mark and accepts into the interpersonal relationship what is better allocated to a field quality.

The state depicted by picture seven is also called the *impregnatio*. The implication is that though the interpersonal relationship feels soulless and though the individuals may feel no inner connection to the unconscious, a mystery is being enacted. In alchemical language, the soul is ascending toward God in the *unio mystica*; this is a state of union with the transcendent Self. *It is a time when projective identification ceases to have interpretive value* and, in fact, has only the value of humbling the therapist in his or her clumsy attempt at understanding. It is a time shrouded in mystery, and there is often a sense of therapeutic failure. What happens here is unknown, *even to the eye of the imagination.* The mystics knew this level, as is evident in the following tale by Rumi, the Islamic mystic and poet of the thirteenth century:

> A seeker knocked at the door of the beloved—God—and a voice from inside asked: "Who is it?" The seeker answered: "It is I"; and the voice said: "In this house there is no I and You." The door remained locked. Then the seeker went into solitude, fasted and prayed. A year later he returned and knocked at the door. Again the voice asked: "Who is it?" Now the believer answered: "It is You." Then the door opened.

The eighth picture, the *mundificatio,* depicts the process of "washing away" lingering inflations that are caused by fusion with processes in the third area. This transformation of negative fusion states continues throughout the entire series of twenty pictures. At this stage in the sequence, the therapist is primarily concerned with the patient's creative linking to the *numinosum,* since the patient's connection to it has been both split off and also fused with his or her ego, causing inflation.

In picture nine, the soul returns, reviving the energy and structure of the interactive field. By now, the field has become relatively stable, and regressions are unlikely to become malignant. This stage leads to the Rebis in picture ten.

In the "Psychology of the Transference," Jung considers the image of the hermaphrodite, known as the Rebis, to be a regrettable product of the alchemist's undeveloped consciousness. He cites the alchemist's lack of awareness of the fundamental psychological process of projection and sees this hermaphroditic image as deriving from the "immaturity of the alchemist's mind" and lack of psychological understanding (1946, par. 533). His assault focuses upon sexuality:

> Freud dug up this problem again. . . . The sexuality of the unconscious was instantly taken up with great seriousness and elevated to a sort of religious dogma. . . . The sexualism of the hermaphrodite symbol completely overpowered consciousness and gave rise to an attitude of mind which is just as unsavoury as the old hybrid symbolism. . . . The sexualism of these contents always denotes an unconscious identity of the ego with an unconscious figure . . . and because of this the ego is obliged, willing and reluctant at once, to be a party to the hieros gamos, or at least to believe that it is simply and solely a matter of erotic consummation. And sure enough, it increasingly becomes so the more one . . . concentrates on the sexual aspect and the less attention one pays to the archetypal patterns . . . I have never come across the hermaphrodite as a personification of the goal, but more a symbol of the initial state, expressing an identity with anima or animus. (1946, pars. 533–535)

The "Psychology of the Transference" contains a strong injunction against enacting negative fusion states that may develop between patient and therapist. One must wonder if this problematic shadow-aspect of psychotherapy, especially sexual acting-out, was responsible for Jung's negative view of the Rebis. And was his aversion to Freud's view of the importance of sexuality a contributing factor? Only in this work on the transference does Jung see the Rebis as negative. In *Mysterium Coniunctionis,* the Rebis is mentioned without negative judgment; indeed, it is praised and noted as an image of the paradoxical union of opposites, of sulphur and the "radical moisture," which are, according to Jung, "the two most potent opposites imaginable" (1955, par. 337). One of many examples we could cite is in Jung's "The Psychology of the Child Archetype." There, the Rebis is not "a product of primitive non-differentiation." Instead, "man's imagination has been preoccupied with this idea over and over again on the high and even highest levels of culture" (1949, par. 292). (For other examples, see Schwartz-Salant 1984, p. 6.)

There is no doubt that the hermaphrodite can function as a negative image. Often it functions negatively in the beginning of the therapeutic process and especially when the therapist is dealing with borderline states of mind. For example, the hermaphrodite may be an image for the kind of fusion state that forms between therapist and patient in a process dominated by projective identification. In this condition two people may feel glued together in one affective body, partaking of the same emotions, while each maintains different defenses and attitudes: one body, two heads! The hermaphroditic self can also be seen shaping the therapist's tendency to act as if she or he were whole, while this "wholeness" is actually a hybrid thing, made up partly of the patient's introjects: we are two, thinking we are one. In this confused mixture, we are easily inclined to make partial interpretations and mistake them as whole. We talk about dynamics to our patients and are then surprised to find out that such interventions have been devastating, for we have failed to note that we had been describing only a part of the ego. Under the dominance of an interactive field structured by the negative quality of the hermaphrodite, we assume, too easily, that the patient has access to certain parts of his or her psyche that are as yet split off from and unavailable to consciousness. Such psychological states can dominate the transference–countertransference process: the self is often experienced as a hybrid object composed of parts of the therapist fused with parts of the patient. Both patient and therapist are easily ruled by this hybrid state.

The negative aspect of the Rebis underlies the confusing splitting processes that dominate the borderline patient. Contradictory and mutually exclusive states of mind are fused. A male patient expresses hatred toward me, then immediately makes loving statements without losing a beat; a middle-aged woman feels sexual toward me if she is feeling young but completely asexual if she feels her own age. The two states exist and define the patient's identity simultaneously; together they are extremely confusing for both of us. Each opposite seems both to deplete and to excite the other. Gender identity also becomes confused when this negative hermaphroditic self constellates.

But the positive potential of this hermaphroditic image also becomes apparent in work with the borderline patient. The patient's lack of an internal, functioning self can be addressed through an interactive field that functions as a conjoined self-image. A self structure can be created between two people without a negative *participation mystique* dominating and without either person losing identity. With proper use of the imagination and with the ability to experience sexuality as an energy field, two people can experience a conjoined self and return to it again and again, just as one person can connect to a unitary self-image. Uplifting spirit, order, and gnosis can be gained from this conjoined self as it can from a unitary self-experience. Significantly, this conjoined self can

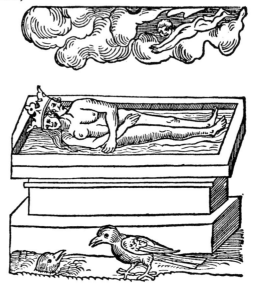

Figure 9.   The Return of the Soul.

Figure 10.   The New Birth.

be introjected to create an inner, hermaphroditic self-structure. Sol and Luna (representative, for example, of rational-discursive attitudes and imaginal ones, or mental and somatic processes, or states of doing and being) have equal value.

The genesis of the positive hermaphrodite includes the experience of the *coniunctio*. When this union state is experienced, an interactive field develops between patient and therapist that has a linking quality and is the source of the therapeutic alliance so crucial for the therapy of borderline conditions and without which psychotic processes can become unmanageable. We can see how the alchemical imagination understood such conjoined states by looking at the tenth woodcut, which depicts the Rebis. This woodcut shows this hermaphroditic figure supported by a lunar crescent. On the one hand, this image represents a state in which the imaginal process has become a ground upon which people can depend, no matter how conflicting their interaction. The dark, persecutory aspect of the Negative Eye Goddess has been tamed. On the other hand, standing on the moon suggests overcoming death (McLean 1980, p. 124). The overwhelming affects of abandonment (including virulent forms of rage, panic, and despair) can become a ground upon which the therapeutic interaction rests. Interactions dominated by persecutory states do not necessarily cease to exist; rather, they cease to destroy the therapeutic alliance. Negative states now exist in a context in which each person's imagination can still function, in which the talion law of revenge has been transformed, and in which each person recognizes how such negative affects are part of his or her natural limitations. Working within the darkness of such states leads to a deepening of union. Yet, without the positive, interactive field stemming from the *coniunctio*, negative fusion states abound, and there is a continual repetitive killing of the imagination as enmity mounts.

Thus in picture ten of the *Rosarium* one encounters a major level of achievement; the creation of a structure that can be a shared self between two people. Of this creation the poet Robert Bly writes: "They obey a third body that they share in common./ They have made a promise to love that body" (1985, p. 19). This subtle body yields wisdom, knowledge, and most crucially, kinship, and has its own autonomy within the third area. It can become a self within an individual, a self with both male and female polarities. Such shared experiences and structures are the proper goal of projective identification.

Figure 11.   Fermentation.

Figure 12.   Illumination.

Figure 13.   Nourishment.

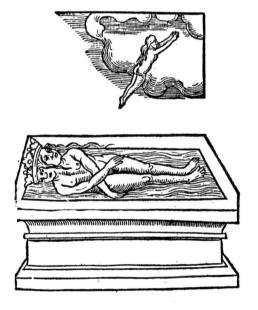

Figure 14.   Fixation.

127

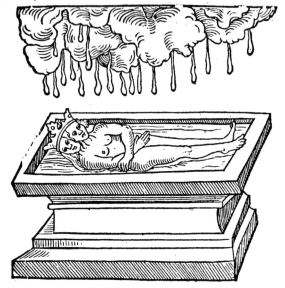

·Figure 15. Multiplication.

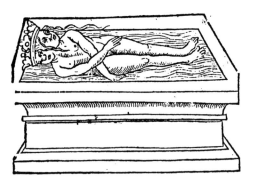

Figure 16. Reviving.

Figure 17.   Perfection.

Figure 18.   Mortification.

129

Figure 19. Coronation.

Figure 20. Resurrection.

CHAPTER FIVE
THE SUBTLE BODY AND IMAGINAL EXPERIENCES
IN THE INTERACTIVE FIELD

. . . the psyche can [have] very real effects which are performed through that something which is called the subtle body. (C. G. Jung, 1935, Part 3, p. 139)

Introduction

The mechanism of projective identification is the means by which a person with a borderline personality attempts to heal his or her connection with the unconscious. In so doing, the person is engaging energies that have to do with what is often called the subtle body, or what I have termed the "third area." Careful attention to this area is therefore crucial to the treatment of the borderline condition. The therapist must learn to facilitate entrances into and exits from this realm, and in general, should be comfortable with this area of the unconscious.

The borderline person has a power problem; he or she is possessed by the need to control the unconscious. Its constellations are so negative that a flexible attitude, or one of proper reverence, is very difficult to establish. This power complex is a source of great distress to the borderline patient, for he or she also knows that it blocks access to an authentic life based upon relationship to others and to the unconscious. The borderline person is likely to feel that his or her power complex is shameful and keeps it a well-hidden secret by splitting it off from the ego's normal, operating consciousness and from other people. Naturally, the borderline person is an expert at sensing power problems in other people. As a consequence of the patient's obsession with power and control, any therapeutic techniques that lead to an awareness of what is happening "in the patient" without also including explicit monitoring of the therapist's own participatory process[1] run the danger of only reinforcing the borderline person's power complex. But to discover an unconscious and autonomous process that captivates both therapist and patient, and then to imaginally relate to it, is a way for the therapist to help the patient to experience the *numinosum*. In this process, both people relinquish an attitude based on power.

The ancient concept of the subtle body is akin to what was known in Newton's day as the aether; this concept was not discarded until the advent of Einsteinian thinking. It is the archetypal forerunner of the field concept in physics and of the interactive field concept in psychotherapy.

The Subtle Body Concept

In his introduction to *The Doctrine of the Subtle Body in Western Tradition,* 1919, G. R. S. Mead stated: "The notion that the physical body of man is as it were the exteriorization of an invisible subtle embodiment of the life of the mind is a very ancient belief." His words are still cogent:

> It is, however, the prevailing habit of skeptical rationalism of the present day to dismiss summarily all such beliefs of antiquity as the baseless dreams of a prescientific age . . . I am persuaded that, the more deeply modern research penetrates into the more recondite regions of biology, psycho-physiology and psychology, the more readily will reason be inclined to welcome the notion as a fertile working hypothesis to co-ordinate a considerable number of the mental, vital and physical phenomena of human personality which otherwise remain on our hands as a confused and inexplicable conglomerate. (1919, pp. 1-2)

The subtle body can be experienced imaginally as a kind of energy field that extends from our physical being.[2] While invisible to ordinary perceptions, it can be seen imaginally. In the context of two people in therapy — therapist and patient — it seems quite clear that their subtle bodies can interact and manifest in a state of fusion, or, the extreme opposite, in a state of separation. The latter state can become

---

[1] I must emphasize that this process does not necessarily mean sharing one's feelings with the patient, but rather that the therapist's statements follow after the imaginal presence of the third area has been established. That is not to say that direct communication of affective states by the therapist to the patient, without such a reference to an interactive field, may not at times be valuable. Some therapists are especially gifted at this kind of direct interaction, which is also extremely important when one is dealing with borderline states of mind.

[2] I would like in this context to refer the reader to A. Mindell's book *Dreambody* (1982). In a sense, Mindell is concerned with Jung's distinction between the psychic and somatic unconscious. In particular, the unpublished *Seminars* on Nietzsche's *Thus Spake Zarathustra* (1934–1939), reveal how psychic imagery can be reflected through the somatic unconscious.

extremely afflicted and persecutory in its soullessness. The third possibility is that the subtle bodies of both can interact in the *coniunctio*.

The question is not whether or not the subtle body exists, but whether or not its existence can be perceived. For when we deal with the subtle body, we are concerned not with ordinary perceptions but with imaginal ones. Those who can *see* will do so; those who cannot will remain skeptical. There are clinicians, however, who are aware of the existence of subtle body phenomena but question the suitability of its use in clinical practice. That brings up far more important issues: is the notion of the subtle body deleterious to therapy, in that it may shift attention away from the importance of the physical body, especially of body energies and associated sexual states? Is the subtle body too elusive to explain in terms that are communicable to clinicians, or does exposure to the concept risk the danger that our clinical efforts might become mired in confusion masquerading as mystery?

Two people can become aware of a state in which their subtle bodies are interacting. This experience is often felt as a change in the quality of space between them, which is experienced as energized and more material in nature. They are then at the threshold of an awareness of archetypal processes, a *mundus imaginalis* as Henry Corbin designated it (1972, pp. 1-19).[3]

The central archetypal structure of the background realm that can be encountered by two people through subtle body experience is the *coniunctio*. When the *coniunctio* is an active, imaginal experience, both people will share the sense of being alternately pulled together toward fusion, then pulled apart toward separation, while in the realm between them there is a continual sense of unity.

Clinical material can be approached with reference to either body or psyche.[4] For example, a twenty-three-year-old male patient, who suffered from occasional impotence, extreme inertia, masturbatory compulsions, and a compulsive use of marijuana, recalled the following childhood experience. At the age of seven, he became frightened by the Popeye character called Alice the Goon. At night he would imagine an immense and terrifying version of her in his bedroom. The only way he

---

[3]Andrew Samuels (1985, pp. 58–59) has persuasively argued that "there is a two-person or shared *mundus imaginalis* which is constellated in analysis."

[4]Attention has been given to the body (Whitmont 1972, pp. 5–16), and this interest has lately increased (Green 1984, pp. 2–24; Woodman 1984, pp. 25–37; Chodorow 1984, pp. 39–48).

could protect himself against her was by pulling the covers tightly up to his chin, so that only his head was above the covers. This ritual continued for the next seven years and subsided only when he began to masturbate and compulsively use marijuana to block his anxiety attacks.

This patient had the look of someone "with the covers pulled up." He would breathe in, then hold his breath for what seemed like an interminable time, and his torso would pull inward toward the back of the chair and recede from view. When he held his breath he seemed to be reduced to a mere head; his rigid body would show no signs of life. He would then spasmodically release his breath. This sequence would repeat itself: the "covers would be pulled up" again, his body would become rigid, and the sudden and forceful release of his breath would eventually follow.

Treatment only marginally addressed this patient's breathing patterns and character armoring. Instead, it focused upon his parental complexes and was especially fruitful when his intense reaction to sexuality (which took the form of a revulsion toward foreplay) was explored. As a result of a brief, one-year treatment, his masturbatory compulsion ceased, he entered into a relationship with a woman his own age, and his addiction to marijuana markedly diminished. His breathing pattern also improved, though he still retained a quality of "pulling up the covers."

This vignette shows how an intense negative mother-complex manifested itself through body and psyche. As a result of my particular training, I chose to work with psychic complexes. Another therapist might have approached this young man's problems through his body armoring and breathing patterns. My approach was moderately successful; a body-oriented therapy would, I am certain, have been at least as fruitful.

The patient employed splitting defenses against the threat of being overwhelmed by psychotic anxieties. In particular, mind–body splitting was his major defense; this was actualized through pulling up the covers—*just to his chin*—in his childhood ritual. This childhood act characterized the way in which he later split from body-awareness. Clearly, his intense anxieties lived, so to speak, in his body and would remain hidden there as long as his splitting defenses worked.

When this patient was not using drugs to temper his fears, his anxiety level would become high, and his body and breathing pattern would be gripped by the kind of rigidity I have described. *Any time a complex is constellated and threatens to assimilate ego functions, the body-ego takes on a pattern associated with the complex.* In relationship to a complex constellation, not only is there an array of physiological responses, such as changes in respiration, heart rate, and galvanic skin response,[5] but there is also a change in the overall body structure. Psychically, this change is experienced through the patient's body image. When the patient I have described was threatened by his negative mother-complex, his body image would shatter into pieces, grow ugly, and become filled with repulsive desires; his physical body would characteristically look as if it were hiding under the covers.

Every complex has a body. The body of the complex is neither the physical body nor a purely mental structure, but an "in-between phenomenon." In Mead's words, it is an "invisible subtle embodiment of the life of the mind" (1919, p. 1). The subtle body can manifest itself psychically in terms of dream, fantasy, and body images, and it can manifest physically in terms of body structure and armoring. *It is both spiritual and physical,* and rather than studying one or the other of these opposites, I shall use clinical material to show that there is much to be gained by attending to that often obscure intermediate realm of which they both partake.

This realm of subtle bodies was a major concern of alchemy. One reads in Paracelsus the refrain "destroy the bodies." He is speaking, I believe, about transforming the body of the complex. In bioenergetic work, the therapist attempts to dissolve body-armoring. That approach engages the physical body, but not the subtle body. If we are to engage the subtle body, the imagination must be employed; this, as Jung said, was the key to the entire alchemical opus (1953, par. 396). If one can successfully work through the subtle-body realm, there is often a chance to transform not only psychic structure but physical structure as well. Mind–body splitting can mend when the subtle-body realm is successfully encountered.

While Jung surveys the use of the subtle-body concept in *Psychology and Alchemy* (1953, par. 394ff.), he develops this concept more fully in his unpublished *Seminars* on Nietzsche's *Thus Spake Zarathustra*. Jung says that projections from the psyche are transmitted through the medium of the subtle body (1934–1939, vol. 3, p. 139) and made manifest in physical and psychic transmissions from one person to

---

[5]Jung demonstrated these physiological responses in his word-association experiments (1918).

another (1934–1939, vol. 10, p. 144). I would like to amplify Jung's thought by stating that the medium of the subtle body may be projected, imaginally perceived, and experienced between two people. Furthermore, this intermediate, subtle body can be a conjoined body, comprising the individual subtle bodies of two people in therapy. This latter form of the subtle-body experience, which is portrayed in the imagery of the *Rosarium Philosophorum,* is our main focus.

Winnicott's discovery of transitional space and phenomena stems, I believe, from subtle-body perceptions. Winnicott says:

> My claim is that [there is] an intermediate area of *experiencing,* to which inner reality and external life both contribute. It is an area that is not challenged, because no claim is made on its behalf except that it shall exist as a resting-place for the individual engaged in the perpetual human task of keeping inner and outer reality separate yet interrelated.
>
> I am here staking a claim for an intermediate state between a baby's inability and his growing ability to recognize and accept reality. I am therefore studying the substance of *illusion,* that which is allowed to the infant, and which in adult life is inherent in art and religion, and yet becomes the hallmark of madness when an adult puts too powerful a claim on the credulity of others, forcing them to acknowledge a sharing of illusion that is not their own. We can share a respect for *illusory experience,* and if we wish we may collect together and form a group on the basis of similarity of our illusory experiences. . . . (1971, pp. 2–3).

One needs Winnicott's courage when attempting to describe subtle-body phenomena. For illusion is the subject, and while a good deal can be said concerning the reality of the imagination and about its potential for enabling one to perceive "the intermediate area between the subjective and that which is objectively perceived" (1971, p. 3), one is then nevertheless confronted by the exceptionally difficult task of communicating this experience. When the subtle-body experience is constellated between two people, both people can experience the kind of phenomenology portrayed in the *Rosarium.*

The experiencing of the *coniunctio* as a here-and-now, imaginal reality can contribute to healing the mad parts of the psyche in which mindlessness dominates, thinking is fragmented, and a sense of personal continuity is lost (Winnicott 1971, p. 97). A mother may cure or mend ruptures in the psychic structure and "reestablish the baby's capacity to use a symbol of union" (ibid.). The *coniunctio,* too, may have this potential when imaginally experienced in the therapeutic setting.

It should be noted that much healing in therapy can occur without the *explicitly* acknowledged experience of the *coniunctio* and without imaginal sight. In the "Psychology of the Transference" Jung says that the *coniunctio* often takes place unconsciously (1946, par. 461) so that its occurrence is unknown to the ego. Healing, as Judith Hubback (1983, pp. 313-327) has shown, can often be understood as the patient's introjection of the therapist's conscious–unconscious union. This process may underlie healing in numerous other instances. It is unlikely that healing stems from an increase in the patient's cognitive mastery of conflict. Nor does it result from the affective experience that a good interpretation may facilitate. These phenomena are relatively visible and tangible.

Instead, the primary source of healing lies in the process that therapist and patient have experienced together, a process whereby the therapist has been able to maintain a self and to repeatedly recover an imagination and capacity to think when bombarded by projective and introjective processes whose very goal is to attack imagination and the linkage (Meltzer 1978, pp. 30-31) thereby engendered. The imaginative thoughts that therapist or patient may have amid such destructive "field phenomena" are rarely the result of a discursive thinking process. Rather they are the "child" of a union, or in Meltzer's phrase, the product of a "combined object" (1978, p. 138; 1973, p. 85).

The imaginal, archetypal couple of the *coniunctio* is the source of healing that can be introjected by the patient and, it should be added, by the therapist as well. The *coniunctio* is much like the unconscious dyad that André Green finds so crucial to therapeutic work (1975, p. 12). It is likely that the *coniunctio* structures the "secured space" that is central to the theory of Langs. In the treatment of borderline states, considerable therapeutic value can accrue from the therapist's and patient's unconscious experience of the *coniunctio*. But there is also considerable value, as my clinical material will exemplify, in its conscious realization as a here-and-now event.

The Somatic Unconscious and the Subtle Body

In his Nietzsche seminars, Jung tells us that the subtle body refers to the unconscious as it is experienced in the body; as one's awareness descends further into body, conscious experience diminishes. For this reason, he explains, the subtle body is exceedingly incomprehensible. But Jung brings the subtle-body concept into his analysis of *Zarathustra* because, as he tells us, Nietzsche's concept of the Self includes the body, *and this Self cannot be reduced to the psychological shadow*. The shadow forms part of the psychological or psychic unconscious, while the subtle body represents the somatic unconscious, which is the unconscious that is experienced as we descend into the body. Thus, having stated his wariness of employing the subtle-body concept, Jung goes on to display a mastery of the subject! He tells us that the subtle body must lie beyond space and time; in fact, it must not fill space. He also reminds us of the importance of the subtle-body concept: "It is marvelous to encounter it in a text which naively comes from the wholeness of man. . . . *Zarathustra* is one of those books that is written with blood, and anything written with blood contains the notion of the subtle body, the equivalent of the somatic unconscious" (1934–1939, vol. 3, pp. 151–152). Here Jung raises an important issue: the subtle body is an important idea, but can it be made comprehensible? For the apprehension of these phenomena depends upon images and hence upon imagination.

Jung's concern with being scientific led him to underplay the subtle-body concept in his *Collected Works*;[6] a few notable exceptions can be found in "Psychology and Religion." He writes: "Our usual materialistic conception of the psyche is, I am afraid, not particularly helpful in cases of neurosis. If only the soul were endowed with a subtle body, then one could at least say that this breath or vapour-body was suffering from a real though somewhat ethereal cancer, in the same way that the gross material body can succumb to a cancerous disease" (1937, par. 13). And, "I have often felt tempted to advise my patients to think of the psyche as a subtle body in which subtle tumours can grow" (1937, par. 36).

At times, a couple may inadvertently find themselves in a subtle-body encounter. At other times, an imaginal technique must be employed to gain access to this realm. The *imaginatio,* in alchemy conceived as "half-spiritual, half-physical," and the "most important key to the understanding of the *opus*" (Jung 1953, par. 396), has an inner logic described by the so-called *Axiom of Maria.* This enigmatic axiom (Jung 1973, par. 68) states: *Out of the One comes the Two, out of the Two comes the Three, and from the Third comes the One as the Fourth* (von Franz 1974, p. 65).

---

[6]Jung explains its significance in alchemy and in the process reveals a mine of information on the subject.

A Clinical Vignette: The Axiom of Maria

"Kate" sat down and said, "Everything is okay. Life was never better." As she started talking I felt uncontacted and noted that I was tending to withdraw and straining to respond in a mirroring way. Halfhearted maneuvers were inadequate and made me uncomfortable. What I could glean from these first few minutes was that our psyches were enmeshed in a perplexing fusion-state in which mutual withdrawal had the upper hand; attempts to overcome its dominance were feeble. I thought of changing the subject and almost said: "How are you doing in your business?" But I quickly recognized that such a choice would only have been a way of trying to create some contact. Instead, I just felt depressed and with that awareness resolved to be receptive.

I then began to make some effort to determine what opposites were at play: she seemed manic, while I felt depressed and abandoned. It seemed that a pair of split opposites was functioning through projective identification, with her depression projected into me. Or was my mania projected into her? Thus, a state of "Twoness" was differentiating out of the "Oneness" of the projective-identification state that had dominated.

As I reflected upon my depressed state, I began to wonder about its manic opposite in Kate and about fusion fears and desires. Now my experience changed. I began to feel the opposites, the manic component and the depressive one. In von Franz's terms, I began to grasp "the Two aspect of the One" by "hypostatizing the Two" (1974, p. 64) into the qualities I have called "mania" and "depression." In other words, a field quality of Twoness had become clear within me. The process of thinking in terms of "her mania" and "my depression" was largely a convenience, a way of grasping the quality of Twoness in an interactive field.

Now I had a choice: what was I to do with the Twoness? Several possibilities emerged. Having been able to contain the opposites, I could have chosen to interpret the dynamic between us as an instance of projective identification. It would have been possible to tell Kate that she had been splitting from depressive anxiety and allowing me to contain it; I could have further related these unconscious choices to the abandonment fears that arose whenever she was on the verge of success. In this instance, an emerging business issue was a source of joy; this joy terrified her, as did her emerging independence from me. If I had communicated these thoughts to Kate, the stage of Twoness would have led to "Threeness" in the form of an interpretation.

Thus, by holding the opposites together in consciousness, I

could have chosen to interpret, and hence to literalize, the Two aspect of the field. Instead, I chose to *see*: I attempted to make imaginal contact with her by seeing, in William Blake's sense, *through* my eyes (Damrosch 1980, p. 16) rather than *with* them. This process involved a shift in the quality of consciousness that had been gained by differentiating the interactive field into the opposite qualities of mania and depression; some of the high-grade energy produced by this differentiation had to be sacrificed. This shift in consciousness can be described as a movement from a "solar consciousness" that readily leads to interpretations, into a "lunar consciousness" that focuses upon images and imaginal perceptions. This shift involves an introverted act in which psychic energy — attention and consciousness — is surrendered to the unconscious and to a symbolic sense of oneness, the "One Continuum."

This imaginal act of giving energy to the One Continuum was a background issue in my interaction with Kate. In the foreground was attention to the imaginal field, a waiting for sight to appear in Kate or in the field between us. In a sense, I was looking at Kate during this activity as if she were a dream image or a process of active imagination (Jung 1916, par. 167). Perhaps this choice of approach can also be understood as a form of "object usage" in Winnicott's sense, which depends upon the transformation of a defensive projective-identification field into a capacity for play (Eigen 1981, p. 415).

When I began to see her differently, I could see that she was terrified. While the opposites were split, imagination had been hindered, and I could not see this terror, nor could I infer it from countertransference reactions. Once again, interpretation could now emerge as the Third; from this vantage point, I could interpret how Kate's splitting was hiding her terror of being seen. But there was another, imaginal alternative. As I focused more attention on the unconscious and a sense of the One Continuum, an energy could be felt to flow upward and back toward the One *and then in a circuit that returned through my heart toward Kate.* It was an effort to focus upon this area, for the affects of the Dyad that precede the potential for Threeness include inertia. A fundamental quality of Threeness is its capacity to enable one to overcome the sense of being leaden and stuck (Jung 1946, par. 404). It is only from this kind of heart-centered act that the field of projective identification can transform and change into a vision of the heart. An unmistakable quality of this experience is its aesthetic element. This has been explored by James Hillman in his paper, "The Thought of the Heart"

(1979, pp. 156–157). A perception of beauty lingers, a beauty of wholeness and mystery that would be destroyed by "making the unconscious conscious."

When I perceived Kate's terror and said nothing, but just *saw* it, she said: "I've been avoiding you, I have been terrified of making contact. I'm frightened of sexual feelings and the vulnerability they bring." And then, as I continued to experience my imagination as heart centered, something new began to emerge. This time it was a vague image, a sense that the energy field or the space between us was changing, becoming more textured and alive. It was neither "in her" nor "in me." We both saw and experienced it, especially its energy that seemed to pull us together; then, just as a physical contact seemed imminent, the field's energy would oscillate so that we became more separate. This rhythmical part of our experience was short-lived because the sexuality that emerged frightened Kate; she became embarrassed and, although she did not deny the importance of what was occurring, she could not continue to explore the experience.

This was a subtle-body experience. The *coniunctio* had emerged "out of the Two." In the *Axiom of Maria,* "Out of the Two came the Three," and the resultant connection to a symbolic sense of oneness was "The One as Fourth." The appearance of the *coniunctio* could be recognized as a synchronistic event because of the simultaneous meaning it had for both of us. It was a sacred event, a moment of grace, and perhaps also a result of faith in a background sense of oneness.

Because of Kate's awakening sexual anxieties, the opposites that had been held together by the *coniunctio* experience dissolved and we found ourselves in the depressive state of the *nigredo.* We were led into a state of soul-loss; there was a lack of contact that was the complete opposite of the union state that had been afforded through the *coniunctio.* These stages typically follow the *coniunctio* experience and correspond to pictures six and seven of the *Rosarium.* But the effects of the *experience* of the *coniunctio* did not vanish; this kind of experience is retained. It leads to kinship libido (Jung 1946, par. 445).

Generally, one does not explicitly follow the logic of the *axiom.* But I believe that it represents the process of dealing with opposites, especially opposites functioning in projective identification. I have emphasized transformative experiences within the subtle-body field. These experiences have an inherent logic. The *coniunctio*, while always an act of grace, can be facilitated by imaginally attending to the interac-

141

tive field. In a sense, psychotherapy is the art of moving from the "Two to the Three."

Discovering Unconscious Couples in the Subtle-Body Field

"Nora" was a talented woman in her thirties. She was professionally competent, having "made it" in the corporate world. Her borderline qualities, especially a considerable masochistic compliance and an abandonment depression (behind which was hidden a delusional God-projection), often undermined her interpersonal relations, including her marriage. She leaned toward fusion states in order to ward off abandonment and was especially prone to introject the projections of others. Generally, her borderline structures contributed to her functioning far below the level that her innate abilities warranted. The following event, which occurred in therapy before the delusional material and abandonment issues had become manifest, played a significant role in the dissolution of defenses against experiencing these painful issues.

Nora began her session with a yawn and handed me a check. I noted that it was in error by one week's fee. In her usual playful manner she said: "Don't make too much of slips like that, I'm just tired. And besides, I have wonderful news about my favorite subject, my supervisor. I finally stopped being a wimp and stood up to her. Her evaluation of my work was awful, filled with envy, and I confronted her on each point and got her to completely change it." Her confrontation was an important event, a landmark in terms of her behavior with authority figures. To Nora it was a culmination of months of therapeutic work oriented toward owning her own authority.

Throughout these months a theme emerged: Nora's consistent contempt for other people. Almost everyone in her past and present, especially her supervisor, had been a target. Refrains such as "their lack of strength," or "their cowardice," or "their refusal to be honest about what they believe" were common. In this session, there was a just-so quality about her story, and the contempt normally present was absent. As she spoke, I continued to wonder about her initial yawn and slip about the check. Her outer success was very important and I acknowledged that, but clearly more was happening than was immediately apparent.

I allowed my attention to turn inward and also began to look at Nora *through* my eyes. As I employed this imaginal process, I was aware of *being in my body*. Throughout this process, a perceptual haziness existed during which my body surface seemed to expand; its energy field seemed to be reaching outward. Another way to describe this imaginal act is to say that the experience of a new field between us slowly developed; there was a sense that the space that separated us had gained in substance, and it seemed to possess its own autonomy in the form of a flickering of imagery. It was difficult to distinguish whether this experience derived from body or from psyche. Both seemed to participate, and imagination seemed to arise out of this body–psyche field. This vision seemed at times to be composed of Nora's intrapsychic process, at other times, of mutual contents in a shared subtle-body field.

During this subtle-body experience, I remembered Nora's initial "slip." What was it about? A dual vision is essential to the imaginal process, as these examples demonstrate. The imaginal act is often structured by history—in this case by the initial data of Nora's slip, its meaning in our process, and its relation to her past. It is also structured by an atemporal process, a spontaneous appearance of imagery through the somatic unconscious. A dual awareness of both timebound and atemporal forms has always formed the basis for imaginal activity; by employing this kind of awareness, one begins to be able to distinguish "true" from "false," or "fantastic," imagination. This dual model is central in mantic procedures (von Franz 1974, p. 198), in Blake's structuring of vision through particularity and the Divine Jesus (Damrosch 1980, pp. 151-152), in alchemy (Jung 1953, par. 360), and in what Bion called "binocular vision" (Meltzer 1978, pp. 49–50).

The conscious and unconscious couple are temporal and atemporal dyads. These two dyadic relations create a quaternity. In "Psychology of the Transference" Jung makes the extremely significant remark that a quaternal structure is necessary in order that the energies of incest are not concretized (1946, par. 430). An awareness of this quaternal structure prevents patient and therapist from merging with energies manifesting in the interactive field.

In the session with Nora, I initially saw her as a woman who was feeling effective in her new state of assertiveness. She was separated from her internal, persecutory images. I also experienced her subject–object clarity; she and I both had the sense that she was contained and her own person. But when I entered into a more imaginal state, I began to see a pocket of contempt in her. There was a sense of glee, quite split off, at the way her supervisor had squirmed under her confrontation.

143

The subtle-body experience is often in the background, a subliminal field of imagery relative to which one forms interpretations and other cognitive acts. In psychoanalytic terms, this experience would be reduced to so-called primary process. But in the kind of therapeutic activity that I am describing the reverse is true: developmental considerations become a background issue, and imaginal processes move to the foreground.

Nora's contempt had been strong in the past; it was now only imaginally perceptible. One would expect some diminution of her contempt, since there is always repression and some splitting in the growth process. One might say that Nora had been able to separate from the shadow (of contempt), which now resided in her unconscious; but the important element here was an imaginal process, not more "shadow integration," nor interpretations of transference or countertransference dynamics.

This imaginal process was experienced in the following way: having seen her contempt, I returned to her initial behavior in the session:

> **Me:** "I think the contempt you have had, especially over the last few months, needs also to be seen as a contempt for me. Perhaps your yawn and underpayment were signs of this contempt."
> **Nora:** "I don't think so. I can follow that with my head but it doesn't feel right."
> **Me:** "You've spoken about how limited our time is together. That could be a link to your father, who spent so little time with you and for whom you have great contempt. Also, we've been spending a lot of time on outer, manifest levels, like talking about your supervisor. I wonder if you experienced that, in part, as a message that I didn't want to directly relate to you. That could engender contempt."
> **Nora:** "I'll think about it, but I don't think so. I think we had to deal on the outer level. Look what's happened in the process! I'm finally standing up for myself."

Throughout these interpretive attempts, which soon felt feeble, I maintained an imaginal eye on Nora's contempt, allowing it to recede into the background. I then entered my body more deeply and waited for an image to emerge.

Nora was now talking about her supervisor's physical size, noting that she was much taller than her supervisor and even overpowered her. In fact, Nora was belittling her supervisor, "putting her down" and dismissing her. She mentioned that she enjoyed making her supervisor cry during their confrontation. After several minutes, something began to vaguely appear to me, a hazy thought combined with what I was seeing in her and between us.

> **Me:** "Perhaps what is going on now is that you and I are like your mother, I mean father talking about your mother." I stumbled, felt confused, and was surprised by my lack of clarity. I had thought I knew what I was going to say but was tongue-tied and got "mother" and "father" all tangled up. I tried to sort this out.
>
> **Nora:** "Wait, maybe we are mother and father talking about Nora."
>
> With that remark she was very reflective; she looked away, immersed in thought. She was experiencing something; I was more an onlooker at this point than a participant. With a suddenness, as if awakening from a dream, she said:
>
> **Nora:** "That's it! I always felt they were contemptuous of me and I completely blocked it out. It seems they were *always* talking about me in the way I just talked about her."

Her experience had a clear ring of truth to it. She had contacted a painful reality about her parental couple—their contempt for her and her lifelong need to deny such an awareness. Now Nora *saw* their contempt.

In the next session, I learned that when Nora turned away she felt she was in a timeless place. This place had a strange quality she had never known before, a sense of mystery; the experience had all the qualities of an entrance into the somatic unconscious. It was also similar to liminal processes, rituals that are enacted in the subtle-body state of awareness.

Nora had the following dream after her vision of the parental couple.

> I am walking along a street. In the gutters are layers of dried eucalyptus or bay leaves and a rich, pure, finely-textured topsoil washed by spring rains. The soil and leaves are light and layered. I look down and see a man-hole cover, which is actually a grille. It is black, wrought iron and octangular in shape. The design is

a Hapsburg *Zweiadler,* a double-headed, crowned eagle with one body. In its claws is a bundle of arrows. I lift it up and look down and across the tunnel. It is well constructed, solid and safe. The other end is about ten yards away. I can see the opening. Outside it is golden and glowing warm, sunny and earthy.

Nora associated the topsoil to the content of her initial dream in therapy, *an Olympic-sized swimming pool filled with shit.* Now the cesspool was transformed into rich, aerated topsoil. An understanding we now gained of that remarkable initial dream was its representation of her psyche as one filled with the projections of others. She was a vessel for the contempt of her surroundings. As a result of Nora's tendency toward idealization and fusion, she could not process these affects; they created psychic (and also physical) constipation, since her psyche swallowed projections but could not expel them. This also explained her contemptuous attitudes toward others. Her contempt of others was an attempt to expel introjects, a lifelong process beginning with her parents' contempt for her.

After her vision and ensuing dream, a change took place. The dream imagery of descent and light at the end of the tunnel indicated the potential for a birth of the self — an anal birth, a capacity to trust her spontaneity and especially her creativity. That proved to be the long-range process, an individuation thread and goal. But the remarkable, immediate gain was facilitated by the double-headed eagle, the hermaphrodite, which is a central image of the *Rosarium. In its positive form it represents, among other things, overcoming splitting.* There is no question that her splitting defenses sharply diminished after this dream. Her need for idealization and her terror at seeing how contempt had ruled her life were faced and changed, and her chronic mind–body splitting began to diminish. For example, she dreamed of a young-girl, about nine years old, who was recovering from an operation for a spinal-cord injury. She had a crescent-shaped scar on the back of her neck. The operation had been a success. The young girl had been in a full-body cast from early childhood. Now she was out of the cast, fragile but recovering.

One further point that merits attention is the way in which we were able to use the contemptuous couple in the work that followed. When projective-identification mechanisms returned, I would recall the couple, often just to myself, at times also to her. This would have the effect of imaginally creating the couple as a third thing between us, which in turn cleared the projective-identification field.

The following material is from another mildly borderline

woman who employed withdrawal rather than fusion as a main line of defense. "Paula" was a professionally successful, forty-year-old woman who entered therapy after many years of Freudian-based psychoanalysis. Her reason for seeing me, a Jungian, was her desire for a therapist who had not only a spiritual vantage point, but also an awareness of Freudian thought. Erotic energies played an especially large role in Paula's life; they also proved to be crucial to our therapeutic work. During the first two years of treatment her withdrawal tendencies had been a main focus; after this period her fear of sexual excitement began to surface. The following exchange occurred between us at this time.

> **Paula:** "I want to be here and stay here today, not wandering in outer thoughts. I need your help."
> **Me:** "How can I help you?"
> **Paula:** "I don't know, I just know I want to stay here. I want to feel the excitement, be with it, not run away."
> **Me:** "You are beginning to split now. (I infer this from the intensity with which I find myself fragmenting at this moment.) Your attention is wandering. Try to stay with the excitement. What fantasy arises?"
> **Paula:** (After a long pause) "It's difficult to just stay here and not split. The word naughty comes to me—I shouldn't feel this way with father."

At this point, with our sexual excitement rising, the atmosphere or space between us began to feel alive, vibrant. Both of us recognized this change; it was an example of an emerging awareness of the somatic unconscious or the subtle body. There was a texturing of space in which we both seemed to be inside a field that was also between us. This flickering awareness of the subtle body was not of a thing localized in space. It was sensed as a change in the feel of space (and time) as perceived during the previous moments. To have called this change a regression would have been completely insufficient. We were inside this experience and also outside of it; we were both aware of its autonomy and of our oneness with it.

We had a mutually implicit reference point in this dialogue; when Paula was between the ages of six and thirteen her father had given her many spankings, and she had vivid recollections of his sexual arousal. She described the event as having an entrance phase that was initiated by her having been nasty to her mother; her father would then

147

tell her to go to her room and wait for him. He would spank her in a prescribed fashion—by placing her over his legs—and then exit as if nothing had happened. The intensity of this sadomasochistic energy created for her a liminal experience; her father's spanking became a profound ritual.

This theme had been the substance of our previous sessions. We had linked the spanking ritual to her history of sexually acting out with nearly all of her previous (male) therapists. She had also begun to feel sexual desires toward me during the therapy session. I interpreted her splitting as a defense against these desires. She feared they would overwhelm her, override any control she might have, and lead to yet another episode of sexual acting out.

Through this form of incest, Paula had had an oedipal victory over her mother. But it was a pyrrhic victory that left her extremely vulnerable to being emotionally and physically flooded by the energies that the incest taboo and the mother normally check. These are extreme sexual, violent, chthonic and archetypal energies that are often associated with Dionysus. A proper relationship to this archetype can lead to healing and renewal of personality. In antiquity, the mystery cults used these energies in this way. In the *Rosarium,* picture four, "Immersion in the Bath," depicts the positive functioning of these energies. But in the "father–daughter ritual," Paula would become identified with these Dionysian levels. As in all such cases of a person's unconscious identification with an archetype, Paula would be so overwhelmed by its forces that she would have to split from the experience to the point of denying its existence. The result was a schizoid quality in her personality, which consisted of an oscillation between being present and withdrawing.

This schizoid quality was rife when Paula entered therapy; and years of work in psychotherapeutic treatments of varying points of view had failed to make a dent in her schizoid character structure. Nearly all of Paula's previous work with male therapists had included her sexual fantasies of impersonal, intense penetration by these men. Sexual acting out occurred with two of them; both were impotent and sadistic in their behavior, both during and after the sexual act.

At the time of the session I have been describing, we had had several weeks of sessions in which a rather stable erotic field existed between us. This was a new development. Previously the awareness of these sexual energies had been attacked by Paula's splitting defenses, making it difficult for me to maintain attention; my consciousness would fade in and out of focus during the hour. At these times our interactive field had a dynamic that recalls Guntrip's idea of the schizoid "in and out program" (Guntrip 1969, p. 36): affective contact and withdrawal alternated with a rapidity that allowed for little reflection. I should also add that Paula's need to defend against sexual feelings was reinforced during the first year of our therapy by her involvement in various sexual affairs. Acting out in this fashion masked her awareness of actual sexual abuse by her father and dissipated the anxiety provoked by her sexual feelings during the therapy session.

Mindful of Paula's wish not to dissociate and withdraw from me, I recalled our previous work, especially as it related to the ritual spankings in her childhood. Our work had led to an awareness that her father's sexual abuse had created an unconscious transference couple comprising Paula (at thirteen years of age) and her father. This couple was our unconscious dyad. During this session, I began to *see* this couple for the first time, but instead of focusing on the unconscious as an inner reality, my attention was on the unconscious "out there," in the subtle body or somatic unconscious that had begun to constellate. My next remark stemmed from the perception of this imaginal couple — Paula and her father — in their spanking ritual.

> **Me:** "Can you sense a kind of energy field between us, as if there is an imaginary couple here composed of you and your father?"
> **Paula:** "I'm not sure. I talked to my father recently. He was so forgetful. I sensed his impotence. I guess that's a loss of the oedipal father. I can sense the couple now, me and my father."
> **Me:** "I'm not sure how you and I and the couple connect. I don't sense the fantasy clearly."
> **Paula:** "I am lying over your lap on my bed. You are spanking me. I'm feeling the tautness of your arm hitting me, the tautness of your thighs and penis, it's all blended . . . the excitement in your body . . . I can't tell whose excitement it is, mine or yours."

My attention was on the imaginal couple between us and also on her. It is essential to grasp the structure of this dual perception. There were two separate objects: a couple composed of the patient and myself, and the imaginal couple, whose presence could be sensed and their form imaginally seen in the space between us. My attention was on both couples at once, oscillating between one and the other or hovering between them. In response to her comment, I, too, felt excited and chose to tell her. But then I was surprised to find myself saying, "What do you want to do?"

This last question was a result of imaginally focusing on the transference couple and the drives and fantasies of this dyad. I felt as if I might lose my boundaries, but I also knew that *not* saying what I did would lead to breaking the field between us. It seemed honest to ask this seemingly seductive question. At the same time, I had a stabilizing reference point through the triangle of Paula, the couple, and myself.

> **Paula:** "I want to *see* your excitement. I want to undress you, to *see* it."

At this point the field intensity rose, and I began to feel somewhat identified with the male in the couple. I was again surprised when the following fantasy emerged in me; I told it to her:

Me: "I want to penetrate you from the rear."

Paula: "Then do it! I want it too! Don't hide it!"

Engaged in my own feelings and vision of the couple, waiting to see what might emerge, the following thought forcefully occurred to me:

Me: "What about mother?"

Paula: "Fuck her—she doesn't matter. All that matters is us!"

Me: "I'm scared."

Paula: "I don't believe it! It's incredible! You'd leave me in it all alone because you're scared! Well I'm not! She doesn't count. It doesn't matter what she thinks."

Me: "But I'm scared."

Paula: "I feel hate, rage, awe, disbelief. You're a fucking bastard—you can't leave me in it alone! I feel a fury, chaos, a splitting in my mind. Oh God, I don't believe it! I feel fragmented by a tornado inside, like my insides were just taken out of me, sucked out of me. You are denying your feelings and desires, and since we are merged, I have to deny mine, or split them off. I can't trust!"

Me: "I think that is just exactly what happened to you with your father."

I said this partly because some clarity seemed useful, but also to dampen what seemed to me to be a rising level of unconscious processes that could be overwhelming. In silence, Paula reflected for several minutes, and in an uncharacteristic manner, she said:

Paula: "So all his other denials [of her illnesses and anger] were just a screen for this primary denial. The only way I could remain integrated was to be engaged in a mutually acknowledged sexual relationship. This is powerful! No wonder I've acted it all out—mentors with unresolved mother complexes and unresolved father complexes. I remember one analyst with whom I couldn't collude and I rationalized that he was incompetent. I continued to experience anxiety in the sessions because there was no mutually acknowledged desire. With my fiancé I feel intact when I'm with him, and then when I'm alone during the middle of the week, my anxiety begins to rise. The only way to maintain cohesion is to be in a mutually desired sexual relationship. Otherwise I lose cognitive skills. I can't think. I only regain them when I have a relationship. I've always thought that I had a learning disorder or, worse, some brain damage."

It is important to underscore the features of our therapeutic work that accounted for our capacity to contain the erotic energy field. I engaged this field—especially with the question, "What do you want to do?"—only after a considerable amount of psychic integration had occurred in Paula; considerable progress had been made toward her achieving mental unity. The difficulty, however, is that mental unity is often achieved *after* engaging subtle-body experiences.

Anyone treating schizoid personality components knows how resistant certain psychic parts are to integration and at the same time how much of the true self they contain. I think that the procedure I am exploring is a possible aid to a treatment that employs a model of regression into early childhood. But I emphasize that a considerable amount of therapy on the level of mental consolidation, especially through transference analysis of projective identification and splitting, is essential before such erotic-imaginal realms can be successfully approached. The expression of erotic desires in the therapeutic process has long been recognized to be extremely dangerous.[7] This method should not be approached by anyone who feels uncomfortable with this material.

---

[7]Consequently, it is only with some reticence that I have allowed publication of the verbatim material in Paula's case. It is certain to shock some people and perhaps will not be universally welcomed. It also will inevitably draw projections onto me, and that is an uncomfortable prospect. But it would be dishonest to withhold this material, especially since it was vital to the successful outcome of the treatment.

I must again stress that the last thing I am suggesting in subtle-body experiences is the free expression of the therapist's erotic thoughts or emotions. That is dangerous and unethical. I have emphasized, however, that such content may spontaneously appear within an imaginal *structure*. One part of this structure is historical, the other atemporal; one part is determined by developmental considerations, the other by imagery. When erotic imagery and affects appear within a proper structure, they can prompt one's entry into a deeper level of transformation, in this case, the central event of the *coniunctio*.

As a result of our imaginal, subtle-body encounter, Paula discovered for the first time the root of her severe anxieties and withdrawal tendencies. She had had a chronic fear of an organic brain disorder that she believed was responsible for the occasional loss of her capacity to think. The intense rage and despair she experienced at her father's denial of his abuse was employed to attack any linking processes, especially in her thinking. By reexperiencing her trauma as we did, she finally understood and eventually gained mastery over her dissociative processes.

In this case, what we had accomplished prior to the session discussed was an awareness of the unconscious couple that had been dominating our sessions and all of her relationships. That couple had been imaginally activated in the therapy. I would like to emphasize the difference of this event from the type of enactments that are employed in Gestalt therapy: I am aware that I actually experienced the desires of which I have been speaking. But *my attention was in two places at once, with one "lens" on the transference couple and another on the patient and myself.* By attending to both couples — the unconscious dyad comprising an imaginal or mythical couple and a dyad comprising the patient and myself, a present-day, historical pair — we could see the truth engendered by our imaginal process. Prior to this imaginal act we had been able to reconstruct the past, but we had not succeeded in revealing the depths of Paula's despair and dissociation. *The reconstruction left us at an oedipal level; the imaginal replay plunged us into the schizoid world of mindlessness that had plagued her being during her entire adult life.*

There is no question that the drama we had entered had been enacted in a transitional realm; it had been a subtle-body experience. The intensity of Paula's sexual and aggressive drives was revealed by this enactment, but she had not yet gone very far toward integrating them. What could aid this? Paula still tended to be overwhelmed by sexual energies; acting out continued to be her means of controlling them. But she now had a suitable partner, and she was far more conscious of her history and psychological process than ever before. In the sessions that followed, there was less splitting, but some fragmenting continued; she was not yet sufficiently embodied. Paula recognized the persistence of this less intense "in and out" dynamic and wondered how it might change. Her first tendency was to believe that her fiancé was the answer. I noted the defensive nature of this approach and expressed my belief that it actually solved very little and was probably fated to lead to an impasse, in which her father and her husband-to-be would become more and more fused.

The transformative possibilities that stem from the *coniunctio* are clear. Paula and I had been aware of a transference couple, an unconscious dyad that had been brought to consciousness. But this dyad comprised personal images; and it may be said to have stemmed from the personal unconscious. Four weeks later, the nature of the dyad became more archetypal; this was expressed by the imagery of a couple in tantric union. I will describe the transformative effects of this shared vision of the subtle body.

A development of particular importance had occurred during this period. Paula had begun to engage in the process of active imagination. In fantasy, she would attempt to return to her childhood bedroom and reexperience what had occurred. That choice often proved very anxiety provoking; she had to substitute a different male figure for her father. An insight also emerged: Paula recognized that when she was hungry she became sexually aroused. At these times she wanted a penis, any penis, to fill her void. She later came to understand that what she really wanted was her father's penis. In the past she had usually eaten to satisfy her longing; now she gained the courage to refrain from eating and, instead, experience her feelings and intense anxieties. This proved to be an important experiment, for while she occasionally succumbed to the desire to eat in order to ward off a painful sense of emptiness, she was usually able to stand her ground and experience her desires. In this way, Paula became more and more capable of entering into her severe anxieties and sexual/aggressive arousal; she began to be able to tolerate the image of her father during these experiences. These same affects could then be experienced with me during our therapy sessions.

In an ensuing session Paula had felt hungry for about an hour prior to her appointment but did not eat. Shortly after she arrived, a mild "in and out" pattern became evident. I noted this and we spoke about it as a sign that sexual desires were present and that she feared they might overwhelm not only her, but both of us. In the past, she would have eaten before the session. Now that she had not acted out by eating, these desires were especially intense. In the prior session these desires were represented by the unconscious couple comprising Paula and her father. Now they were no longer confined to the unconscious dyad, and were even stronger.

As we felt the power of these energies, a new quality emerged: Paula became deeply embarrassed. She had the sense of an inner void and wanted to fill it with my penis, not with me. What was most embarrassing to her was the intensity of her desire and its amoral quality; she had great difficulty containing the tide of impulsivity. It was essential that we both stay in this intensely charged erotic atmosphere and simply experience it.

This stage is depicted in the *Rosarium* as "Immersion in the Bath," picture four. We were experiencing the sexual energies that can dominate the subtle-body field. Generally they are highly impersonal and often have a strongly compulsive nature. The purpose of this highly-charged libido is to effect an immersion in the unconscious. The couple, *primarily their unconscious dyad,* must be transformed. Jung writes:

> (In the Bath) the immersion is effected by the rising up of the fiery, chthonic Mercurius, presumably the sexual libido which engulfs the pair and is the obvious counterpart to the heavenly dove. . . . Thus the pair are united *above* by the symbol of the Holy Ghost, and it looks as if the immersion in the bath were uniting them from *below,* i.e., in the water which is the counterpart of the spirit. . . . Opposition and identity at once. . . . (1946, par. 455)

The sexual energy we were experiencing held the possibility Jung describes, the emergence of the *coniunctio,* "opposition and identity at once," and hence it was vital not to interpret it as a form of acting out or as a defense mechanism.

But these correctives were an afterthought, not a conscious reflection. While we were in the "Bath" together, I recalled little of what had previously occurred. The main focus was on our experience and not, for example, on the unconscious couple with which we had previously worked. The session felt as if it could have been our first. Only gradually did our previous process begin to filter into our awareness. Paula began to speak:

Paula: "What can I do about this? What does one do with these feelings? They seem so cut off from anything human. Do they change?"

Me: "You can talk about them. You can feel them, feel how they link to your father. They can't be solved by acting on them."

I soon realized that the words I spoke made sense and were somewhat calming to her. But I also recognized that I was repeating something like Freud's recipe of sublimation and repression. What I said took me away from the experience of the "Bath" and from affective contact. My approach had been a superego ploy, a shallow escape from her question: "Do they change?" With this recognition I stopped "problem-solving" and waited instead. Only then did I begin to recall the session in which we had experienced Paula and her father as an imaginal couple. I mentioned this to her.

Soon something new began to occur. We could both imaginally see and experience a couple, but one very different from the previous dyad. The couple seemed to hover in the space between us, engaged in a tantric embrace that determined the energy field we experienced. This field was now typified by the *coniunctio,* picture five of the *Rosarium;* it had its own rhythmic energy. Through it, our subtle bodies were pulled toward, but not into, fusion; then they rhythmically separated. Prior to the manifestation of the *coniunctio,* the energies we had felt were primarily sexual. Now a change occurred. The *coniunctio* experience brought us a sense of closeness; Jung refers to this closeness as "kinship" (1946, par. 445), Turner calls it *communitas* (1974). Importantly, sexuality no longer dominated our contact. It was as if the libido rose upward and opened our hearts. Our contact became primarily heart centered.

In "Psychology of the Transference" Jung discusses a case that illustrates the appearance of the transference. While working with a woman's dream about a very special, six-month-old child, Jung asked what had happened six months prior to the dream. He found that another archetypal dream had occurred, and further, that upon writing it down the woman had had a vision of a golden child lying at the foot of a tree. This sequence indicated that a "child" was being formed in the unconscious and led to the next question: What happened nine months before that vision?

> She had painted a picture showing, on the left, a heap of coloured and polished (precious) stones surmounted by a silver serpent, winged and crowned. In the middle of the picture there stands a naked female figure *from whose genital*

155

> *region the same serpent rears up towards the heart,* where it bursts into a five-pointed, gorgeously flashing golden star. . . .

And Jung adds:

> The serpent represents the hissing ascent of Kundalini, and in the corresponding yoga this marks the first moment in a process which ends with the deification of the divine Self, the syzygy of Shiva and Shakti. [A footnote here adds:] This is not a metaphysical statement, but a psychological fact. (1954, pars. 376–380 and n. 31; my italics)

The heart is the central issue of the transformation process. Often people are afraid of sexual energies in their intense, impersonal form *because* acting on them destroys the process of opening the heart. It is often quite wrong to think that a fear of these energies is based upon concerns over emotional flooding. Fear of flooding is often a manifest issue, but a far deeper one is the fear of destroying a sacred process that can lead to the *coniunctio* and the opening of the heart.

It was clear that an answer had been given to Paula's question: "How do the energies change?" They change by working their own transformation, by opening the heart chakra. As always in the *coniunctio* experience, but especially in a heart-centered vision, both people feel a kind of linking of their bodies, as if flesh and blood were being exchanged in this subtle-body experience.

I must add that Paula's experience was also one of all the chakras opening, while her (and my) heart was the major and most energized of these centers. She spoke of a column of energy rising up her back and also through her. This is the well-known imagery of the rising Kundalini.[8]

From a clinical point of view, we must be concerned with the effects of such subtle-body experiences. The fact that they occur is commonly known. The fact that people know they have been through something utterly unlike any previous experience is also common. But we often hear of people having similar reactions with drugs, though these prove to have little effect upon behavior and the sense of self once the person has returned to normal consciousness. We know something about the profound impact of subtle-body experiences by the observation of a person's behavior (in therapy sessions, for example) and also by the person's own disclosures of other life changes. But the dreams that follow the subtle-body interaction are especially diagnostic of a depth trans-

---

[8]This imagery was probably prefigured in my earlier desire to penetrate her from behind.

formation of personality. For without dreams that register inner, structural change we have no basis from which to proceed.

The following is the last in a series of four dreams with the theme of change in Paula's inner relationship to a male figure.

> I am in a boat, steering it. I don't know how it is propelled, but it moves slowly and gently in water that is aqua blue. Beauty and stillness are all around. I can see no land, just water; I feel safe, moving slowly ahead. I look to my left and I see a man is swimming in the water next to me. He seems like a composite of my father and fiancé but his eyes are different from anyone I know. He swims gently, carefully alongside me. He seems like my father at times and when he does he is about 40, my age. I see land ahead and continue steering. I think to myself that when we get to land he probably won't stay with me but will keep on his way. This feels okay. As we approach land I ask him about this and he says, "I'll come with you." It feels safe, like he is a partner. I awake to the jolt of the boat hitting up against the shore.

This dream came after I told Paula about wanting to use her material for publication; in the process, I explained about the *coniunctio*. After the dream Paula said, "You gave what happened a cognitive quality." It is important to note that Paula's dream figure not only represented the sum of the figures current in her life, but offered something new as well: he had unfamiliar eyes.

Thus, the result of the *coniunctio* experience culminated in the integration of an inner figure, the animus, neither a synthesis of introjects, nor an autonomous image of the objective psyche, but a combination of both. As a consequence of the changes indicated by this dream, when her fiancé left her for several days, or when she left therapy sessions, she suffered no strong experiences of loss, nor feelings of a "hole in her stomach" accompanied by frantic wandering or the need to sleep. These reactions had been diminishing all along, especially after the imaginal experience of her father and herself as an unconscious dyad. But they declined sharply after the *coniunctio* experience. Moreover, after the subtle-body experience her attention was even more fully focused on the therapy, and fears of sexual flooding were no longer an issue. Finally, Paula's newly won sense of being embodied was firm. Prior to her subtle-body experiences the only time she had known embodiment was during sexual intercourse. Now she could experience it alone while doing everyday things. After the animus/birth dream she had a relatively constant inner companion for the first time, and the depressive or persecutory anxiety that had plagued her was vastly relieved.

The dream I have cited is the culmination of a series of dreams in which Paula's relationship to her animus developed. Other dreams included one of a man and a woman stabilizing each other on an icy path and another of a man leaving on a bus but throwing his wallet and money to her so she could follow; there was no panic of loss on her part in this second dream. During the many years of earlier analytical work, she had never had dreams of inner, supportive figures. After the *coniunctio* experience through the subtle body, dreams and ego integration often change. Mutations of inner structure and the foundation of the conscious personality lead to far-reaching transformation.

CHAPTER SIX
VISION AND THE HEALING EDGE OF MADNESS

The field of battle is the hearts of people. (Dostoyevski, *The Brothers Karamazov*)

Introduction

In this chapter I continue to explore the unconscious dyad in relation to borderline states of mind. Although experiences with borderline patients can be understood in terms of transference or countertransference projections that repeat early continual traumas (Kahn 1974) and developmental failures, this perspective nevertheless falters. These experiences should also be envisioned in terms of field dynamics that engage atemporal forms. These field experiences are larger in scale than purely personal dynamics comprising our mutual projections.[1] For in some mysterious way the therapeutic interaction constellates, creates, or discovers—no one word will do—some "third thing." Jung's description of the alchemical god Mercurius is apt: "The elusive, deceptive, ever-changing content that possesses the patient like a demon now flits about from patient to doctor and, as the third party in the alliance, continues its game . . . " (1946, par. 384).

We can say that the archetypal transference is constellated by the reactivation of early introjects in the transference and countertransference, and that this new material projects outward to yield the wondrous imagery of the hermaphrodite, the combined or double-sided object that Jung's alchemical research illuminated. But are we simply dealing with a

---

[1] The following statement by Claude Lévi-Strauss describes an approach to psychic material that precisely mirrors Jung's model, and, indeed, my own:

Many psychoanalysts would refuse to admit that the psychic constellations which reappear in the patient's conscious could constitute a myth. These represent, they say, real events which it is sometimes possible to date. . . . We do not question these facts. But we should ask ourselves whether the therapeutic value of the cure depends on the actual characterization of remembered situations, or whether the traumatizing power of these situations stems from the fact that at the moment they appear, the subject experiences them immediately as living myth. . . . The traumatizing power of any situation cannot result from its intrinsic features but must, rather, result from the capacity of certain events . . . to induce an emotional crystallization which is molded by pre-existing structure . . . these structural laws are truly a-temporal (1967, p. 197f.).

replay of earliest mother-infant interactions where "archetypal" and "personal" designations are of little value (Eigen 1986, 1987, pp. 59ff.), or are these new processes and energy fields that are not reducible to infant or even prenatal life? This is a crucial theoretical question, for therapists who believe that experiences in psychotherapy replicate early failed or aborted developmental experiences would do well to consider whether this approach is adequate to the nature of the psyche and its archetypal or objective dimension. Often psychotherapy reveals bewildering and bizarre introjects stemming from the patient's early childhood experiences. The therapist then identifies these through reflecting upon fusion states and participation in projective identification. But this approach is too limiting. An imaginal focus is required if one is to effectively engage the borderline person. The therapist must begin to think differently—that is, he or she must imaginally focus upon interactive fields that are structured by atemporal forms (Lévi-Strauss 1967, p. 198).

The interactive field can be comprehended only as a third presence, which often takes the form of an unconscious dyad; it should not be viewed through a structural model of projections that must be integrated. The object-relations model is not unimportant; its value is unquestionable. But though it is indispensable, by itself it is insufficient. Both models are required: the projection model, which is concerned with early developmental issues, *and* the imaginal model, which incorporates the alchemical imagery of the *coniunctio* and its attendant stages.[2] We need to adopt a model that is two sided: one aspect pointing toward a space-time world and the other toward a unitary world structured by archetypal processes. These aspects intertwine. As M. Eigen has emphatically noted (1987, p. 61), they cannot and should not be split into separate and opposing categories of "personal" and "archetypal." The unconscious dyad may be seen to stem from both the patient and the therapist *and also to be* part of a larger, interactive field. Once it is

---

[2] André Green's discussion of what he calls "tertiary processes" is pertinent here. He defines these processes as not materialized but made of conjunctive and disjunctive mechanisms in order to act as a go-between of primary and secondary process. It is the most efficient mode of establishing a flexible mental equilibrium and the richest tool for creativity, safeguarding against the nuisance of splitting, an excess of which leads to psychic death. Yet splitting is essential in providing a way out of confusion. Such is the fate of human bondage, that it has to serve two contrary masters—separation and reunion—one or the other, or both" (1977, pp. 41–42).

Green's "tertiary processes" occur in the interactive fields I have described in Chapters Four and Five. This process, as he says, links "conjunctive and disjunctive mechanisms," or, in our terms, the separating and conjoining aspects of the *coniunctio*. The need for interpretation, which always involves some degree of splitting, should also be recognized.

sufficiently seen and experienced, the unconscious couple can eventually lead patient and therapist to an experience of union. This union experience is precisely what the borderline person lacks.

Discovering the Borderline Patient's Unconscious Dyad: Projections and Field Dynamics

"Ed" was an exceptionally intelligent and multitalented thirty-eight-year-old man. He entered treatment for several reasons. He employed his intellectual and creative gifts only marginally in his career; in general he was plagued by a lack of purpose and commitment to any goal. Other people were getting along in life, and he was not. A major theme in his life was an obsession with actions that others had taken toward him which he often found to be immoral; he was also absorbed with his own behavior, of which he was a keen critic. He would spend hours alone engrossed in wondering why people treated him as they did, or why he was so emotionally paralyzed and unable to be forthright during interaction with another person whose malevolence would later become quite evident to him.

At the outset of our work, Ed seemed to be suffering from a narcissistic character disorder. An idealized transference combined with the controlling dynamics of his grandiose-exhibitionistic self was present, so that I felt compelled to have answers to his questions (Schwartz-Salant 1982, pp. 50 ff.). My responses were usually well received, but I had an uncomfortable sense that he was merely being polite. It was soon clear that his narcissistic character formation was a defense against a deep and chaotic part of his personality. His transference did not differentiate into idealized and grandiose-exhibitionistic strands as it might have if he had had a narcissistic character.

My work with Ed demonstrates a complex interactive field that is exceptionally difficult to apprehend. In fact, my compulsion to act out a pattern of unrelatedness — by talking without much reflection — could at times nearly nullify my observing ego and his as well. During these periods, all my attempts to bring coherence or consciousness to the session resulted in pain for both of us and led only to role reversals. I then felt a pressure to "get it right"; often I could not refrain from speaking. I would attempt to make interpretations, though even scant reflection would have shown me that I had only shallow comments to make. During these times, however, I was not disposed to self-reflection, but would proceed with my commentary, all the while feeling dull-witted and hoping that what I had to say would be accepted. Since Ed was intent upon being truthful he did not accept this behavior from me. He had suffered too many years of being tortured by frustrated mental and creative gifts and previous unsuccessful therapeutic experiences to allow our work to fail, too.

Often, I felt that Ed was the truth-seeker, whereas I was the liar, just barely able to survive. Survive what? That is not easy to describe, but I can say that soon after our work began and the strength of Ed's narcissistic transferences diminished, our unconscious psyches became meshed together in such a way that a searing and tormenting energy field was established that nearly destroyed my capacity to think and reflect. Each time Ed arrived, I would have a brief period of optimism and feel that we might establish a good connection and proceed with our work. I would then become emotionally and physically limp, and it would be difficult for me simply to remain embodied and be with him. Instead, I usually felt obliged to talk and thus to *act* rather than *be*. Often I could not tolerate the absence of meaningful content between us, and sometimes I was frightened of this man. At times I felt that he might strike me, but my usual afflicted state was one in which I believed that he was the one dedicated to the truth and that I was a fraud. This condition persisted despite Ed's torment about being the subject of his own lies.

For over a year we could barely relate to one another, though there were many desperate attempts to create a sense of connection. During this period, my work with Ed primarily consisted of my showing him that I could survive amid his attacks. Every word I used, each tone of expression I chose, came under his scrutiny. During this process, Ed began to form a growing alliance with me. One day, he spoke of some reading he had been doing and, to my surprise, asked about the nature of our unconscious couple. This represented a crucial shift in his psyche toward an attitude of more cooperation in the therapy; I was then able to reflect imaginatively upon what might be structuring our interactive field. I arrived at a hypothesis that made sense to both of us: that a couple who did not want union was our major obstacle. The state of nonunion (see picture seven of the *Rosarium,* "The Extraction of the Soul") is described by Jung as a loss of the soul and has an impact similar to that of schizophrenic dissociation (1946, par. 476). Our *soul-less* interaction manifested in ways that seemed to catapult us into completely different universes. At such times, I would believe that we were relating

162

well to each other, yet we were really not communicating at all. Upon reflection, it became clear that my interpretations were strained; I was not connected to Ed and had been speaking to avoid the pain of emptiness, despair, and a feeling of impotence. In fact, the level of dissociative intent was so profound that we might each as well have been talking to ourselves.

The *Rosarium,* commenting upon picture seven, offers the following recipe for healing this disconnected state: "Take the brain . . . and grind it in most sharp vinegar, or in children's urine until it is obscured, and this being begun again as I have written it, may again be mortified as before. . . . He therefore that maketh the earth black shall come to his purpose and it shall go well with him" (McLean 1980, p. 45). Notably, the *Rosarium* adds that in searching for this black earth "many men have perished" (ibid.).

"Grinding the brain in sharp vinegar" is by no means a poor metaphor for the way I functioned with this man and he with me. Many of his nights were spent trying to recover from sessions that destroyed his ability to think and left him totally confused and enraged. The *Rosarium* implies that there is a purpose to the tormented states of mind that afflicted both of us. This purpose is suggested by the creation of the hermaphrodite (picture ten, "The Rebis"). The alchemical Rebis is a combined male–female object and represents the creation of a fertile and stable interactive field. But illustration seven, "the ascent of the soul," warns of a great danger—perhaps the death of the therapy, and perhaps activation of the patient's tendencies towards self-destruction, a possibility that always exists with the borderline patient when levels of extreme dissociation and despair are engaged. In Ed's and my work together, there was some ground for believing that the states to which we were subject had some purpose; it was equally clear that our *nigredo* would not become fruitful if our therapy process was to be dominated by acting out and unconsciousness.

Over the course of many trying sessions that took place within a period of approximately two years, the nature of our problem began to emerge. Our interaction was structured by an unconscious couple dominated by a drive for nonunion; each half of the couple desired to destroy the other through lies and malicious envy. At the same time, the parts that comprised this couple were stubbornly and inextricably bound to each other. Thus our interaction was dominated by the characteristic borderline quality of simultaneous drives toward fusion and separation, which together produced great confusion.

As a very young child, Ed had experienced his parents in ways that resembled the dynamics of this dyad. He recalled feeling persecuted by his parents' false implications that they actually *saw* him and had his best interests at heart. He would be repeatedly perplexed by their antagonistic behavior toward one another and their fraud and deception toward him. Apparently, they had functioned as a double-sided object, each half contributing to a persecuting dyad. The young, extremely intelligent, and sensitive child would earnestly lecture them on their behavior and would be repeatedly upset and unhinged by the accumulating knowledge that he had had no effect at all, except as it rebounded onto him in the form of his father's rage or his mother's martyrdom.

This unconscious parental dyad had been split off from his otherwise normally functioning personality in order that Ed could survive. Consequently, he developed the typical borderline split between a normal–neurotic and a psychotic personality — a split that was also a fusion state. James Grotstein writes:

> In approaching a psychoanalytic conception of the borderline I should like to offer the following understanding: What seems to give the borderline personality (and borderline state) its uniqueness in differentiating itself from psychoses on one hand and neuroses on the other is not so much its midplace on the spectrum but is instead a qualitative difference. This qualitative difference is characterized, in my opinion, by the presence of a psychotic personality organization *and* a normal or neurotic personality organization which have undergone a unique interpenetration with each other so that a new amalgam emerges which can well be stated as 'psychotically neurotic' or 'neurotically psychotic.' It is as if a collusive symbiosis exists between these two twin personalities which allows for an unusual tenacity, stability, and cohesion compared to psychotic states generally (1979, p. 150).

When Ed's defensively idealized transference waned, his psychotic parts (largely conveyed by the unconscious dyad) entered the therapy process and nearly usurped it. This led to what could be called a transference and countertransference psychosis; its intensity was extreme. Yet unless therapy contains a transference psychosis (and a countertransference psychosis as well, though hopefully to a lesser degree) there is little chance of healing the borderline person. By countertransference psychosis I do not imply the therapist's blatant loss of reality or decompensation, but rather the emergence of parts of his or her personality that are unintegrated, thus having an autonomy beyond the organizing domain of the self. These "mad parts" of the therapist can take over the therapy in subtle and diverse ways; the patient may introject them and begin to act quite mad, even to the point of engaging dangerous situations. For example, after a therapist had seductively shared his personal material with a borderline patient, the patient dreamt that he was being driven in a vehicle by a madman. The patient's outer-life situation reflected this psychic state: as a result of his irrational behavior he was nearly fired from his job. This sequence was a consequence of the therapist's denial of his own psychotic parts — unintegrated and compulsive qualities of his personality — which he was "sharing" in the hope of creating a "holding environment."

To convey the extent to which Ed and I were dominated by an unconscious dyad, I will relate material taken from sessions that took place two years after our work began. At this time, Ed dreamed that he was gently embracing two women, one black, the other white. I understood this to be the image of opposites combining, an image which I, too, could now carry in projection because there had been sufficient reparation on my part for previous therapeutic errors (for example, talking too much and acting rather being embodied). I felt that Ed thought me more reliable than heretofore; it seemed to me that he no longer was obliged to split me up into "good" and "bad" parts, which he then had to scan from both a conscious and an unconscious perspective.

The dream of the two women was soon followed by another in which he and another man (which he associated with me) were flying in an airplane very close to the ground in order to gain a view of the earth below. At first, the other man was guiding the vehicle, but then the patient was taught by the man to guide it himself. This dream seemed to indicate that the therapy was now based on mutual cooperation. Indicative of the potential of our interactive field was the emergent image of a fruitful coital couple. The dream image of the airplane symbolizes a vessel; since this vessel hovers near the earth, we can say that the image indicates both spirit and a capacity for a solid therapeutic alliance. Such understanding had been sorely lacking during the prior two years; Ed had suffered as a consequence and had taken great pains to make me understand that *I* was the cause of his great distress.

Soon after this dream, I was surprised to find Ed once again in a state of extreme agitation and doubt about my role as therapist and about the therapy itself. Yet this should have been no cause for surprise. My desire to see our process progressing and free of Ed's searing criticism was a tendency that, he said, "drives me crazy." His comment led me to examine why I was driving him crazy and whether or not I wanted to do such a thing to him. To use his phrase, which I found unpleasantly apt: why was I (again) "operating in bad faith?" But, before the examination could proceed, a row occurred that left both of us in a state of doubt over whether or not it would be possible to continue therapy.

I will be specific about the session in question. Ed arrived on time and even before sitting down asked me a question about a previous remark I had made. His question felt like an attack, although it was not expressed angrily; I became very defensive. But my response was far stronger than usual: I lost sight of my defensiveness as I felt my body fill with an agitation that was disintegrating in its affect. I felt that I was under an attack of global nature. I was anxious, inwardly shaking, yet I found myself trying to act as if everything were okay. In effect, I was denying the state of nonunion that existed both between us and within myself. Clearly, I was behaving in a borderline way. I had previously experienced this state with him, though not so intensely as in this time. Ed always accused me of operating in bad faith when I behaved in this way. The seriousness and prominence of this accusation gradually increased during the course of the therapy.

The session I am describing cannot be understood without a clear comprehension of the evolution of this theme. In this instance, the illusion that a viable and helpful connection now existed between Ed and myself was part of the underlying deceit; the fact was that in significant ways I did not want emotional contact with him. The awareness of my desire to *not* have any form of union with Ed was slow in arriving; in retrospect, I am both chagrined and astonished at the ingenuity of the tactics I employed to avoid this discovery. Certainly, a subjective countertransference was present, but much more was operative in this interaction. There was a field quality inherent in our process, in which nonunion was the main ingredient.

One of my unconscious strategies to avoid contact with Ed was to remain anxious. My fear of the malignant energy field evoked by our mutual presence would thereby allow *him* to take the lead in understanding any material the therapy process was engaging. When I was at my worst, I would present Ed with an extremely toxic double-bind by denying the madness between us and electing to see him as strong and adept; these qualities are usually carried by the normal–neurotic self. I often found myself dull and unable to think clearly. Worse, I would find myself immersed in an imaginative and creative void, a leaden state that combined heavy Saturnian authority and the compulsion "to know." In contrast, Ed would seem bright, sharp, and intelligent. It was as if his ownership of these qualities meant that they were unavailable to others — specifically to me. I would submit to the sense of having lost all acuity, all creative energy. In any other case I had at the time I would have capably employed these countertransferential reactions syntonically and unearthed an "other side" of chaos, despair, and helplessness; in this case I did not. Nor did I recognize that Ed needed me to be able to think with him if not for him. I later came to realize that there was a *choice* involved in this countertransference, though this choice was not evident to me at the time. Leon Grinberg has described the course of this countertransference as follows:

> From a structural point of view, one may say that what is projected by means of the psychotic mechanism of projective identification operates within the object as a parasitic superego, which omnipotently induces the analyst's ego to act or feel what the patient in his fantasy wants him to feel or act. I think that this, to some degree, bears comparison with the dynamics of hypnosis as described by Freud. According to Freud, the hypnotizer places himself in the position of the ego ideal, and hypnotic submissiveness is of a masochistic nature. Freud further holds that in the hypnotic relation a sort of paralysis appears as a result of the influence of the omnipotent individual upon an impotent and helpless being. I believe the same applies to the processes I am discussing in that the analyst, being unaware of what happened, may later rationalize his action, as the hypnotized person does after executing the hypnotic command. By means of the mechanisms of obsessive control, the inducing subject continues to control what he projected onto the induced object. The subject's omnipotent fantasies thus acquire some consistency, as they seem confirmed by the object's response (1977, pp. 128-129).

In time, I began to shake myself out of this hypnotic involvement with the patient and was able to recognize a state of nonunion. This emerging awareness combined with Ed's concerted efforts to contain me resulted in redeeming the therapy.

I have emphasized that I "chose" nonunion because I have no doubt that a choice was involved, although I was unaware of it at the time. But the fact that a choice existed meant that a moral issue was involved: I had lied to Ed about understanding him, and about being in the same psychological universe with him. I must emphasize the aptness of his complaint that I was acting in bad faith; the recognition of its truth was shocking. My self-image had been that I was a person who deeply wanted union, indeed, who held it in the highest esteem.

It was against this background that I finally was able to recover my bearings in the therapy. It was abundantly clear that transferential elements were involved, and that my behavior was a representation of Ed's interaction with his mother and father and, particularly, with the parental couple that their psyches evoked: a couple in intense, antagonistic disunion, each out to destroy the other through envy and hatred. My bad faith and lies reflected his parental experience. The state of being overwhelmed and barely able to retain my thoughts replicated the feelings Ed had when his parents denied his perceptions. His parents also represented deceitful behavior, of which he was certainly capable — indeed, he could treat his friends and acquaintances with the very lack of truthfulness that he found so distressing in others. But I, too, was driven to behave in immoral ways; and while I can attribute this compulsion to countertransferential acting out, which it certainly was — especially the resistance to experiencing despair — something else was involved. We were both participants in a process that was not merely a repetition of past history but was also a creation in its own right.

In my therapeutic work with Ed I was often thrust into a masochistic position.[3] In part, this was a matter of choice, based upon my belief that the borderline person *sees* what the therapist does not wish him or her to see. By acknowledging Ed's perceptions (for example, that I had *chosen* to act in ways injurious to him), I was obliged to recognize unconscious shadow aspects of my personality that I had allowed to guide my behavior. This helped him to begin to gain faith in the correctness of his perceptions. I could easily have dismissed his complaint as a paranoid distortion that was picking up only a shred of truth. This perception would have been comforting to me, but very undermining of Ed.

I also wish to note that there were times, though perhaps too few of them, when I reacted to Ed in ways that were not masochistic. For instance, at times I expressed how much I hated the way he was treating me, especially his criticism of my words and behavior, which he mercilessly scrutinized as being careless and incompetent. This expression of hatred was possible — and was not an assault — when I could feel how much his attacks (even though they may have been premised upon truth) were painful and frightening to the small child within me. I was standing up for this child when I could talk about my hatred without attacking Ed. Indeed, this direct response was a relief to Ed, for it showed that I

---

[3] For an important discussion of masochism see R. Gordon, 1987.

was real and perhaps even trustworthy, despite the fact that a good deal of what occurred between us was dominated by an intense drive to disrupt contact.

The clinical material that relates to this patient depicts some of the more difficult aspects I have encountered when treating the borderline person. It is impossible to clearly separate the personal transference and countertransference from the archetypal field-dynamics that are so richly constellated within these levels of treatment. The therapist treating the borderline patient must acknowledge the experience of nonunion. He or she must also be capable of accepting its existence and of respecting it as a state that carries a meaning beyond what can be gleaned from the immediate experience. Hence, successful therapy will depend to large measure upon faith and the therapist's capacity to repair the errors incurred amid his or her denials of the pain of nonunion.

Ed and I engaged a transference couple that desired nonunion and was so split from awareness that neither of us had any idea at all what the other was saying. An active force placed us in what felt like separate universes. Was he responsible for this state? Was I? Was he out to defeat me or to see if I could be tricked by his duplicity? (For example, I would obligingly act as if things were going well just as he often did as a child when he had to split from his real perceptions and instead try to believe that his parents were doing the best they could.) Was our interaction doomed because of its destructive nature, or, as the *Rosarium* suggests, was it a process through which a new self was being formed? Often our therapeutic endeavor seemed possessed by a demonic, trickster-like force that toyed with me as if I were its infant.

How can one understand this demonic force? Can it be reduced merely to the component of envy; that is, *my* envy attacking our connection by "misunderstanding" him? Or, was I acting out his introject of parental envy? Such interpretations have value; other equally valid interpretations could also be made. But if we do not also possess an archetypal viewpoint, we are likely to overlook the essential fact that something of a significantly different nature has been operating: an archetypal process much larger than the two of us.

A subsequent session revealed other aspects of our unconscious process. Ed began with a question: "What is your relationship to my inner couple?" It seemed as if his plight was encapsulated in this question, and I acted as if there were no time to lose, feeling pressed and harried to "get it right." I began to lecture him: "The inner couple is also an image of the relationship of your consciousness to the unconscious. If the couple is in disharmony, you will be in disharmony as well." To this assertion he bristled, as usual, with the insistence that I was being as impersonal as a textbook. And of course he was right. There were other instances of my intellectualized attempts to answer his question during this session; all were spun from my haste and a refusal to take the time to listen to what he was saying—to truly understand instead of pretending to understand. My behavior perpetuated my erroneous belief that I was connected to him. We also exchanged roles: at times I felt the need to slow down and be utterly precise, whereas he galloped along, moving too quickly for me to be able to understand him in a full, grounded way. Suddenly, Ed returned to the question: "What is your relationship to my inner couple?"

The fact that I was feeling somewhat depleted helped me to orient myself in a way that I knew might be helpful—back toward what had been happening between us. I allowed myself to become more centered, more fully embodied, and I surrendered much of my control. Only when I finally succeeded in returning to my own feelings was I able to recognize that I had been afraid of being physically harmed. My fantasy had been that I had better have the right answers or Ed would hit me.

Then I began to realize that I had been experiencing and reenacting Ed's early life with his parents, for when he failed to create harmony between his parents, he was in danger of being hit. He experienced his parents' disharmony and antagonism as dangerous to both the family unit and to himself, and he had to set it right, lest he be attacked. His solution was, in effect, to attempt to force his mother and father to behave differently—both toward one another and also toward him. It appears that I had been acting out an introject of his child-self as it compulsively attempted to create union. In this particular case, the urgent demand was that I create harmony between us by answering the question about his inner couple. And the compulsion to do so overrode the underlying awareness that a basic lack of connection—a prevailing nonunion—was the dominant factor in our relationship.

I expressed these thoughts to Ed and this interpretation proved somewhat effective in leading us to a deeper understanding. He suggested the possibility that he was attacking me for acting in disunion with myself, adding that I could be seen to represent both his own couple in disunion, *and* his child-self frantically attempting to change the situation. Alternatively, I could be seen as a person who incorporated the potential to evoke the disharmony that he found so devastating. Whenever I would evoke disharmony by being out of harmony with myself, Ed would become aggressive and have the urge to hit me. The verbally abusive negative inner couple (his parental images in their state of disunion), which was constellated in me, severely affected him.

There was a definite improvement when we became able to objectify the interactive field in terms of a couple engaged in battle, while paradoxically desiring no contact at all. We were also able to observe this same couple as persecutory of the small child within each of us. Containment for these persecutory affects grew as we became able to imaginally identify the couple. Perhaps this containment is the element that enabled the therapy to continue and even reach the point in which our interactive field was able to transform into a unified field and a working alliance. At that point, the significance of transference and countertransference dynamics diminished, and Ed could begin to make substantial changes in his life. In the *Rosarium,* picture seven is followed by a regenerative state depicted by falling dew. The soulless couple, washed and revitalized by the dew, is eventually renewed in the form of the Rebis, the hermaphrodite (picture ten). The hermaphrodite (as discussed in Chapters Four and Five) represents the creation of a linking structure, akin to what Jung calls the transcendent function and what Winnicott calls transitional space. As a result of our linkage, the therapy gained a playful and exploratory quality that had previously been absent. In an important sense, Ed's individuation process began anew at this juncture, and the significant life changes that he was able to make further contributed to his growth.

The following example illustrates how an unconscious dyad not only structures the interactive field, but also one's mind–body experiences. It also reveals how the therapeutic apprehension of the unconscious dyad in its form of nonunion can lead to a field of union.

"Mallory," a thirty-five-year-old woman, began a session by relating the following dream: "In an ancient stone atrium I was doing an erotic dance with an eighteen-year-old boy. He knew more than I ever will." I sensed that she wanted me to be excited about the dream; I felt awkward about having absolutely no response at all. I reflected upon the previous day's session, which had dealt with Mallory's fears that I would be angry with her because she was emotionally distant. I felt disconnected from the dream; it also felt dismissive to sidestep my thoughts about yesterday's session. I attempted to link these feelings by saying:

171

"Since the dance with the boy and the stone atrium seem to be such positive symbols, perhaps you had the dream to affirm how vital it is to stay on the track of what happened yesterday, and to encourage you not to withdraw out of fears of my anger."[4] To this Mallory replied, "You'll have to help me, I don't know where to go from here."

Suddenly I felt dull and flaccid, as if all the structure and alertness had vanished from my body. I was mentally engaged and expectant, waiting for something to arise either from her or from me. But I could not readily contain the dull and flaccid feelings and almost immediately began to recount yesterday's experience, recalling how frightened Mallory had been. With this, her countenance changed abruptly and she bitterly reproached herself: "I never do it right. You're cold, angry with me. I can feel it." I had difficulty at that moment distinguishing "me" from what felt like a "them," that is, her parents.

It was clear that something important was going on, and I realized that Mallory might be using the session to repeat a family pattern. I asked: "Where are you with your parents now?" "I'm at the dinner table, she is to my left, he to my right. I'm terrified, constantly alert, scanning for danger. I have to be, I have to make sure everything is okay. She's a bit drunk and stuffing herself with food; he is passive, simply waiting. But I know he will explode at any moment. I have to prevent this somehow but I don't know how. I try to humor them; it barely works. I know his anger will eventually come out, he'll explode. Then she'll withdraw and be a martyr, terrifying everyone with her martyrdom. He'll then be frightened, and her martyrdom will turn to anger against me."

With this information, I could play with the following possibility: when I had initially heard Mallory's dream, my silence had stemmed from the fact that my mental processes had replicated her silent father's dullness; and my awkward and flaccid body feelings probably resembled those of her drunk mother. I was somewhat intimidated by this patient's capacity to put me into such uncomfortable states. I did not feel any recognizable anger, but it was difficult to allow myself even minor feelings of irritation in working with this patient, since I feared they might trigger a paranoid reaction that could lead to a delusional transference certain to doom the therapeutic work. This aspect of our interaction was a mixture of mutual neurotic and psychotic parts. I had split off from the

---

[4] This interpretive attempt was clumsy, useless to my patient, and primarily to relieve my own discomfort.

rage I was feeling and as a consequence did not adequately embrace the nature of the couple I had introjected; instead, I avoided the anger embedded in my dull state by absorbing it, behaving like her martyred mother. I recognize that I could have interpreted this state as a response Mallory might naturally have anticipated. But Mallory's paranoid scanning was too intense for me to have hazarded such an interpretation; it would have been too fragmenting for her.

The parts of Mallory's inner parental couple were split from each other and also at war; my mental and somatic selves reflected this state. When I was well-connected, Mallory felt at ease. She would keep me centered by telling me stories about her life. At such times, Mallory was able to create in me a unified inner couple that did not terrorize her. But this endeavor was always strained by her foreboding that the future would bring further persecutory states. By "fixing me" Mallory could only temporarily avoid the battle that would certainly come. Just as her parents would fight with each other in spite of her best efforts to entertain them, so my two natures would eventually fall out of harmony. In a way they already had, for Mallory could only attain cohesiveness through our mutual splitting—she from her fear and I from the omnipresent tension and anxiety.

The feeling-tone of the session would immediately change when these moments of disunity occurred. If I did not know what to say or do, or if I felt muddled, Mallory would think I was angry with her. She would experience me as if I were her father at the dinner table. "What's wrong?" she would ask; she would then feel that she could not "fix" me, and would become very frightened and complain that she "never does it right."

When I was able to become aware of how my own unconscious was being influenced and structured by Mallory's internal parental couple, several advantages accrued. Firstly, she participated in a corrective emotional experience, in the sense that she could experience me as embodying her parental couple but could see that I did not retaliate. I also required less "fixing" than they did, especially as I grew more conscious and did not act out the splitting process, thereby losing sight of the opposites. Mallory now had the possibility of freeing psychic energy that had hitherto been in the service of an incessant scanning process that had remorselessly energized her negative parental couple. Secondly, Mallory gained the possibility of introjecting a more harmonious dyad when she experienced how I could maintain my own mind–body union while she was in a state of disunion.

In the sessions that followed, we had a sense of connection, of working well together. Mallory said that it "felt good, but what about the other stuff?" She meant, of course, the disunion we had previously experienced but she was also referring to her fear of my rage. I noticed that she was scanning me, for I felt a pressure, as if her vision had a substantial quality that exerted a force. I encouraged her to express what she saw, and she reported that I was defensive. It was a struggle to accept her finding, and I asked how she recognized my defensiveness. Mallory responded by saying, "Maybe you're worried about something." I was aware of an inner tightness and had a sense that I was withholding my feelings. Mallory wondered aloud if these feelings were sexual, saying "that's usually the root of things." Here was something new and important, for Mallory had dared to imaginally see me and express her feelings about me.

The borderline person concretizes imaginal perceptions inwardly. For example, at the beginning of a session, he or she might perceive that the therapist is tired and withdrawn but will say nothing about it. After some contact has been made in the session, the patient, provoked by an inner attack, might comment on how he or she is being "too much of a burden for you, or for anyone." The patient's vision, which may be regarded as a psychic organ or structure that the person refuses to acknowledge, will become demonic if he or she cannot dare to communicate through it.

Mallory had dared to share what she had seen; I could then respond to her vision by indicating where her perceptions were accurate and also by indicating areas that were beyond her perceptual lens. Thus, her imaginal perception was tested, and she was able to depart from a feeling of omnipotence, namely, that what she saw was the truth. On other occasions, Mallory split from what she could see by relegating her accurate perceptions to her madness. What one sees is often very disturbing. In fact, a person's imaginal perception is usually denied early in life because what is perceived by the child (for example, a parent's hatred) is too searing to absorb. Many borderline persons begin to integrate split-off psychotic parts when they become able to dare to see that they had been hated by their parents. Being able to share one's imaginal perceptions is extremely important, though this ability is rarely available to the borderline person. Instead, as dreams often reveal, the imagination usually becomes mired in matter. The dreamer may attempt to jump over a stream and will be able to get only halfway across, or try to enter a room only to encounter a lead-sealed door. There are endless variants of such themes, in which the linkage of two different states is severely hindered.

In Mallory's case we continued to explore her scanning process, noting everything she saw. She began to experience the virtues of her sight and came to enjoy the fact that it could be a relational, rather than merely defensive tool, one that operated like a kind of psychic warning radar. She could also experience how my seeing her, as well as her seeing me, had the effect of enlivening our interaction. This, in turn, produced the experience that something autonomous was coming to life between us: a union with a characteristic rhythm that both joined and separated us. In following sessions, Mallory and I began to grasp aspects of her negative inner couple and also began to experience the release of a positive couple that began to structure our interactive space.

The *coniunctio* is not only an event but a pattern; inharmonious aspects of that pattern soon began to emerge with Mallory and myself. In the session following the union experience something was askew; the positive couple was absent, we were not working well together, and it felt terrible. In an effort to recover our good connection, I actually said: "What about us?" No longer passively scanning with paranoid defenses, Mallory immediately sensed what was "off" in my remark. "The *us* feels slimy," she said. "That's how my father was but he would always deny it. It was never in the open. If you had said, 'How about you and me?' it would have been different — clear, honest. The *us* feels terrible!" This remark led to our awareness of the existence of an incestuous couple. This couple also appears in the *Rosarium* following the *coniunctio* (Jung 1946, para. 468). Our *coniunctio* had served to attract more unconscious material and to perpetrate the kinship quality between us. It also led Mallory to another stage in the integration of her vision.

Integrating one's imaginal sight — that quality which is usually split off and has taken up domain in the patient's psychotic part — is often accomplished only after the therapist sees this sight operating in the patient; in effect, it is as if the therapist is being spied upon. For example, after I had worked with a male patient, "John," for six months I recognized that while he constantly scanned me, he also idealized me and would sacrifice his vision, or attempts at vision, to that idealization. Usually, the scanning was a very subtle background phenomenon, which was barely perceptible unless I made an extra effort to be embodied and emotionally present. But his idealization induced me to bask in the self-approving light of what a good therapist I was, rather than reach out to contact him sufficiently to perceive that he saw.

Once I was able to focus upon his background scanning-process, John began to speak about his fears of women. The world, he claimed, is "a batch of piranhas." I was not included in this assessment, however. I was different, safe. Indeed, how else except by idealizing me could he face his fear? John asked if the piranhas were real, then quickly affirmed their reality and their power to fracture his sense of identity. It became clear that his idealization separated me from destructive energies and allowed him to split from his negative inner images. Any attempts John made to confront these negative images had an "as-if" quality that conveyed the falseness of his effort.

John volunteered that each time I saw him scanning me he felt a physical tension in his chest, stomach, and throat, and would feel the reality of inner persecutory attackers. When I did not employ my imaginal sight, his splitting defenses of idealization would remain intact. When I would communicate to him this idealization strategy, its defensive function would temporarily abate, only to be replaced by a masochistic defense. John would agree with everything I said and even add examples to help me prove my point. He would explain that my reflections made him very anxious. It was clear that in these strenuous efforts to keep me "ideal," he was splitting from what he really saw — namely, the knowledge that I often did not *see* him or the intensity of his fear. Over and over he would complain that his smooth exterior hid his true feelings from everyone *except from me*; only *I* knew that he was really very young and afraid. He would simultaneously attack and soothe me: he would tell me that I did *not* see him, but would continue to split from his own perception by insisting that I was different from other people.

Imaginal sight is like active imagination, *but when using imaginal sight in therapy, it is essential that the unconscious of the therapist be constellated through his or her countertransference.* For example, only after I became conscious of my splitting tendencies and of a somewhat flattened affect that did not engage John's psychotic parts, could I begin to make use of this countertransference reaction. By consciously submitting to this induced countertransferential state and becoming embodied, I could allow imagination to lead me to perceive his background scanning.

The imaginal realm does not necessarily manifest through visual images; feeling and the kinesthetic sense are also natural conduits. Possibly the nature of the imaginal act is colored by the therapist's inferior function, so that one therapist will see "visibly," while another therapist will see "feelingly." In any event, the process requires that the therapist allow himself or herself to be affected by the patient's material without having to resort to interpretation, which would at best prove to be a defensive maneuver.

Imagination is an act born of the body. It arises out of a matrix of confusion and disorder. Faith, rather than the mastery of understanding, is its midwife.

Madness, Religion, and the Self in Borderline States of Mind

The borderline patient has a core of madness that must be uncovered if successful treatment is to be achieved. The patient's self, or soul, is enmeshed in psychotic mechanisms of splitting and denial. This true self might be represented as a child living in filth, locked up, petrified, or frozen in ice. There are countless images that depict this state. The following clinical material is drawn from my work with "Amanda," a forty-eight-year-old borderline woman. Amanda's psychotic parts could only enter the therapy after I was able to end her obsessional control, which manifested by her reading to me from a notebook. Her explanation for this controlling behavior was that she might "otherwise lose her thoughts." Amanda functioned quite well in daily life; to a large measure her madness intruded into an otherwise competent, functioning personality only during therapy session. A relatively condensed psychotic transference, in which delusional processes are contained by a sense of alliance, is highly desirable in treatment (Grotstein 1979, p. 173).

Amanda's confusion was dominant in our therapy process; this confusion was disorienting for both of us. As a three-year-old child she had suffered an overwhelming trauma: her father left the family.[5] He had never said goodbye to Amanda, ostensibly because the family felt that she would be better off without so explicit a closure. Yet her father had been her only source of love and comfort as well as the only barrier between her and her mother and grandparents, whom Amanda experi-

---

5 In this discussion I have not focused upon the patient's maternal experiences, which certainly contributed to her splitting defenses. My impression is that they may have had less developmental significance than abandonment issues with her father.

177

enced as cold, aloof, and harsh. Amanda recalled an early incident of her mother sending her to play outside on a rainy day. Her mother had dressed her in new white shoes, but had then scolded her for getting them dirty. This memory is a paradigm for her early individuation experiences: separation from her mother was undermined by the implicit demand that she remain fused with her mother's narcissism. This included the demand that she be perfect. With such a maternal background Amanda had only minimal positive internal resources. She thus had little support to help her contain the intense anxieties that erupted when her father abandoned her. She had lost her only love object.

This incident had been so traumatic for Amanda that no therapeutic work on her relationship with her father could occur for several years. Up to that time, Amanda had never mentioned him. Eventually, she began to refer to him as a "nice person." She would also say that "he preferred my mother." Even though he returned to the family fold after a nine-month absence and was present in her life for the next forty years, there was almost nothing she could find to say about him; her mind would become blank.

Gradually, Amanda's abandonment fears entered the transference, and session endings became very painful for her. Between sessions, Amanda's image of me was often effaced, but occasionally she was able to suffer my absence consciously, rather than by splitting and becoming manic. It became possible to begin the reconstruction of what had happened in her inner world when her father had left. One memory she was able to salvage was that she "became hysterical and hid under the bed" after she discovered that he had left. Her conscious memories of this event began and ended here, however; even this recollection felt uncertain. In fact, all of Amanda's recollections had a strange uncertainty to them. Our reconstruction of what may have happened upon her father's return nine months later includes the hypothesis that Amanda believed that the returning father was an imposter. Moreover, she had, in effect, created an inner, idealized father who would someday return and truly love her. In the transference, Amanda split me into several "fathers," including both the imposter and the idealized father. The latter existed only outside the therapy sessions in her imaginary conversations with me.

A severe reality distortion occurred when Amanda's father deserted her: she denied her love for him and his very existence. Since Amanda's positive inner world was of such little worth, she could not mourn his loss. A delusional inner world came into play, one that was structured by both the idealized father and its negative split-off polarity, the imposter father. She did not experience either of these images consciously; life with her real father continued as if he had never abandoned her. Amanda would say that he was "nice." Inwardly, however, her perceptions were dominated by severe distortions: her father was/was not the man who had returned to her. That is, he was neither her real father, nor an imposter.

In the transference, I was initially regarded as the imposter to whom Amanda had to learn to relate. She would insist that I list the rules of patient behavior. "What should patients say or do with the therapist?" Amanda would ask. I was depersonalized by her, but not completely. She always was always able to maintain a sense of humor, which represented her observing ego; at the same time, she was extremely serious.

When I succeeded in interpreting her splitting, she suffered the loss, outside of the therapy sessions, of my image; a painful deadness eclipsed her imagination. "Out there you don't love me any more," she would say. A long period of depression and acute suffering of abandonment feelings ensued. At these times, Amanda's psychotic parts would become enlivened, for she could not be sure the real "me" would return.

After we had worked with Amanda's abandonment feelings for some time, it became clear that yet another "father" existed—one who carried the depth of her abandonment experience. This "father" was identified with money, although the very mention of this theme released an almost immediate hysterical flooding. She recalled that her father had left the family home because he had not been able to earn a living that matched family standards. Amanda's understanding was that her mother and grandparents had kicked him out because of his financial dereliction. In her unconscious, money was the root of all her loss. In daily life Amanda would do everything she could to "forget" how much money she had. An inheritance she received was traumatic because it forced her to think about money; her only recourse was to hide the money in a bank account and forget about it completely. To invest it, or even to draw interest from the principal, was beyond her capacities. Money had little reality for her other than its connection to abandonment.

For many months, the mere mention of money evoked such overwhelming abandonment feelings that the continuity of memories and insights was disrupted. After my persistently confronting this issue during many therapy sessions, Amanda's capacities to deal with money issues gradually began to improve. As she grew more capable in this area, a fog seemed to clear; the fact that money was unconsciously identified with the father who had deserted her became more clear to her. We could then recognize three fathers: the imposter father, the idealized father, and the abandoning father who was represented in Amanda's psyche by money.

Amanda's splitting in therapy sessions lessened, but it still served to dull her pain; she remained extremely confused. A "blanking-out" of her mental processes often occurred. As she put it, "the head doesn't work." Each thought or memory would immediately produce others, so that a multiplicity of centers would each compete for her attention and thoroughly confuse both of us. Amanda would then reject all my attempts to explain what was happening. These experiences truly reflect Harold Searles's statement:

> I often have the sense that one or another patient is functioning unconsciously in a multiple-identity fashion when I feel not simply intimidated or overwhelmed . . . but, curiously and more specifically, *outnumbered* by him. (1979, p. 448)

Qualities of confusion, splitting, and reality distortion all form parts of the borderline person's psyche. Rarely is there a complete distortion of reality, although the behavioral stance often possesses an autonomy that is like a state of demonic possession. The quality of near-psychotic behavior is often stressed in the literature on the borderline personality. But there is a strange kind of order in this "possessed" behavior. We can begin to glimpse it in this clinical material as we consider the way in which Amanda often rejected interpretations.

Amanda would say something like, "that's not quite it," or "maybe." Her response was always frustrating because I had usually put a great deal of effort into trying to create some coherence for her and for myself. As a result of her denial I would often become irritated. At times, this reaction would be quite strong; it was often clear that projective identification was involved. This led me to attempt to examine her anger with me for "disappearing outside of the sessions." Such interpretations were somewhat effective. But this enterprise did not reach Amanda's psychotic parts.

It should be noted that when Amanda gave me such conditional answers, though I was irritated, I did not feel that my interpretations had been completely negated. In fact, Amanda was often at her best at these moments, and her mode of rejection rarely displayed a strong intention to defeat me. If my interpretations were grossly inaccurate she would become confused. Then "other thoughts" would fragment her attention, leaving both of us in a muddle that also obscured her anger toward me. But when my interpretations were relatively sound, they elicited a reaction in her that revealed a depth not usually apparent. If, regarding an interpretation, I asked the question: "Does that seem right?" Amanda would reply, "Not exactly." If I asked, "Is it wrong, off the mark?" she would answer, "No, not completely." At these moments, it seemed that she was using my interpretation to get close to something. But what? Apparently, Amanda was able to find value in the same interpretation that she was negating. What I said was considered by her to be neither true nor false. She would suspend choice, but not for defensive purposes. A process was at work inside her that could only express itself by her suspending choice. I discovered that if I "hovered" in the suspension without trying to amplify the interpretation she would often remember a detail from the past, or have a new insight. She would have to balance each statement she made with a second statement that revealed the confusion or incompleteness of the first. There was no possibility of saying, "This is right," but only, "It is neither right nor wrong."

The French psychoanalyst A. Green, whose thinking has influenced my approach to this clinical material, has described the borderline person's "logic" as follows:

> According to the reality principle, the psychic apparatus has to decide whether the object is or is not there: 'Yes' or 'No.' According to the pleasure principle, and as negation does not exist in the primary process of the unconscious, there is only 'Yes.' Winnicott has described the status of the transitional object, which combines the 'Yes' and the 'No,' as the transitional is- and is-not-the-breast. One can find precursors of Winnicott's observations in Freud's description of the cotton reel game and in his description of the fetish. But I think that there is one more way of dealing with this crucial issue of deciding whether the object is or is not, and that is illustrated by the judgment of the borderline patient. There is a fourth possible answer: *Neither 'Yes' nor 'No.'* This *is* an alternate choice to the refusal of choice. The transitional object is a *positive refusal*; it is either a 'Yes' or a 'No.' The symptoms of the borderline, standing for transitional objects, offer a *negative refusal of choice*: Neither 'Yes' nor 'No.' One could express the same relation in experiential terms by asking the question: 'Is the object dead (lost) or alive (found)?' or 'Am I dead or alive?'—to which he may answer: *'Neither Yes nor No.'* (1977, p. 41)

When in acute distress, the borderline patient can never be certain if the therapist is truly present in a flesh-and-blood sense. One could also say that the patient is uncertain if the therapist is alive or dead. This state of uncertainty always exists in the patient's unconscious and manifests itself in bewildering ways when splitting defenses fail to dispel abandonment anxiety. Hence, the patient can never answer the question: *Is the therapist alive or dead?* since it would appear meaningless and confusing to do so. Moreover, if he or she were to be asked: *"Is the therapist both alive and dead?"* the patient would continue to be confused, for it would mean that the therapist was a transitional object, that is, something both created and found.

The patient cannot experience the creativity of transitional space while in a state of confusion. Indeed, the possibility of play is usually absent for the borderline patient. The therapist, who tends to become so embroiled in countertransference reactions that his or her foremost desire is simply to survive each encounter, often feels either depressed and dull, or manic; like the borderline patient, the therapist will then *act* by using commentary to fill space rather than undergo the experience of *absence* (Green 1977, p. 41). This state is a difficult one to bear; to be able to sustain it requires the supporting faith that if one delays action and simply waits, the patient will not become destructive and the psyche will become enlivened. At crucial moments in the therapeutic process, the therapist's supreme act of faith in relation to the borderline patient is to trust that this patient will not "kill" him or her. To render the therapist ineffectual and mindless would be one way by which the patient would effect such a "killing."

In Amanda's case it was not a matter of her needing my interpretations to become more cogent or of her needing me to augment and deepen them. Instead, what Amanda needed was that I be able to register and accept her sense of paradox. This sense of paradox was only able to manifest when I could remain in an embodied and receptive state amid the experience of her absence. Her dialogue would now be in sharp contrast to her more usual confused and fragmented discourse. For fleeting moments I would be privy to a depth in her that was normally hidden by her splitting defenses and an infantile ego that "just wanted to feel good." Thus, Amanda's remarks conveyed her awareness that my interpretations were only partially satisfactory. Her response to my interpretations was that they were "not correct" *and* "not wrong." However, on a deep and subtle level it was not a question of whether or not a statement was right or wrong but rather that it was *neither* completely right *nor* completely wrong.

The subtleties of madness are often only perceived through feeling and observing our own states of confusion. In the case under discussion, more overt forms of madness also began to be uncovered. Some of these forms were not very subtle, and their perception merely required an empathic observer who would be sensitive to the patient's shame at carrying such fears of madness. For example, Amanda revealed a considerable paranoia when she expressed fears that her money would be stolen by the bank, or that her checks were only the bank's way of cheating her. She was also persecuted by fears that her grandchildren would be stolen from her while she accompanied them to school. But Amanda's more subtle forms of madness, in which confusion and reality distortion coexisted as part of a "Neither-Yes-nor-No" logic, were more difficult for me to decipher; this was so because of my tendency to deny the existence of these states.

There are a number of reasons for the therapist's having countertransferential reactions of confusion and irritation. Firstly, the therapist is not being overtly asked to add or subtract content from what he or she has said, although that wish may be implicit in the patient's communication. More important is the frustrating sense of coexisting opposites: one has the feeling that he or she is both approaching and at the same time failing to apprehend the patient's process. This process is not a sum of discrete parts; it can be known only in its wholeness. Generally, the borderline person hates partial interpretations; the therapist often feels persecuted for not being perfect and may even complain (sometimes aloud to the patient!) that he or she is always being criticized. Often, the therapist's best efforts are diminished by the patient's outright anger and rejection.

Amanda's splitting began to further diminish when she became able to experience her abandonment anxieties; our confusion lessened and her imagination slowly began to function. Gradually, she began to be able to "find" me outside our sessions. I was becoming more of a "real" object and less an "idealized father." The therapy became lively, though the outside world (in which she functioned well but took little interest) remained a place that held little value for her. All of Amanda's interest was concentrated on returning to the therapy.

Amanda's external object relations were becoming more realistic. Her husband, who for years had carried her idealized projection and had betrayed her through affairs with other women, gradually became to be seen more realistically. Previously, his inner deadness had persecuted her, but once she came to know and respect her own angry feelings, she was able to rail at his lack of relatedness. Gradually, and without necessarily liking it, Amanda could begin to accept him as he was. There was also a substantial improvement in Amanda's relationship with her mother. This change was a result of her learning to recognize when she was angry with her mother. At first she could feel this anger only with therapeutic help and often it would take many days to do so. Gradually, the interval between incident and anger decreased until finally her inner response coincided exactly with the outer provocation. Amanda began to confront her mother more assertively and was able to forge a better relationship with her. The gradual emergence of a functioning self was epitomized by her greatly diminished tendency to split; her imaginative capacities grew, and she became more able to find value and meaning in the pain of her abandonment anxieties.

The split between the "dead" external world and the lively therapeutic world represented not only Amanda's good/bad dichotomy but also an entrance into the Kleinian depressive position, which she now experienced in relation to her father. Our process prior to this development had largely taken place within a paranoid-schizoid realm where splitting and persecutory affects dominated. As the process moved to a level of the depressive position, Amanda's hatred of me as the transference father was displaced onto the dull, outer world, and her love of me, as the transference image of the once-loved father, was more fully experienced in our work together. This splitting, however, was more manageable than it formerly had been, and interpretation could now be more effective. She could now face the split between love and hatred; with great trepidation, she began to express her hatred to me. Its first appearance took the form of a jocular remark: "Out there I hate you." Gradually, she could begin to join with the affect while in my presence.

This new-found courage had a continuing positive effect. Amanda's capacity for the play of imagination had previously been severely limited and she had been especially prone to split her emotional life between feelings of love and hate. This splitting now diminished and she gained an imaginative capacity that could be communicated to me and that was more complex than her previous flow of fantasy that had circulated around the idealized father projection. This distinction is important and registers the difference between what alchemists called true and fantastic imagination (Jung 1953, par. 360). The borderline person often experiences either an imaginative lacuna or else a torrential flow of imagery and affect in countless passive fantasies *that destroy the capacity to experience feelings*. The false imagination functions to split a person from his or her feeling; it also furthers mind–body splitting and often manifests in somatic complaints. But true imagination, according to the alchemical metaphor, is far more realistic; it engages feelings and nurtures the growth of consciousness and the awareness of the suffering of one's soul.

There is one other important issue that should be mentioned in relation to this case. About a year before Amanda's abandonment anxieties and imagination became the focus of treatment, she dreamed of a small girl who was frozen in ice. The ice began to thaw and the child began to come to life. This dream was a critical juncture in our work, and it was preceded by a strange occurrence. At the close of a particular session, Amanda suddenly turned around and spoke to me in French, which she had never done before. In the next session Amanda asked me about "sub-personalities," since she had realized that "another person" had spoken French to me. We discovered that this "personality" carried her sexuality for her. For the first time, an erotic feeling existed between us. I believe that the "sub-personality" in her dream material was the first appearance of a self structure; its appearance had a synthesizing effect that overcame dissociation. Previously, this "personality" had been split off and had existed in a frozen, schizoid state.

The loving and erotic quality between us remained for several months, then vanished with the emergence of her abandonment anxieties and depression. It appears that in order for the self in this patient to embody and become part of space-and-time life, she first had to be able to experience and suffer acute feelings of abandonment. Schizoid self-parts are always present in the borderline person, and their integration is essential if a positive self is to emerge.

The borderline person's emerging self will make use of an interpretation in a way that is bewildering to the therapist. When an interpretation is accepted, he or she will often return to the next session with responses that seem to deny it. The therapist may feel confused or angry and will often *act* through intervention or withdrawal. "Acting," as A. Green says, is "the true model of the mind. . . . Acting is not limited to actions; fantasies, dreams, words take the function of action. Acting fills space and does not tolerate the suspension of experience" (1977, p. 41). The therapist may feel as though the patient has denied what has been previously communicated, but this "perception" actually serves to block perception of his or her own emerging state of confusion and incapacity to tolerate the state of psychic *absence*.

185

At this point it would be worthwhile for us to examine the discrete parts of this process. If the therapist is unable to contain the pain of the patient's absence and says something like, "But last time we came to an understanding that you now seem to be denying," the patient might say, "What have I said to indicate that?" The therapist may then feel angry because his or her sense of reality has been attacked. Yet the therapist has misunderstood the patient's communication and has taken it as a negation of his or her interpretations. But the therapist has in fact made an assumption that an agreement has been reached: this assumption has been made in order to dispel his or her own confusion and to avoid undergoing the suspension of experience. At the point when the patient says, "What have I said to deny what we did last time?" the feeling of confusion will often dissipate and leave the therapist with the sense that he or she had acted badly by assuming that the patient has denied real insights.

At this point it will seem to the therapist that the patient has been merely reflecting by setting aside what has transpired. Yet the therapist had taken this "setting aside" to be an attack on the work of the last session; he or she may view it as a "negative therapeutic reaction." In fact, the patient has been trying to make use of the interpretation *by temporarily denying it*. This act can appear to be a complete denial. The therapist's narcissism is attacked, since he or she wants a given interpretation to be definitive; he or she does not want it to be merely a stepping-stone to a deeper level. What must be understood is that the patient is attempting to disengage from the therapist's narcissism by employing this "neither/nor" logic. To do this is terribly risky, for it means he or she is beginning to show more of the true self and is thus daring to ignore the therapist's narcissistic needs.

The negative logic of the borderline patient so aptly described by Green can also be understood conceptually through the system of the *via negativa* of the fifteenth century cleric and mystic, Nicholas of Cusa. The *via negativa* is a metaphysical system that provides a mode of perceiving both the nature and the goal of the borderline person's use of negation as a path to self-emergence. In this system, every positive statement stands in opposition to another that demonstrates its finitude or incompleteness; thus, each statement yields another that can be added to the previous one. God, the unknowable object of this dialectic, is unified; He is a *coincidentia oppositorum*. Hence, the state in which opposites are united, and painful and deceitful splitting may at last be overcome, represents the unconscious goal of the borderline person. To reach the goal, however, a journey through a territory of madness is demanded. This domain of madness is one in which the inner life suffers fragmentation and confusion; in other words, it is the complete antithesis to unity and the harmony of opposites. Moreover, madness itself seems to guard against the psychic intrusion of others. Madness is a process belonging to a self that has survived persecution, and which, however weakly, manifests in paradox. This paradoxical mode is the fulcrum of the borderline person's peculiar logic.

Moreover, the therapist can err by failing to embrace the "neither/nor" logic of the borderline patient. He or she may attempt to understand the meaning of a patient's communication by interpreting feelings encountered in the countertransference. For example: "The anxious feelings I am having with this person inform me that he may be dominated by abandonment anxieties." This is what Frederick Copleston describes as the level of the senses, which simply affirm (Copleston 1985, p. 237). Or, the therapist may try to gain knowledge of the patient by determining what *is* or *is not*; for example: "She is in a manic state, but this may not be the core issue; instead, the mania may be a defense against her abandonment depression." Copleston refers to this form of reasoning as one in which "there is both affirmation and denial" (ibid.). The madness of the patient must be faced; the therapist must learn to continue to *be*, without necessarily *knowing*. In this way, the therapist respects the unknowable.

In Nicholas's thought, sense perception corresponds to what Green has called primary process thinking, and discursive reasoning (*ratio*) corresponds to the reality principle. The borderline person's logic, which follows the model of *neither Yes nor No,* corresponds in Nicholas's system to the *intellectus.*

> Whereas sense-perception affirms and reason affirms and denies, intellect denies the oppositions of reason. Reason affirms X and denies Y, but intellect denies X and Y both disjunctively and together; it apprehends God as the *coincidentia oppositorum.* This apprehension or intuition cannot, however, be properly stated in language, which is the instrument of reason rather than intellect. *In its activity as intellect the mind uses language to suggest meaning rather than to state it . . .* (Copleston 1985, p. 237, italics mine).

One can never *understand* a person's mad parts, *but one can know that one does not know.* Translating the state of madness into a discursive process (such as causal sequences of untransited developmental stages) fails to grasp the nature of madness and also fails to provide a symbolic sense of containment for the borderline person. Such reductive thinking turns the borderline person's madness into a *thing* to be ordered, instead of admitting it to be as vital and alive and characteristic of self as the person's other more "acceptable" qualities. The reductive method cannot circumscribe the phenomenon of madness, which is beyond the province of rational knowing.

The only knowing that is useful in the treatment of borderline disorders is the knowing which is reached through a negative logic. The patient's madness has the capacity to distort and destroy his or her own and the therapist's perceptions in such a way that seemingly benign interactions, or interpretations that were formerly accepted by the patient and have been introjected, turn into persecutory objects. But it should be clear that this change from the benign into the persecutory is not the result of the patient splitting from abandonment anxieties, since abandonment experiences are *neither the cause nor not the cause* of the person's madness. We need to be able to tolerate the suspended state of *not knowing* and at the same time not negate the attempt to know. This form of waiting can provide a deep experience of a person's psychotic parts, even if it is not possible to become truly comfortable with the feelings of oddness and terror, absence and mindlessness they are apt to provoke.

Madness: Personal or Impersonal?

Is the madness one experiences in another person personal or impersonal? Certainly, it can feel like a soulless thing that terrifies subject and object by its very absence of form and by the experience of the void that is part of it. For madness is imbued with *absence* or *blankness* rather than the affirmative presence of any thing. In therapy, the madness one begins to see seems like an alien Other that has nothing to do with the patient *with whom one wishes to be.* Certainly, it is difficult to accept the mad parts a patient brings into the room. To avoid these parts, we tend to cling to explanations of projective identification dynamics and to manufacture interpretations that may even include the therapist's fear of being abandoned. But these choices are all defensive strategies to fill a void, an absence of experience, a space where thought and experience do not exist.

It is easy to think of madness as matter to be organized. A therapist may communicate the following: "You are fleeing from an abandonment anxiety and fear that I, too, will abandon you in the process." This rationale may be true, but it is also defensive, a way of avoiding the absence and blankness that can characterize madness. Yet the patient, assaulted by "well-intentioned" interpretations, quickly flees into extreme states of mind–body splitting and the therapist's intrusion goes unnoticed. Indeed, the patient is as happy as the therapist to have something to cling to—in this instance, the interpretation of an anxiety state. The patient's anxiety becomes a *thing* to be ordered and understood. It becomes a substitute for madness and reduces it to an impersonal energy.

How can madness be considered to be personal? Can I, or need I, love my patient's madness? The image of St. Theresa drinking the pus of her sick patients seems relevant in its excess. How can this madness, which often succeeds in turning both people into automatons, be part of one's humanity? To bear a saintly attitude toward it, to be the "wounded healer," or the doctor who wears the mantle of suffering, will not be experienced by the patient as embracing and containing of the patient's process. Indeed, if the therapist identifies with this saintly image of the wounded healer a disjunction between patient and therapist will be certain to occur.

A quite different situation emerges if the therapist is able to succeed in encompassing the phenomenon of a patient who now reveals *his or her* madness. The patient has been terrified of exhibiting this madness. The realm of madness is a no-man's-land, a place where meaning, imagery, and all relational potential is destroyed.[6] When the therapist is able to comprehend madness as an aspect of the patient and becomes able to experience the patient and the patient's madness in a personal, human way, a change can occur: as one enters into the alien territory of the patient's madness, one's personal orientation fails. A solely personal relationship to this phenomenon cannot fully contain it. One has the feeling that madness must be apprehended through a more comprehensive perspective. As a larger container for madness is allowed to develop, a sense of an impersonal dimension becomes prominent. The patient's madness begins to seem autonomous; it can appear like a machine or a deity, a separate force that not only rules the patient, but can also rule the encounter between patient and therapist. The

---

[6]See M. Eigen's *The Psychotic Core* (1987) for a masterful discussion of psychosis. I would like to call special attention to his work on distinction-union as a basic structure of the self (pp. 306–312 and Chapter 4).

impersonal/archetypal perspective can become too extreme, and stray too far from human levels. One must then return to the smaller personal framework, though this soon feels too confining and again requires expansion.

Thus one's perception of madness oscillates between the polarities personal–impersonal, or personal–archetypal. I cannot say that I relate to the patient's madness in a personal way, but neither can I say that I relate to it in an impersonal way. Yet if I say that the relationship is both personal *and* impersonal I have abstracted my experience in an intellectual way that destroys the experience of madness. I resist destroying the strange and even awesome way in which personal and impersonal qualities are coupled—a coupling that seems to become manifest only when the phenomenology of madness *as part of the patient* is deeply engaged. What I can say with certainty, however, is that the patient's madness is *neither personal nor impersonal.*

This distinction between the personal level and an impersonal transcendent level is also revealed when the mystic is asked the question: Is the God you experience personal or impersonal? The mystic will answer that the God experience is intensely personal. Once this observation has been voiced, it will seem incorrect; the mystic will then speak of God as sublimely Other and say that his or her experience belongs to a realm that is intensely impersonal. It will not do to say that the God experience is both personal and impersonal. To do so would bind and falsify the experience. One can only say that the God experience of mystic reaches is neither personal nor impersonal.

The mystic's paradoxical expression embraces his or her experience. The borderline person's *neither Yes nor No* rarely has the fluidity of paradox but instead caricatures it. The mystic's paradox communicates a sense of wholeness, while the borderline patient's paradoxical logic—when its elusive and underlying truth is not apprehended—can trigger feelings of emptiness and confusion in the therapist.

The borderline person's *neither Yes nor No* seems to cancel whatever has been achieved. For example, a session may approach clarity, and confusion will wane. The following session may begin with an attack. The patient's attack is his or her way of guarding against the therapist's tendency *not* to see in a paradoxical way. What the patient would wish to say to the therapist—if the therapist has not eliminated all possibility of communication by precipitous talk or action—is that the insights gained in the previous session are neither correct nor incorrect.

By attacking the therapist the patient is simply expressing an inability to grasp the paradoxical nature of the therapeutic experience. If the therapist can suspend action and create a space for confusion and an absence of knowing, *then* the patient may be able to say that a previous interpretation was neither complete nor incomplete.

The soul of the borderline person and Nicholas of Cusa seem to have a common approach to the *numinosum*. It is as if the person were saying: "You cannot fully know me. I am beyond any rational comprehension. You can only know that you do not know. If the knowing you possess is authentic and hard won, I will allow you to approach my soul, but only if you always know you do not know. Your need to know and your arrogance are the greatest threat to me, as is your being anything less than your best as you try to understand me." As one approaches the soul of the borderline person, one transits the territory of madness. Jacques Lacan has written: "Not only can man's being not be understood without madness, it would not be man's being if it did not bear madness within itself as the limit of his freedom" (1977, p. 215). (See Eigen 1986a for an elaboration of this theme.) Unless one can delve into the borderline person's madness one will never be able to understand him or her.

The borderline person's madness accrues from experiences of extreme pain, confusion, and bewilderment. To a degree, madness is created (though it is also an *a priori* state, like the chaos of myth and alchemy) by denial, splitting, projective identification, and identification of the ego with archetypal images. Madness defends against the pain of being hated, scapegoated, and attacked by parental guilt and envy for any individuation effort. Madness also serves to dull the experience of pain. The soul, in its exit from the territory of madness (when, for example, it is *seeing* and *daring to be seen*), is always attended by the pain that accompanies the process of overcoming splitting.

The borderline person often acts in ways that appear mad because the pain is so deep and the risk of having it touched so great that all avenues to his or her soul are full of roadblocks, detours, and warning signs of danger. The borderline person is always testing, for example, by asking an "attacking" question. When the borderline sector in any individual is approached, the danger light goes on. The *coniunctio,* with its capacity to heal splitting, always touches upon the insufferable pain endemic to it. This pain and its attendant madness is at the core of the borderline person. The patient will "go on alert" in order to ascertain whether or not the therapist realizes and is capable of handling the depth of his or her pain and sensitivity. If the therapist assertively states his or her understanding, while the patient sees the assertion to be incomplete if not false, then a detour must be taken until the risk of exposure is diminished. These detours engage madness and lead to "nothingness" — a state of suspension and waiting; the patient watches to see if this time his or her pain will be apprehended and understood.

Borderline and Religious Experiences

Is there a relationship between the thought processes of the borderline person and genuine experiences of the *numinosum* as in mystical experiences or in Nicholas of Cusa's *via negativa*? A mystic experiences union with the divinity as a *complexio oppositorum*. The soul's immersion in and subsequent separation from God is a reality, and that union then lives on in the soul of the mystic. But for the borderline person *loss of union* is the critical issue. Whatever union experiences with the *numinosum* there may have been, especially during the first months of life, and whatever union experiences in later developmental stages may have taken place, the borderline person has not been able to sufficiently own or incarnate them.

Often, the borderline person may serve as a link to the *numinosum* for other people; for example, he or she may be psychic, or be a therapist. The *numinosum* may be alive and remarkably healing for others when the borderline person serves as its conduit. But it has not incarnated *for the person*. When he or she is alone, the *numinosum* disappears; it is no longer experienced as a healing Other, but instead constitutes a reminder of painful absence and abandonment that can barely be tolerated. Somatizations and mind–body splits eliminate the capacity to differentiate feelings and to experience conflicting opposites; a bewildering simultaneity of contradictory feeling-states occurs.

There is a link between borderline states of mind and a genuine experience of the *numinosum*. The manifestation of borderline states of mind within religious experiences is well known. For instance, St. John of the Cross suffered from a terrible sense of emptiness and depression. In his experience of "The Dark Night" his mind was often blank and his thoughts fractured; he lived in despair, feeling abandoned by God and by people. He had profoundly difficult experiences that caused him severe suffering. He was ostracized by his community and imprisoned. Yet he was also able to remain calm, even serene, in the belief that all of his suffering was for the purpose of the purification through which he might receive God (Williams 1980, pp. 159–179).

The story of St. John's life evokes diagnostic reflections over borderline phenomena. The workings of John's "psychotic twin" are evident in his mental blankness. The persecutory anxieties he suffered are manifest in the responses of the world his behavior elicited. Borderline persons generally thrust their madness into the environment. John's severe states of abandonment are characteristic of the borderline person, as are his feelings of emptiness, and his proclivity for seeking pain. Moreover, John's vision of suffering as a way to God might be seen as a symptom of good–bad splitting and manic and omnipotent defenses; these states would then be viewed as defenses against his feelings of worthlessness. John may have been a borderline person, but his influence upon spirituality and his understanding of complex meditative states of mind has made him an invaluable source of wisdom.

But one does not need to examine borderline logic and its relationship to various mystical systems to recognize the link between borderline phenomenology and religious pursuit. Consider *The Diagnostic and Statistical Manual of the American Psychiatric Association, Third Edition* (DSM III),[7] which offers the following eight diagnostic criteria for the borderline personality disorder:

(1) Impulsivity or unpredictability in at least two areas that are potentially self damaging, e.g., spending, sex, gambling, substance use, shoplifting, overeating, physically self-damaging acts.

(2) A marked pattern of unstable and intense interpersonal relationships, e.g., marked shifts of attitude, idealization, devaluation, manipulation (constantly using others for one's own ends).

(3) Inappropriate, intense anger or lack of control of anger, e.g., frequent displays of temper, constant anger.

(4) Identity disturbance manifested by uncertainty about several issues relating to identity, such as self-image, gender identity, long term goals or career choice, friendship patterns, values, and loyalties, e.g., "Who am I?", "I feel like I am my sister when I am good."

(5) Affective instability: Marked shifts from normal mood to depression, irritability or anxiety, usually lasting a few hours and only rarely more than a few days, with a return to normal mood.

(6) Intolerance of being alone, e.g., frantic efforts to avoid being alone, depressed when alone.

(7) Physically self damaging acts, e.g., suicidal gestures, self-mutilation, recurrent accidents or physical fights.

---

[7]The criteria for borderline personality listed in the updated version, DSM III-R, do not change the argument that follows.

(8) Chronic feelings of emptiness or boredom.

But these same criteria are also a profile of the Old Testament creator Yahweh, who certainly possessed at least five of the stated criteria! He was impulsive and unpredictable in ways that were self damaging. His relations with his people, Israel, were unstable and marked by idealization and devaluation. His anger was intense and often uncontrolled, and he could behave ruthlessly and with complete disregard for his chosen people. He destroyed his own creation with a flood. His identity was diffuse, for he needed constant mirroring. His moods often changed capriciously.

Diagnostically speaking, Yahweh is a borderline personality. This fact is instructive: Yahweh may indeed be a borderline personality, but he is also the supreme light, the source of the *numinosum*. In the Old Testament, Yahweh has a personality that includes not only numinosity, creativity, and wisdom beyond that of any mortal, but his personality *also* includes borderline characteristics. Perhaps it is not possible for a human being to bear a creativity that touches a divine level without his or her also suffering borderline states of mind. In the figure of Yahweh, light and the dark are united, albeit in a bewildering fashion. But the combination of the positive *numinosum* with borderline characteristics is a mark of the creative genius of the Old Testament. This should not be forgotten amid our efforts to separate light and dark qualities of the *numinosum* from each other, an essential task that must be performed in order that the light may incarnate.

The therapist learns to see the dead or blank self of the borderline person and to survive persecutory attacks upon any form of linking as well as the suspension of mental processes that its neither/nor logic induces. Although it is important to uncover chronic states of abandonment in working with the borderline person, this task is only a first step along the path of encountering states of mind characterized by blankness and mind-destroying fury. *The torment of abandonment may thus be seen as a rite of passage for an incarnating Self.* But abandonment issues do not sufficiently explain the borderline condition. To focus upon them at the expense of engaging deeper levels of the *numinosum* results in enhancing the patient's capacity for repression, but does not facilitate the embodiment of the self as a center that is in contact with the *numinosum*.

Treatment Issues

The following reflections on the borderline psyche and treatment considerations derive from various sources. These are Bion's concept that there are both normal and psychotic parts to every personality; Jung's researches on alchemical symbolism; my own clinical experience of positive and negative manifestions of the *numinosum*; and my emphasis on the importance of the unconscious dyad. The psychotic part of a person may be thought to contain the image of a child, who represents the true self or soul. This child image often appears in a depleted or helpless state; it is a *dead self* not unlike the dead Osiris, who languished in the Underworld and was attacked when he dared arise. Another image representing the person's psychotic part is of a couple who are fused yet in a state of radical disunion. This couple violently rejects separation, yet the parts of the couple are at the same time without any genuine contact. I have found, in my clinical work with patients, that the unconscious couple often assumes a violent form, with each member striving to attack the other; the female part often has a powerful phallus, and the male part is engulfing and mutilating. This unconscious couple often manifests in interpersonal relations and causes confusion or a sadomasochistic interaction between therapist and patient. But this interaction is a defensive operation engaged by both patient and therapist to prevent them from experiencing the actual nature of the unconscious couple, which is especially hateful toward the soul. The couple, locked in a deadly and cruel combat, is actually a single double-sided object (Green 1977, p. 40) that is deeply antagonistic to the child held captive within its territory.

Thus the psychotic part of a person contains the soul as well as an extremely persecutory dyad, a couple existing "before the creation" and prior to the separation of opposites. The dynamics operating within this dyad are complex, but Jung's researches into alchemical symbolism provide some guidance for an understanding of them. Should we regard the extremely destructive affects that accompany the psychotic part of the individual to be a result of developmental traumas? Or might these destructive affects instead be a consequence of union experiences that include but are not simply reducible to historical antecedents? Jung amplifies alchemical texts that illustrate how union experiences at first create very destructive contents; in alchemical language these contents are called thief or devil, and often they assume such animal forms as the rabid dog, snake, basilisk, toad, or raven (Jung 1955, par. 172). The borderline person's shadow, which houses these destructive contents, commonly will appear in the form of the renegade, which seeks to destroy anything positive or life-giving. Another prominent shadow configuration is the seductive death demon (which Neumann calls uroboric incest), who lures the soul into a regressive fusion and plays upon the soul's memories of its original experience of the *numinosum*.

It is important to have a dual understanding of these shadow elements. On the one hand, they can be perceived as part of an introjective structure, born from the patient's ongoing need to deny the horror of his or her early perceptions. A kind of inner fifth column is thereby created—what Bion represents as the lying *fiend* (Meltzer 1978, pp. 106ff.). This image of the fiend is clearly identical with the devil, who carries the destructive function in many religions. On the other hand, *extremely destructive states of mind can be created through the experience of union*; these dark creations attempt to destroy the memory of union experiences with the positive *numinosum*. The so-called negative therapeutic reaction is susceptible to containment when both patient and therapist become conscious of the fact that a union experience, though barely perceptible, has previously occurred. Such union experiences are registered in dreams, and may also be experienced as processes between two people.

The union experience is of special significance when one is working with the borderline person. Through it, the therapist introjects the person's previously split-off, helpless self, which, as I have noted, commonly takes the form of an injured or tormented young child. Such union experiences, including their resulting demonic products, can bring to light the patient's constant inner struggle: a battle between life and death in which the opposing forces are God and Satan. When this conflict is unconscious it will manifest in sadomasochistic dyads that structure the patient's inner life and relationships. This sadomasochistic style creates a relatively safe territory for the patient, even though he or she must pay dearly for it. The toll is taken in terms of relational failures and an undermining of creativity and all forms of self-assertion.

When the truly demonic parts of a person become conscious, a new stage is set, one in which death through suicide, illness, or accident becomes a serious concern. At this stage, the therapist will often wonder if the patient's previous unconscious use of splitting devices were not a better state of affairs! But if the patient can be helped to confront the death-drive within the context of union—that is, by seeing its relationship to positive experiences—he or she may discover new self-images and thus find a reason for living. In alchemy, forms that at the outset are dangerous (such as the "rabid dog" and the "thief") later become protective of the "child," which represents the new self. In some mysterious way, demonic aspects may be necessary for the destruction of structures in the old personality that have outlived their usefulness.

Throughout this process, a grave danger lies in the therapist's need to be in control, for if this need is not surrendered, he or she becomes aligned with the "old king" who rules the normal, competent personality. This neurotic need may severely undermine the healing process by creating more splitting in the patient and between patient and therapist. *One needs the patient's help*, otherwise the healing process cannot stand against the powerful forces of death and destruction that emerge from the psychotic parts of both patient and therapist.

To be able to *see* that the psychotic part is also the link to the *numinosum* in the borderline person is crucial for the initiation of the healing process. But once the person's madness begins to be more fully uncovered and mutually acknowledged, then the *numinosum* may be directly encountered as the transcendent Self. I believe this experience is what Grotstein calls the "Background Object."[8] One would hardly expect to discover the *numinosum* amid the confusion, splitting and denial that can dominate treatment. But the *numinosum* is present nevertheless. This transcendent Self is not created through interpersonal relations, but is rather an *increatum* (an *a priori*) and the patient's birthright. When the *numinosum* incarnates, healing is nearby.

But the forces of death or destruction must never be underestimated. The devil works at this stage of potential healing as a trickster, luring the therapist into thinking all is well and often seducing him or her away from an encounter with the patient's madness. Once the *numinosum* becomes part of the patient's (normal–neurotic) functioning personality, we enter a phase in which the patient aligns with life and against death.

The linking of the normal–neurotic to the psychotic part of the patient is a crucial treatment issue. I have underscored the importance of imaginal sight in this process. Also, the therapist must remain vigilant;

---

[8]He writes that this "corresponds to the most archaic organizing internal object which offers background support for the infant's development. . . . it is one which is awesome, majestic, unseen, and behind one. It 'rears' us and sends us off into the world. In moments of quiet repose we sit on its lap metaphorically. In psychotic illness and in borderline states it is severely damaged or compromised" (1979, p. 154n).

he or she must be careful not to split the patient into separate functioning and psychotic parts. The patient's splitting and denial can be so strong that the "normal" part may be favored by the therapist. Both parts must instead be seen as fragments of a whole.

Discovering the existence of the unconscious dyad and entering the imaginal process it engenders can lead to the transformation of the interactive field so that an ability to play and an experience of the transcendent function (Jung 1916) can emerge. This transformed space is crucial because it allows the patient and therapist the possibility of making a connection between the normal and psychotic parts of the personality that cannot be achieved through acts of interpretation (Grotstein 1979, p. 175).

The borderline person lacks a transcendent function. This is not to say that a link between conscious and unconscious does not exist; in fact, the person may have a channel through which the unconscious may be freely brought to consciousness. According to A. Green and others (see Meissner 1984, pp. 55ff.), borderline people do not manifest *functional* transitional phenomena:

> Borderline patients are characterized by a failure to create functional byproducts of potential space; instead of manifesting transitional phenomena, they create symptoms to fulfill the function of transitional phenomena. By this I do not mean to say that borderline patients are unable to create transitional objects or phenomena. To say such a thing would be to ignore the fact that many artists are borderline personalities. In fact it can only be said that from the point of view of the psychic apparatus of such individuals, transitional objects or phenomena have no functional value, as they do for others. (Green 1977, p. 38)

The borderline person has little capacity to play with the unconscious, to affect it by consciousness or to allow the conscious personality to be affected by the unconscious. Instead, the unconscious will pronounce itself by presenting the patient with extremely concrete associations to dreams that rarely lead to other associations, or with a random flood of ideas, or, conversely, with a total incapacity for free association or imagination. The borderline person may be a psychic or a creative and gifted person, yet he or she is usually only a "receiver" for this information and can rarely interact with it in a meaningful way. Borderline persons can often use their psychic gifts to help others but can do little to aid themselves. Subject to the unconscious, they feel completely helpless when confronted with its contents. Therefore, the transcendent function is crucial for the therapy of the borderline person.

I suggest a model of a psychotic part of the personality which contains a parental couple that is a single object (a negative state of the hermaphrodite); within it the soul is terribly afflicted by the death-force (which incarnates as the renegade). Yet, by imaginally working with the unconscious dyad manifesting between patient and therapist, a transcendent function can emerge that will link the normal–neurotic and psychotic parts of the patient. Throughout the process, vision will be severely curtailed unless there is a profound recognition of the *numinosum*. That uncreated element — often perceived in the background or fusing with the normal personality to create a polluted state — must be seen as the patient's birthright and an essential source of healing.

CHAPTER SEVEN
PASSION AND REDEMPTION AS REFLECTED
THROUGH *THE GOLDEN ASS*

It is, to my mind, a fatal mistake to regard the human psyche as a purely personal affair and to explain it from a personal point of view. (C. G. Jung 1937, par. 24)

Introduction

In "Psychology of the Transference" Jung explained why he chose so arcane a system as alchemy to study the transference:

It is only possible to come to a right understanding and appreciation of a contemporary psychological problem when we can reach a point outside our own time from which to observe it. This point can only be some past epoch that was concerned with the same problems, although under different conditions and in other forms (1946, p. 166).

In this work I have employed alchemical symbolism to view borderline conditions as aspects of the archetypal pattern of the *coniunctio*; in this way borderline conditions are seen to be situated within a larger archetypal pattern that subsumes the personal perspective (Jung 1937, par. 24). *The Golden Ass* provides another illuminating context for reflecting upon borderline conditions.

The Golden Ass was written in the second century A.D.[1] Jack Lindsay, whose translation I shall be following, summarizes the tale:

Apuleius tells the story of one Lucius who through his overweening curiosity and magic-dabbling is turned into an ass. Lucius goes through an odyssey of misfortunes and suffering, till at last he eats the redeeming rose-petals and regains his

---

[1] "It is one of the three great works of imaginative prose narrative that we own from the ancient world. Petronius's *Satyricon* is the first, with its turbulent realistic ironic and poetic picture of the successful philistine world of the first century A.D. . . . The second is *The Golden Ass*. The third is Longus's *Daphnis and Chloe* (in which) the Greek spirit looks nostalgically back over its lost chances and creates an image of 'paradise regained' . . . out of the poetic essences of the fertility-cults" (Lindsay 1960, p. 13). "*The Golden Ass* . . . sums up its epoch and at the same time remains a timeless fantasy to which men can always return for images and symbols of their earthly life. In one sense it records the breakdown of Graeco-Roman civilization; in another it prophetically looks to the reconstruction of the fourth century . . . but beyond all such points of reference, it has an inner vitality which makes it symbolic of the life of man here and now, in the twentieth or any other century" (Lindsay 1960, p. 28).

human form. The theme of the tormented man-inside-the-ass (the beast of burden bearing the weight of the unintelligible world, as Christ bore a crushing
burden till he reached the foot of the Cross) is one that enables Apuleius to
achieve a new and startling focus from which to look out on human activities and
judge them. Lucius has been avid to grasp the forbidden lores and practices that
will enable him to get behind the appearances of things; as a result he becomes
the victim of the dark forces he has invoked. His odyssey is a long struggle
towards a new level, a new integration of life, in which his old hungers and
compulsions are overcome (Lindsay 1960, p. 13).

In *The Golden Ass*, the torments that the hero Lucius endures
are created by the great goddess Isis; they have the function of transforming his inflated personality into one respectful of archetypal forces.
When employing developmental theories we also recognize the healing
function of suffering. But when the borderline person can experience an
archetypal reality lying behind his or her suffering, not only is the ego's
identification with archetypal processes dissolved, but a new orientation
to these processes can emerge. The issue we are addressing is essentially
religious; a connection can be made to the *numinosum* through "worship
of the Goddess," that is, recognition of the religious aspect of the Feminine, and especially of embodied life.

Lucius is a self-possessed and self-centered young man of good
family. We meet him as he embarks upon a journey; his purpose is to
learn the secrets of magic. Lucius has a well-developed intellect, a solar
consciousness, and a heroic, if somewhat arrogant, bearing. His narcissism keeps him aloof from the feelings of others. That he tends to make
excessive use of projective identification and splitting devices can be
deduced from his numerous encounters with people who one after
another recount tales filled with sadomasochistic events, demonic possession, good–bad splitting, sexual perversity, and terrifying episodes of
abandonment. These are all qualities of Lucius's own self that he will
later be forced to encounter. Indeed, Lucius encounters a profile of his
own psyche in the very first tale.

In this first story, Lucius is presented with aspects of his psyche
that he haṡ denied. He meets a pair of travelers; the first is a rationalist
who vehemently argues against the views of his fellow companion, Aristomenes. Aristomenes was also originally a rationalist who had rigidly
defended himself against the Goddess, but now he is a believer in her
powers. Aristomenes' tale concerns his friend "Socrates" who has been
completely overwhelmed by the psyche's dark powers of seduction and
persecution. These images, of the rationalist and of Aristomenes (and

Socrates), represent a split between patterns of denial and patterns of engulfment; they are conflicting aspects of the structural foundation of Lucius's ego. At this stage in his development, his "as-if" personality affords him a functional aloofness from the experience of the underlying terrors that have resulted in his elemental splitting. The source of these overwhelming affects is the dark aspect of the Goddess (who in this tale appears in the person of the witch, Meroe); she forms the fourth element in a quaternity composed of Lucius (the central or reality ego) and the denial–engulfment oppositional pair.

Lucius remains emotionally untouched by Aristomenes' tale of wretched possession, brutality, and abandonment. This tale is a prefiguration of what will eventually befall him when he succumbs to the power of the dark aspect of the Goddess; however, he does not take seriously the warning inherent in this tale. This "as-if" quality of his personality is thus presented to us at the beginning of the novel, and his lack of compassion and engagement continue as dominant themes of his character throughout the ensuing tales. He is not able to feel the reality or see the true meaning of the stories he hears. When we first meet him in his quest for the knowledge contained in the black magic of the feminine forces, he is intensely preoccupied with the idea of power. His "heroic" arrogance causes him to behave rashly; as in all such cases, he gets what he thinks he wants. Wishes do come true, though they are not usually granted in the form expected by the ego.

Lucius, acting like a person suffering from a borderline personality disorder, becomes submerged in deeply persecutory states of mind as a result of the impact of the reactions of others to his sexual-aggressive desires. His affair with Pamphile's maid, Fotis (a relationship that is typically "borderline" in its considerable pregenital quality and lack of personal relatedness), eventually undoes his defenses. Fotis subtly turns on him through the "error" of giving him the wrong potion to drink. As a result, he becomes an ass rather than the bird he hoped to become. Lucius's troubles begin when he finds himself unable to return to human form. His borderline nature is evident: his splitting, already apparent from the earlier tales, is now concretized by his reduced state. He is a human being inside of an ass; his human consciousness is totally split from his bestial qualities.

Lucius's desire to understand the mysteries of the dark side of the feminine principle incorporates itself in his wish to change shape and to cast spells that will affect others. This suggests a capacity to consciously create and manipulate states of projective identification. The *process* whereby imagination is set in motion and then affects others (through projective identification) is contained in what was known in antiquity as the mystery of the Goddess.

The Golden Ass reveals ancient attitudes, both healthy and pathological, toward such psychological processes as projective identification and imagination. In this tale both imagination and body are media for the perception of and relationship to the *numinosum*. The main focus of the story is the pre-Aryan magic that was practiced in Thessaly. The problematic nature of this form of magical practice—the tendency for an individual to identify with powers that he or she has gained rather than respect their Otherness—is emphasized in this work; magic's relationship to the *numinosum as it is experienced through the body* is equally stressed. An evolutionary form of this type of magical practice appears in the "left-hand path" of tantrism, and in the *Rosarium Philosophorum*, which was used by Jung as his model for the transference. From a contemporary clinical point of view, *The Golden Ass* can be viewed as a document outlining borderline states of mind. It is a record of behaviors and attitudes held by many individuals of the time toward the psychic and physical energies that are linked to the central mystery of union, the *coniunctio*. Concerning this relationship, Maria-Louise von Franz, who is the only Jungian author to write a complete psychological interpretation of *The Golden Ass*, says:

> [If] one compares the attempts at an incarnation of the Father God in Christianity, one sees that God comes down into man. He comes down from the heavenly sphere into a human body, carefully purified from any *macula peccati* and, to some extent, takes on human form. In the parallel attempts at an incarnation of the Goddess, it is not the same thing. Venus does not come down and incarnate in a feminine being, but an ordinary feminine being becomes, or is regarded as, a personification of Venus, and she comes slowly up. In the development of the Catholic Church, the Virgin Mary is first an ordinary human being who slowly, through the historical process, is elevated to nearly divine rank. Thus, in the incarnation of the male God there is a descent into man, and in the incarnation of the female Goddess, an ascent of an ordinary human being to a nearly divine realm. I could not say whether this is a general law, but I think it is meaningful to think about (1980, p. 83).

While in some cultures there are goddesses who descend (for example, the Shinto sun goddess), and while there are also patriarchal god-images that were human before they were divine (for example, Gautama Buddha), von Franz's differentiation between masculine and feminine relations to the *numinosum* is useful. However, her analysis should not be taken as definitive of the ways that men and women relate to the sacred. The distinction that must be made is that between an "earthly-lunar" relationship to the *numinosum* and a "heavenly-solar" one. Both men and women can experience each form of relationship to the *numinosum,* but for the last several thousand years, patriarchal culture and its emphasis on the heavenly-solar form has dominated both men and women. The earthly-lunar form has been projected onto women by men in order to defend against "the left-hand path." This projection is, however, more than a defensive maneuver; it is also a route for the "return of the repressed." This allocation to women of the experience of the *numinosum* through the body is culturally determined; this particular relationship to the *numinosum* may also be rooted in woman's very nature. There are two ways in which the *numinosum* can be experienced: one can experience it as emanating from above and eventually incarnating in a downward path, or as incarnating upward from below. It is less than useful to ascribe a gender differentiation to these two forms of relationship to the divine.

At the time Apuleius wrote *The Golden Ass,* patriarchal repression was gaining strength, the "left-hand path" would soon be repressed, and rational attitudes were in ascendence. These attitudes supported the suppression of "feminine" relationships to the *numinosum* and the *coniunctio.*

When the *numinosum* is experienced as emerging through the body from below, a transformative realm can be entered that is unknown to the patriarchal worldview, which imposes order upon disorder. Whether the sources of that order are divine illuminations from ecstatic visions, or principles of science and the equations deriving from them, or developmental theories of individuation, the patriarchal model uses order to subdue what is viewed as disorder. Thus disorder is undervalued; it is a state to be conquered, not one to be accepted for its own mystery.[2]

From the point of view of the *Golden Ass,* the borderline dilemma is created by a wrong, power-oriented attitude toward the "left-hand path" of the energies of the Goddess. This misappropriation of

---

[2] In the great feminine mysteries of Eleusis, the event of the birth resulting from the union between Persephone and Dionysus was announced as: "Brimo gives birth to Brimos!" (Kerenyi 1949, p. 143). Brimo is one form of the Goddess; her name means "the power to arouse terror . . . to rage" (ibid., p. 142); she was closely associated with Pluto and Dionysus, and her image refers to an attitude that values imaginal sight and body consciousness. The experience of terror and chaos was understood by the initiates to be inextricably linked to the birth of a new consciousness.

power includes using imaginal and body energies in subtle ways; such a person may control others through manipulation, or unconsciously employ abandonment threats that are communicated through projective identification. He or she may also act out sexual and aggressive drives for manipulative purposes. Lucius's splitting, sadomasochistic persecutions and perversions and intense abandonment experiences continue until he learns to recognize and respect the Dionysian energies of this "path." Through these energies he experiences the death of his power complex and also the demise of his solar-heroic ego that denies pain and suffering.

The negative aspect of the left-hand path is a desire for continual fusion and for the power this fusion engenders. One must disengage from fusion states, yet how is it possible to do so without rejecting the value of this path and its attunement to the *numinosum* (as experienced through the body)? Lucius's "solution," which is reflected in the initial tale of Aristomenes, is to create a delusional relationship to the Goddess, one that does not recognize or value her dark and earthly qualities, or her humanity. The Goddess, when viewed in this way, is partially denied; she becomes the "all-good" Mother. Lucius's "solution" of splitting and denial is shown to be destructive. He exemplifies the borderline person's fusion–distance dilemma. On the one hand, he is driven to possess the magical powers associated with feminine energies, and on the other, he approaches the mysteries of the Goddess through inappropriate attitudes of ego control and power.

Comments on Stories in *The Golden Ass*

The first tale describes archetypal aspects that underlie the borderline personality. The cheese-and-honey merchant, Aristomenes, finds that his old friend "Socrates" is now a pauper and in rags. Aristomenes is a person with a "positive mother complex." He has an attitude that denies negative aspects of the feminine.[3] This attitude is exemplified in this tale by his tendency to minimize Socrates' ordeal. Socrates tells him that he had been beset by robbers and had barely managed to escape with his life. He had then found his way to the house of an old woman named Meroe. Meroe had taken possession of Socrates, and he had been obliged

---

[3] This Jungian terminology covers the same phenomenology as the concept of Rewarding Part Object Relation (RORU) in the Masterson-Rinsley schema of the borderline personality (Masterson 1976).

to serve her every desire. He had tried to escape and in the process discovered Meroe's dark identity:

> She is a witch. . . . She is superhuman, able to drag down the heavens or to lift up the earth, to harden running water or to dissolve mountains, to raise the dead or to tumble down the gods, to poke out the stars or to light up the darkness of hell (Lindsay 1960, p. 37).

Socrates provides us with the classic description of the witch of antiquity. This witch can create overwhelming confusion and catastrophe and halt or reverse the play of opposites (von Franz 1980, p. 22). Of particular interest is the witch's manipulation of opposites; the borderline person's psychic state is composed of confusion, splitting, and self/object oscillations. From one moment to the next, opposites will shift from "inside" to "outside" and from "good" to "bad."

Meroe kills Socrates and frames Aristomenes as the murderer. At the end of this tale Aristomenes says: "Trembling, terrified, I rode through many strange and desert places, as if driven by the guilt of murder. I abandoned my country and my home. I exiled myself and came to Aetolia, where I have again married" (Lindsay 1960, p. 44). Terrified that he will be found guilty of the murder of Socrates, and collapsing under the pressure of being the scapegoat, Aristomenes describes the abandonment of himself and his family. The result of this meeting with the negative mother is abandonment, and a flight reaction by the "heroic" Aristomenes. This is not a positive ending, to be sure; yet many a borderline person has such a tragic end—that is, a life dominated by abandonment threats and the pain of being chronically scapegoated.

After hearing this tale, Lucius then continues his travels. On the way, he stops to ask an old woman for directions to Milo's home. She answers:

> You come upon his house . . . even before you enter the city's bounds. . . . Look over there, at those last windows that face on this side towards the city, and that door on the other side opening up upon a blind-alley in front. There lodges Milo, a man with heaps of money and other good things besides. But he's got a bad name for miserliness and dirty griping ways. . . . And there, shut up in that poky house, poring over his hoard, he lives with a wife that shares his miserable life. He won't have another servant but a single wench, and he stalks about as ragged as a common beggar (Lindsay 1960, p. 45).

The setting of the house is noteworthy: it is near a dead-end alley and beyond the boundaries of the town. Milo himself is described as dirty, unkempt, and miserly. His house, the place to which Lucius is attracted and which will be the setting for the eruption of his borderline pathology—his metamorphosis into an ass—is a masterly description of the state of anal fixation, a condition common in borderline personalities. Anality is filled with overwhelming energies because it is a bridge between the personal and archetypal polarities (see M. Milner's discussion of anality and creativity, 1957). Milo's house is situated at the "border," that is, between personal and collective unconscious levels. The borderline patient, a liminoid patient, is stranded between these levels.

Milo represents negative attributes associated with many borderline persons, who often feel themselves to be dirty; to support their anal self-image they will often secretly be physically unclean, as well. Such persons are often outsiders, existing at the fringe of groups or even of society itself; they often thrive upon the misery of others, and are at times appallingly lacking in concern for other people. That Milo fears envious attacks can be inferred from his dress, his tendency to hoard possessions, and his essential misogyny. His obsession with money indicates that he secretes his energy in order not to lose any precious libido. This is common borderline behavior, although we sometimes encounter an opposing tendency, whereby the person's energy floods others.

Lucius finds Pamphile (who is a powerful witch) seated at Milo's feet. This means that the witch is in a position subservient to masculine power attitudes. Such anal–obsessive power attitudes function in a manner that denies the witch: through these attitudes only a bare minimum of libido can be given to life and to people. Milo's house represents obsessive control and withdrawal; these defenses offer Lucius an illusion of retreat from the terrifying realm of the witch, a realm he had previously encountered in Aristomenes' tale of Meroe and Socrates. Thus, at this point, Lucius's defenses continue to operate, and he is able to keep the persecutory energies of the dark side of the feminine at arm's length. But his defenses are beginning to crumble. Narcissistic or obsessive character structures will often keep the borderline person at a distance from persecutory affects, although eventually these defenses will fail.

The next day, Lucius awakens and explores Thessaly. His description is typical of a borderline state of mind wherein archetypes strongly impinge upon reality:

> In fact, there was nothing that I saw as I walked about the city which I did not believe to be something other than it was. Everything seemed to me to have just been struck by some fatal incantation into a quite contrary image. I thought that the stones on which I trod were petrified men, that the birds twittering in my ears were enchanted men with plumes . . . and that the waters of the fountains were

flowing human bodies. I thought that the statues would step down and walk, that the pictures would move, that the walls would speak . . . (Lindsay 1960, p. 50)

Lucius is bewildered by this invasion of the unconscious, but is able to repel it: at this point in his journey he is still able to retreat from the state of being engulfed by the unconscious.

In the house of Milo and Pamphile, Lucius has an affair with the slave girl, Fotis. His lack of feeling for her typifies the borderline person's sometimes ruthless lack of concern for others. Jung said that *concupiscentia,* uncontrolled desire, is an open door to psychosis (von Franz 1980, p. 31). In Lucius's affair there is no evidence of respect for the source of erotic energies, there is only an exhausting play of them. Such a lack of observance of the numinous is dangerous and can only lead to trouble. Fotis is offended by Lucius and later unconsciously acts against his desires in the episode in which he becomes an ass.

So the tale shows how uncontrolled erotic desires become the doorway for Lucius's descent into the torments of the borderline person's universe. The tale continues to reveal structures as they typically unfold in the borderline person. Lucius now leaves Milo's house to pay a visit to his aunt Byrhaena. In contrast to Milo's hovel, Byrhaena's house is an ostentatious dwelling. There Lucius sees a bas-relief in which Actaeon is spying upon Diana, who is about to take a bath in the woods. The relief hints at the grave dangers Lucius will be facing, for he, like Actaeon, is disrespectful of the Great Goddess. Actaeon is depicted in the act of entering Diana's sacred grove, startling the nymphs attending her as they attempt to hide her from his gaze. Ovid describes the power of the Goddess and her wrath:

[T]he goddess stood head and shoulders over all the rest. . . . Though she would fain have had her arrows ready, what she had she took up, the water, and flung it into the young man's face. And as she poured the avenging drops upon his hair, she spoke these words foreboding his coming doom: 'Now you are free to tell that you have seen me all unrobed—if you can tell.' No more than this she spoke; but on the head which she had sprinkled she caused to grow the horns of the long-lived stag . . . and clothed his body with a spotted hide. And last of all she planted fear within his heart. . . . When he sees his features and his horns in a clear pool, 'Oh, woe is me!' he tries to say; but no words come . . .

But while he stands perplexed he sees his hounds. . . . The whole pack, keen with the lust of blood . . . follow on. He flees over the very ground where he has oft-times pursued; he flees (the pity of it!) his own faithful hounds. He longs to cry out: 'I am Actaeon! Recognize your own master!' But words fail his own desire. . . . The whole pack collects, and all together bury their fangs in his body

> till there is no place left for further wounds. . . . They throng him on every side and, plunging their muzzles in his flesh, mangle their master under the deceiving form of the deer. Nor, as they say, till he had been done to death by many wounds was the wrath of the quiver-bearing goddess appeased. (*Metamorphoses*, Book III, pp. 137–143)

A lack of respect for archetypal powers can be disastrous, for when the *numinosum*, in either spiritual or body-erotic form, is carelessly encountered, as is often true in the case of the borderline person, it will turn into a life-destroying force. Von Franz says:

> The dogs would stand for the dissociating aspects of animal passion. This motif is really a very deep one, for if man transcends his human level—either goes above it into the realm of the Gods, or below it into the realm of animals—it is the same thing. . . . So we can say that the picture which Lucius meets at the entrance of the house of Byrhaena anticipates his whole problem: you are entering the realm of the Great Goddess and the realm of animal life; you will have to pay in classical form" (1980, p. 32).

A positive manifestation of the dog motif appears in an Egyptian myth where dogs help Isis to find the scattered members of Osiris (Harding 1934; Mead 1906, vol. 1, pp. 197f.). In this myth the dogs represent body-consciousness and they function here in sharp contrast to Actaeon's bloodthirsty hounds. Egyptian religion permeates Apuleius's story, and is particularly prominent in his account of Lucius's initiation into the mysteries of Isis and Osiris. This myth will provide us with another context for viewing a process essential to the redemption of Lucius.[4]

In the myth, Isis collects the scattered parts of Osiris (who has been dismembered by the devil Set). Set can be seen as a being who might personify the affect-storms that plague the borderline person and threaten to destroy any sense of coherence that may have been gained. When the borderline patient's complexes are constellated, for example through a fantasized or actual abandonment threat, he or she becomes inundated by negative affects resulting in a state of near-chronic psychic dissociation. The borderline patient's complexes have a perseverating quality that is the result of the lack of cohesion that results from an

---

[4] I have elsewhere discussed it as a description of processes of the somatic unconscious (Schwartz-Salant 1982). As I have described in Chapter Five, Jung employs the term "somatic unconscious" to describe experiences of the unconscious that occur during one's descent into the body. He thus distinguishes this process from mental–psychic perceptions that can occur through reflection, intuition, and even ecstatic states, all of which may exist with minimal body-consciousness.

absence of a functioning self structure. The dismembered Osiris represents the self in its helpless, dissociated state. Isis, Osiris's wife and sister, eventually comes to his aid. She is led first by babbling children, next by dogs, and finally by the underworld spirit of Anubis.

The babbling children may be conceived of as the many thoughts and fragmented ideas that so easily dominate the therapy session. If we follow the myth's logic, we see that these fragments are not meant for interpretive, interventive, or even empathic concerns. Instead, the therapist may use them to evoke associations and also see them as indicators of a confusion that should not be subdued by the use of reason. The children also represent the ability to play amid chaos, and they offer a means by which the therapist may disidentify with a power position based upon knowledge. The children are also vulnerable, in contrast to Set, who is impervious to feelings and whose rage easily disrupts the therapy experience.

The dogs, who are the next figures to lead Isis, represent the capacity to listen to the body. Since the borderline patient employs mind–body splitting, the act of listening to one's own body and assisting the patient to do the same is an important vehicle for healing. If the therapist allows himself or herself to become embodied (a state not easily achieved with the borderline patient due to the infectious nature of splitting), the therapist's *relation* to the body can then be introjected by the patient. When the therapist is using the body as a frame of reference he or she will wait for perceptions provided by various somatic states. These perceptions guide us to the patient's dissociated areas. If the therapist is able to use and reflect upon his or her body feelings, rather than push them aside by interpreting the patient's material, he or she will often discover split-off anxieties and fears that might otherwise go undetected. Thus, one can use the body as an imaginal vehicle to follow the patient's process while also reflecting upon the various complaints, fantasies, and other "babblings" that occur. Out of this mixture of perceptions a synthesis may occur, a thought or image that can bring all the fragments together. This synthesis has a mythical representation in the image of Anubis, who in the Egyptian underworld guides the souls of the dead.

There is a special logic to this process (Schwartz-Salant 1982), one that plays with opposites, weaves them back and forth, and resists interpretations that go beyond them. Interpretive modes belong to the rational-discursive, or problem-solving approach, whereas mythical consciousness waits for a synthesis to appear. In the Isis myth, coherence is aided by Anubis. His appearance emphasizes the importance of spontaneous body experiences.[5]

The Golden Ass depicts how the ego's fusion with the realm of passions, rather than maintenance of a respectful relationship with them, results in the loss of the positive quality of body consciousness. However, an opportunity for Lucius to gain wisdom is provided by Byrhaena's warning him that Pamphile is a witch and a nymphomaniac who tries to possess any young man:

> She is a witch of the first rank, and is accounted Mistress of every Necromantic Chant. By merely breathing on twigs and pebbles and suchlike ineffectual things she knows how to drown the whole light of the starry universe in the depths of hell, back in its ancient chaos. . . . And those who do not comply [with her lustful mind] at once she loathes, and in a flash she whisks them into stones or cattle or any animal she chooses—or else she simply wipes them out (Lindsay 1960, p. 53).

But when Lucius hears this warning he is even more enchanted, and the desire to learn Pamphile's magic consumes him:

> Byrhaena . . . merely excited my interest. For as soon as I heard her mention the Art of Magic, than which nothing was nearer to my heart's desire, I was so far from shuddering at Pamphile that a strong compulsion made me yearn to attain the described mastery, though I should have to pay heavy fees for it, though I should fling myself with a running jump into the very Abyss . . .
>
> Trembling with distracted haste, I extricated myself from Byrhaena's grasp as if from shackles. . . . And while I scurried along like a madman, I was saying to myself, 'come now, Lucius, keep your wits about you, and look alive-O. Here is the desired chance' . . . (Lindsay 1960, p. 53).

The borderline person does not respond well to interpretations, even if these contain wisdom that truly applies to the patient's conflict. Dreams can be adequately interpreted, yet the patient, though sincere in the wish to accept the therapist's insights, will behave in a way that completely undoes the interpretation. It seems that there is a path that the borderline person is destined to take and that a therapist's intellectually formulated understanding, even if it carries wisdom, will only obscure it. The path always involves torment. There is often a hidden wisdom in the borderline person's actions, which impulsively reject ana-

---

[5] Within this context, pelvic armoring associated with the borderline patient's anal fixation easily induces a rigidity in the therapist, making it difficult for him or her to feel open, embodied, and alert to imaginal processes arising from the body.

lytical insight. Certainly this is true for Lucius. *The borderline person must develop an ability to learn from experience.* Only then can he or she accept the greater wisdom of the unconscious.

In another vignette in the novel Thelyphron, a guest in Byrhaena's house, tells a story about himself. As a young man in Thessaly, he had undertaken the job of protecting a corpse from witches during the night before its burial. When a weasel creeps in, Thelyphron tells it to leave but then he falls into a deep sleep. He awakens to find that all is well with the corpse; he then receives his money. The next day, the dead man's widow is accused of having poisoned her husband. The old man who accuses her produces an Egyptian priest who brings the corpse back to life. The erstwhile corpse says that he was indeed poisoned and that though his body was ostensibly being watched, a witch disguised as a weasel had entered the site. Thelyphron now realizes, to his horror, that he had fallen asleep during his watch and that his nose and ears have been bitten off by the witches for use in their magical rites. That he had great confidence in his abilities to stay awake during the night represents his "solar" attitude, which is neither cognizant nor respectful of the powers of darkness.

The weasel is a marvelous image of the negative and terrifying kind of cunning (von Franz 1980, pp. 38f.) that undermines the borderline person as well as those with whom he or she interacts. The weasel is foxlike but much more cruel. It was believed to be a witch's animal and was thought to possess a merciless and inhuman cunning. The weasel aspect of the unconscious can undermine a person's instinct, which is symbolized by the nose and ears — organs that are central for a person's survival. Loss of these organs implies that what has been heard is not properly heeded. These organs of perception are undermined by the negative aspects of the unconscious, represented here by the weasel. They become channels for paranoid perceptions, even though these perceptions always contain a kernel of truth.

The weasel hunts for food beneath the earth's surface and the weasel aspect of the unconscious hunts for that which underlies a person's defenses. Hence, the weasel generally represents a function of the unconscious that makes available to the ego perceptions of the negative aspects of life such as lies, perverted sexuality, and seduction (von Franz, ibid.). These necrophilic secrets can undermine a relationship. Rather than face this dark side of existence, the borderline person splits from it, and often relegates its demands to a secret life of fantasy and behaviors that are repulsive to the person's "normal" personality; he or she thereby loses the instinctual wisdom that is also provided by the weasel.

The weasel aspect of the unconscious becomes evident through interactions with borderline persons. For example, a patient may begin a therapy session with a question such as "What am I accomplishing here?" This is an interesting question but one that will tend to arouse the therapist's anxiety. The therapist may or may not answer. Both choices of response seem inappropriate. To answer the question will create a mind–body split in the therapist. But to withhold an answer may seem sadistic. Either choice feels cowardly. *When one finds oneself in this dilemma, the tendency is to ignore body feelings and to mistrust intuition and imagination.* But such a response merely indicates the clever working of the weasel, who eats away our trust in body consciousness and instinct. When the therapist is influenced by the weasel aspect of the unconscious he or she will not uncommonly make disembodied, confessional statements — for example, "I feel confused now," or, "there's such an attacking energy here" — and will believe that both he or she and the patient are honestly sharing feelings. Through such statements the therapist implicitly lays blame upon the patient.

If the therapist answers the patient's question without employing *imaginal sight* and without listening to the body, confusion will only be amplified. Consequently, therapy can be mutilated, and what is expressed by the therapist can return to haunt both patient and therapist or even lead to the termination of treatment. When the weasel complex is dominating the session, it is difficult to answer even a simple question because the patient will intuit aspects of the therapist that the therapist would prefer to avoid. This includes the therapist's split-off shadow qualities. While optimally the therapist should be able to process such contents of his or her psyche, under the ruthless assault of the negative sight of the weasel, the therapist's countertransference resistance rapidly escalates. This can severely undermine the therapeutic process. Yet the weasel is only a dark aspect of the Goddess; the art of therapy is to recover true sight and instinct within this dark aspect's negative manifestations.

Lucius is blind to the warnings that flow abundantly from the world, which should alert him to the dangers inherent in the powers he is courting. The story of the weasel fails to awaken him. What follows is a brilliant vignette that foreshadows Lucius's fate and encompasses many of the themes elaborated throughout the tale.

The witch, Pamphile, is attracted to a certain young man and sends Fotis to obtain a lock of hair from his head so that she may perform a magical incantation to inflame him with desire and bring him to her door. Fotis is unable to secure the lock of hair and instead brings Pamphile goat hairs that she has taken from hides being prepared for wineskins. Meanwhile, Lucius leaves Byrhaena's house in a drunken state, no wiser for having heard the weasel story. Lucius has proclaimed his desire to assist in the following morning's festivities honoring the god of laughter. He then chances upon the goat skins. By now, Pamphile's potent magic has done its work, and Lucius in his drunken state believes the wineskins to be robbers attempting entry. Drawing his sword, he overpowers them; he then stumbles into his room and passes out.

The next morning, we find Lucius bemoaning his fate. His heroic valor has vanished; rather than acting like a man who is proud of his deeds, he is whimpering with fear and cowardice. He is immersed in fear of being attacked for having committed a brutal murder, and he miserably descends into impotent defenses. Lucius has lived his aggressive shadow in an *abaissement du niveau mental,* but once his "normal" consciousness returns, he is unable to sustain his chthonic masculinity and is overwhelmed by the scapegoat complex that plagues every borderline person (Perera 1986).

The festival story now unfolds: Lucius's inability to laugh at himself is directly linked to his lack of vision. At first he does not suspect what is going on, despite obvious clues evident in the behavior of those around him. He cannot distance his perceptual faculties from his preoccupation with "how bad his situation is." In the tradition of the Risus festival, he is accused of murder, but when faced with the truth—that he has stabbed and "killed" three wineskins instead of three robbers—the humor of this situation evades him, he is so self-involved with feelings of humiliation and anxiety. This perceptual limitation becomes more serious, for by his insistence upon maintaining a point of view centered upon his own maligned feelings, Lucius effectively refuses to honor Eros, the god of the festival, or to accept the honor bestowed upon him of being the focus of the festival's merriment.

Lucius's attitude represents a concretization of the imagination. He cannot distinguish between imaginal and literal reality. The tale reveals the roots of this typically borderline dilemma: Lucius is split from the power of the imaginal world, represented by Pamphile. Had his sense of humor been operational, he would have had an opportunity for self-discovery. But Lucius remains mired in his need for power and control. He is unable to respect Eros; consequently his ego has insufficient imaginal quality to extricate him from his morbidity. Lucius's behavior thus prefigures his metamorphosis into an ass. Effectively, he *is* an ass; his narcissistic myopia makes him behave like one. It is inevitable that this condition will become concretized, and this is what occurs in the next scene.

Borderline patients who have a sense of humor can undergo their ordeal of suffering more easily. The lack of a sense of humor can affect the therapeutic process in disturbing ways. For example, a patient may begin a session with a complaint that seems so outrageous it is hard not to foolishly make a lighthearted comment about it. For example, the therapist may say, "It's not the end of the world." The patient's complaint will be made with great seriousness (even if it seems to the therapist to be of a very minor nature), as if the patient were bemoaning an offense to a god. In actuality, he or she really needs to be able to laugh at this inflation, which, through induction, often appears instead in the therapist's lightheartedness or joking. Often, months later, the therapist will be surprised to hear the patient say, "the last time I talked about my feelings you laughed at me!" There is no question that the patient had been and continues to be in real distress over the therapist's remark.

Therapists also tend to take themselves far too seriously when dealing with borderline patients. Often, there is a failure to realize how absurd one can be; there is a tendency to be overly serious and obsessive about errors of insight. Preoccupation with one's own fallibility and ignorance of one's absurdity exclude an awareness that healing, if it comes at all, will come from the depths.

The story continues with the literal metamorphosis of Lucius into an ass. Fotis tells Lucius that she is responsible for his plight and promises to make things better by showing him Pamphile's witchcraft. Together, they spy upon Pamphile as she rubs herself with ointment and turns into a bird. Lucius craves the same experience. He begs Fotis to get the ointment for him: "Do this and I shall stand at your side a winged Cupid by my Venus" (Lindsay 1960, p. 83). Fotis gives him some ointment and he rubs it on his body. But she has made a "mistake" and given him the wrong ointment. Instead of becoming a bird, Lucius turns into an ass. Fotis says that she is terribly sorry and prescribes a simple antidote: Lucius needs only to eat roses to return to his human form. But no roses are available nearby and there is no time seek them, so Lucius spends the night in the stable.

Lucius's real troubles begin here, for robbers break into Milo's house and take Lucius the Ass with them. He dares not eat the roses which he now sees, since returning to human form now would mean certain death at the hands of the robbers. Indeed, if Lucius becomes himself he will be killed; this part of the tale is a comment on the precarious nature of the borderline person's relationship to exhibitionism. Lucius must now live in a state far below that of his human potential, as an ass. This reduced state is a great problem for the borderline person, whose only possible safety seems to lie in being less than what he or she is; otherwise, he or she becomes subject to envious attacks and abandonment.

At the time Apuleius wrote his work, to be an "ass" had specific symbolic connotations (von Franz 1980, pp. 46ff.). One was concupiscence, since the ass symbolized, among other things, an uncontrollable sexual appetite. The ass was also a symbol for the Egyptian devil, Set, who dismembered Osiris. Thus to become an ass would be to become identified with Set, the god of overwhelming aggressive and compulsive emotion. The ass was also sacred to Dionysus. To be merged with affects belonging to these underworld gods means to undergo torment and dissociation, for these affects are far too large for any human being to carry. Inflation of this nature is an underlying factor in psychosis.

Is it a sign of a psychosis to be turned into the ass? Some people who have emerged from a psychotic period speak of how they felt themselves to be like animals during their psychotic episodes. Lucius, however, does not lose his reality sense; he is alert to the actualities of his life and does not distort them. While he cannot be said to have entered a psychotic state, he is assuredly swallowed by a complex characterized by unbridled emotions.

Lucius's experience can help us to see how it feels to be in a borderline state. Allegorically speaking, the borderline person often makes an ass of himself or herself. This person rarely lives up to his or her true capacities; if the borderline person were to use his or her abilities and strengths it would feel as if life itself were being risked. Certainly, this phenomenon is demonstrated by Lucius's adventure. Also, a person in a borderline state is often overrun by sexual and aggressive affects of great intensity (or completely split from them). Like Lucius, the borderline person is subsumed in affects. From an inner vantage point, the borderline person may be able to actually see what is happening, but is unable to overcome the afflicted state.

In antiquity, the ass was associated with Saturn, the planet representing depression, confinement, and restriction of all kinds. So another aspect of being changed into an ass is that one is captured by an abandonment depression. The borderline person is not only subject to abandonment states but also lives in a perpetual state of entrapment in a depression. Life itself often becomes oriented toward avoiding these persecutory states.

Lucius the ass is tormented by the robbers and falls into the nadir of an abandonment depression from which there seems to be no escape. Actually, the split between his normal–neurotic personality and his psychotic side is beginning to lessen. This phase of the story represents the dissolution of Lucius's narcissistic and obsessional defenses (which are so overtly present at the Risus festival) and the emergence of his underlying abandonment depression.

In a neurosis, a person's energies are drained by a complex that impinges upon the ego and captures some of its functions, but leaves it relatively functional. In borderline states, however, a complex will capture the entire ego and encapsulate it. The person does not become lost in delusions, as would be the case in a psychosis, but, like Lucius, is trapped inside his or her defensive shell, and in a sense, is on the inside looking out. To the casual observer, the person suffering from a borderline condition may seem normal, but this is not in any sense true. The borderline patient is possessed.

Another dimension appears as we reflect upon borderline conditions through the medium of *The Golden Ass*: redemption for Lucius consists in the act of eating roses, the sacred flowers of the goddess Isis. This means of salvation is essentially religious. Von Franz has written that Lucius primarily repressed his earthly, religious passion (1980, p. 49). The rose that Lucius must eat, symbolic of the Goddess, represents the energy of love *that does not belong to any individual.* Instead, it represents a level of erotic and aggressive energies (the rose also has thorns) that are impersonal. These levels cannot ever be fully embodied; nor can they ever be exhausted in human encounters. Desires to fuse with them and possess them, when acted upon, lead to interminable sadomasochistic involvements. An alternative to fusing with these energies is found through respecting the mystery of the *coniunctio,* the sacred marriage of opposites. As I have emphasized, the *coniunctio* experience combines the opposites of fusion and distance, which are the states that so plague the borderline person. The *coniunctio* is a central, archetypal healing image; it is not surprising to find this image in *The Golden Ass*. Lucius's path to healing is an emotional journey through religious structures concerned with union and associated in antiquity with the Goddess.

But Lucius's ego is fused with the energies that are necessary for this union; thus inflation, the polluted state of being identified with inhuman powers, is his great problem. He wants to be a god. In one incident, Lucius in his ass form is purchased by a band of people who carry with them an image of the Syrian goddess Cybele. These people seem to be whirling dervishes and offer prophesies, ostensibly produced by the heavenly breath of Cybele; actually they are fakes who are only pretending to be in a state of ecstasy.

Borderline persons are often attracted to charismatic persons who have a spiritual connection and who seem to be guided by higher forces than mere power drives. The religious leaders to which the borderline person is drawn may be authentic, but their (borderline) followers can rarely incorporate spiritual values, and instead become fixated on an idealization that often cracks when a flaw in the leader's personality is revealed. The quest for a spiritual dimension to life becomes a substitute for religious experience. In authentic religious experience, the ego is overwhelmed, cast aside by a greater power that evokes images commonly associated with the *numinosum* — those of awe, terror, beauty, light, and infinity. In a pseudoreligious quest, the ego gains a sanctuary in which it may take refuge, but the travails of daily life, including the experience of emptiness and the terrors of abandonment, continue. The borderline person on this quest for the spirit may have a childlike innocence that discounts the dark shadow aspects of life. For a time, these dark forces may be forestalled, but eventually they will eclipse such innocence.

In extreme instances the borderline person's process of splitting from the psyche's dark aspects will manifest in mutilation of the body. If the therapist comments to the patient that a symbol is being concretized, he or she is met with resistance. Often the patient will respond in a way that shows that he or she is very confused by the therapist's attitude and may say: "Why shouldn't I cut myself? Why should it be symbolic?" The patient seems to be in a universe of archaic beliefs, as if he or she has been transported into a primitive culture, in which mutilation has a sacred significance. It must be recognized that what is manifesting here is a phenomenon that is completely beyond present-day collective values. The borderline patient's self-mutilations cannot be understood simply as perversions; acts of self-mutilation can often have a lifesaving quality. If the patient does not enact them, he or she may be lost in a schizoid wilderness. Indeed, acts of self-mutilation often seem to be the only means by which the patient can retain contact with the body and continue with life. These acts can also have an even greater significance; they often form a container for the patient's passion. These acts of self-mutilation elude precise interpretation and, in essence, remain a mystery.

Mutilation is an extreme state on the borderline behavioral spectrum. Far more common is a passion for union, for the *coniunctio*. The level of passion that is fixated in sadomasochistic levels and fused with impersonal and archetypal energies is surely an aspect of Lucius's personality. The religious level may be found in Lucius's passion for a union that is more than fleshly. In antiquity, the *coniunctio* was considered to be a mystery; it retains this quality today, even though it is experienced by many people.

Once, during a telephone session with a woman patient, as I interpreted a dream that had images of union in it, I felt a qualitative change in the feeling between us, as if a kind of energy flow could be felt. This energy was erotic, but also strange and numinous, and led me to an awareness of the uniqueness of the communication, which was in no way limited by the fact that we were talking by phone at a distance of over a thousand miles. I asked this patient if she had noticed any change at the time; she described a similar response. I pursued the subject and asked if she had ever had an experience like this before. She recalled that some twenty years earlier, when she was working on her doctoral dissertation, she knew a love for her work that was like a union; she experienced this love between herself and her work as having its own life. She had never had the experience since and said she had decided that it was probably a once-in-a-lifetime event and that she would never know it again.

The night after this experience, she had the following dream: *The Queen of cockroaches and her Consort were returning to earth from outer space.* Her association to cockroaches was that they survive everything. As a result of our phone conversation and the dream experience, the image of union became central to our work. Prior to this, I did not think that this woman had any familiarity with these levels. She had appeared mildly schizoid, diligent, compliant, intelligent, and interested in becoming more conscious. She was, in general, a patient for whom therapy seemed useful and appropriate. She had also made progress through assimilating dream interpretations. But only after this *coniunctio* experience did she truly begin to flourish and become empowered. Her deeply rooted feminine values began to emerge, and only then did I learn that I was working with someone from whom I could learn a great deal.

Such is the way the *coniunctio* is hidden, though it is ever ready to reappear. It has survived centuries of patriarchal suppression and the overvaluation of cerebral illumination.

I will again emphasize a crucial shadow issue: no one can *own* this coniunctio image and its energies. It is neither wholly archetypal nor wholly human. It belongs to a liminal, "in-between" realm. In *The Golden Ass,* the major problem is always Lucius's desire to possess the energies that create union states. Jung says that greed makes the *coniunctio* impossible (von Franz 1980, p. 58). In another tale a young girl, Charite, who has been captured by the same robbers who had abducted Lucius, is set free by Tlepolemus, her beloved. But Tlepolemus is brutally murdered by Thrasyllus, whose name means "rashness, or the impiety that comes from presumption and envy" (G. Knight 1985, p. 122). In turn, Thrasyllus is killed by Charite, who then kills herself. So this *coniunctio* dies because of the characters' unassimilated chthonic drives, brutally envious desires to either possess the *coniunctio* or to destroy it. Lucius's metamorphosis into an ass is the fate of anyone who identifies with an archetype. In effect, he is swallowed by the archetype. The torture of Lucius is a potential purification, much like "The Dark Night of the Soul" endured by St. John of the Cross, for Lucius has lived in a state of pollution, merged with powers that he should have recognized and respected as Other. The above-mentioned tale concerns the tragic consequences of the ego's identification with archetypal powers that would otherwise be available to assist in the creation of the *coniunctio.*

Unless the therapist has sufficiently integrated the chthonic shadow, he or she will be unable to create the atmosphere of containment required by the patient. That is, I do not believe it is possible to make progress in the confrontation of the borderline patient's possession by a demonic death force without a "street-smart" embodied shadow—one that can act as an inner reflector and source of strength for the therapist. The demonic power basks in interpretations and reflections that exclude direct contact with instinctual feeling. When the therapist is pitted against the rabid intensity of the death force, he or she quite easily becomes disembodied and cerebral. The temptation is also to treat the patient as an equal, as if both people would together devise a strategy to deal with this death drive! This death demon (or ghostly lover, vampire, satanic spirit, etc.) creates an interactive field that must be encountered by the therapist's self that neither fuses nor argues by means of the intellect, but instead supports the patient's soul when the patient is helpless to do so. Such vigilant attention is not maintained by means of gentle reflection and acute intelligence. It is a state of quiet alertness sustained with the help of our most chthonic qualities — those states that might appear in dreams as threatening figures. When Set is overcome by Horus he carries Osiris on his shoulders: only when the chthonic shadow is integrated can the self exist as a solid nucleus.

I shall not deal in detail with the Cupid–Psyche myth, for to do so would only repeat much of the work of von Franz (1980), Neumann (1956), and Hillman (1972). Each of these authors approaches the story differently, and significant new approaches to this remarkable tale continue to appear (e.g., Ross 1988). I only wish to emphasize that the Cupid–Psyche myth is a focal point of *The Golden Ass* and that it represents a remarkable archetypal pattern that thrives in the phenomenology called borderline. All of Psyche's tasks represent states of mind and issues that are typically encountered in the treatment of borderline patients. Psyche's despair, when manifesting in the setting of therapy, is rarely seen to be the plight of the suffering soul. The requirement that Psyche sort a nearly infinite number of seeds may well represent the extreme confusion that is so commonly evident in treatment. And her task of securing the golden fleece from dangerous sheep may signify not only uncontrolled impulsivity, but also the common therapeutic dynamic of impulsive, rational interpretations that must be forestalled (Psyche is told by a reed to wait to gather the fleece until after the sun sets). Moreover, Psyche's task of obtaining some of the water of the river Styx requires intervention by Jupiter for its successful completion; this may represent the patient's and/or therapist's abandonment to creative inspiration in the therapeutic encounter. Psyche's final task is her descent to the underworld Persephone so she may obtain Persephone's beauty box. Perhaps the greatest divergence of critical interpretation concerns the meaning of this task and the event that follows, the ascent to heaven by a united Cupid and Psyche. I would like to offer the following reflections on Psyche's descent to Persephone, since they seem to me to have bearing upon ways in which this segment of the story illuminates the archetypal background of healing in the borderline person.

Persephone, the underworld aspect of Aphrodite/Venus, indicates a strong connection between the Goddess of the Underworld and the Goddess of Love. Persephone is best known in her role of the maiden, or Kore, who was abducted by Hades and later became Queen of the Underworld. Persephone, then, is the abducted goddess who must overcome the loss of her mother through experiencing the lower energies of Hades; she thereby gains her own feminine power. Hades was identified in antiquity with Dionysus; consequently, one may see in Persephone the image of a figure who is abducted by the ecstatic powers of life, and especially those powers that serve to ignite the imagination. Dionysus's cult, especially in its early Minoan form, was visionary. Persephone appeared to those being initiated in the Eleusinian Mysteries in a flickering vision that the Greeks called *elampsis*, a "flaring up" (Kerenyi 1949, p. 114). Note, then, the following attributes of Persephone and her realm: Dionysian vision experienced through sexually rooted ecstasy; a feminine deity who rules the somatic unconscious (the underworld) and who is penetrated by this Dionysian power; a level of psychic reality experienced through a "flaring up" of vision. Persephone's realm is seen to be part of the somatic unconscious, and its visions, as mediated through erotic energies, belong to the cults of the *left-hand path*. Persephone's domain is the realm of death, persecution, loss, sexuality, and *vision*.

Persephone's realm, analogous to the "Lower Waters" of the *Rosarium,* can be properly approached only through the *coniunctio* experience. A person may know this experience through interaction with another person, or through an introverted act in which he or she is guided by inner Self-images. Such relatedness with an Other is essential if the experience of Persephone's energies is not to be destructively overwhelming.

The Cupid and Psyche tale provides us with a means for entering a space in which *relations* are the essence. Persephone's beauty box contains the lifegiving substance that brings inert matter to life. This substance has the capacity to kill one form of existence and engender another. But only if its potential for death is understood and revered can it be approached at all. Such issues are extremely pertinent in the treatment of the borderline person, whose central issue is the resurrection of a dead self.

We might describe the substance in Persephone's beauty box as the fullness of passion that annihilates our accustomed sense of space and time and opens us to a timeless space in which the *coniunctio* can occur. We are within the realm of a transubstantiation mystery between two people. For within the energies of the *coniunctio,* the interactive space becomes alive and textured; its processes and energies that had previously been beyond awareness become available to consciousness. The "Lower Waters" are necessary for this process to occur; Dionysian sexuality and mystical joy exist within the dynamics of the *coniunctio* as a "third thing" that is of and between two people. The result of this experience is the death of an old consciousness and the birth of a new one in which *relation,* symbolized by the *coniunctio,* is the central unit.

The Golden Ass helps us to understand borderline states of mind; its sequences reveal a way of viewing the borderline condition within a larger context than that afforded by developmental models. Lucius is redeemed only when he submits to Isis, the Great Goddess, and is willing to die. But only after his many ordeals does he finally turn to the feminine quality of the transcendent dimension. He turns to the *numinosum* as it manifests from below, through the body, and surrenders to a power greater than himself. There is a beautiful prayer at the end of the book, a part of which follows:

> Queen of Heaven, whether you are fostering Ceres the motherly nurse of all growth . . . or whether you are Proserpine, terrible with howls of midnight, whose triple face has power to ward off the assaults of ghosts and to close the cracks in earth . . . illuminating the walls of cities with beams of female light . . . O by whatever name, and by whatever rites, and in whatever form, it is permitted to invoke you, come now and succor me in the hour of my calamity. . . . Remove from me the hateful shape of a beast, and restore me to Lucius, my lost self. But if an offended god pursues me implacably, then grant me death at least since life is denied me. (Lindsay 1960, p. 236)

The approach toward the feminine side of the *numinosum* is central to Lucius's path of healing and is also central to my emphasis on the interactive field, which possesses its own archetypal dynamics. This approach includes the therapist's willingness to sacrifice interpretations or insights. Indeed, these solar perceptions should be sacrificed to the goal of enlivening an interactive field in which two people may discover together the imaginal world that is affecting their work.

The borderline person's suffering can only be resolved by the discovery of the imaginal realm and by a special focus on the *coniunctio*. Jung wrote:

> Neurosis is intimately bound up with the problem of our time and really represents an unsuccessful attempt on the part of the individual to solve the general problem in his own person. (1942a, par. 18)

The life of the borderline person "is intimately bound up with the problem of our time." Until the person's life is redeemed through the energies of the *coniunctio*, his or her life will be tormented by states of fusion and distance, which are "an unsuccessful attempt on the part of the individual to solve the general problem in his [or her] own person." The *coniunctio* is a complex process that includes not only the state of union, but also states of despair, chaos, and mindlessness—the madness of the "Dark Night of the Soul." Redemption is only possible if the patient and therapist are capable of (re)discovering those domains of imaginal truth that have been severely repressed by Judaeo-Christian attitudes toward the feminine aspect of the *numinosum*. By resurrecting the power of the imaginal in human relationship and by opening interactive fields in which the basic unit is *relation per se*, we orient ourselves to feminine attitudes and values both in life and in psychotherapy. The borderline person's suffering has a *telos*, and this purpose, which is achieved by some but tragically eludes others, is also the *telos* of humankind.

REFERENCES

American Psychiatric Association 1980. *Diagnostic and Statistical Manual of Mental Disorders, Third Edition,* Washington, D.C.: APA.

Apuleius, Lucius. ca. 200 A.D. *The Golden Ass.* Robert Graves, translator. New York: Farrar, Strauss and Giroux, 1951.

Apuleius, Lucius. ca. 200 A.D. *The Golden Ass.* J. Lindsay, translator. Bloomington: Indiana University Press, 1960.

Bamford, C. 1981. Introduction: Homage to Pythagoras. *Lindisfarne Letter* 14. West Stockbridge, Mass.: Lindisfarne Press.

Beebe, J. 1988. Primary ambivalence toward the self: Its nature in treatment. *The Borderline Personality in Analysis.* Wilmette, Ill.: Chiron Publications.

Bion, W. R. 1967. *Second Thoughts.* London: Heinemann.

———. 1970. *Attention and Interpretation.* London: Maresfield Reprints, 1984.

Bly, R. 1985. A third body. In *Loving a Woman in Two Worlds.* Garden City, N. Y.: The Dial Press, Doubleday.

Bohm, D. 1980. *Wholeness and the Implicate Order.* London: Routledge and Kegan Paul.

Brown, N. O. 1959. *Life against Death.* Middletown: Wesleyan.

Bychowski, G. 1953. The problem of latent psychosis. *Journal of the American Psychoanalytic Association* 1:484–503.

Charlton, R. 1988. Lines and shadows. *The Borderline Personality in Analysis.* Wilmette, Ill.: Chiron Publications.

Chodorow, J. 1984. To move and be moved. *Quadrant* 17/2.

Comfort, A. 1984. *Reality and Empathy.* Albany, N.Y.: State University of New York Press.

Copleston, F. 1985. *A History of Philosophy.* Vol. 3. New York: Doubleday/Image.

Corbin, H. 1969. *Creative Imagination in the Sufism of Ibn Arabi.* Ralph Manheim, translator. Princeton: Princeton University Press.

———. 1972. *Mundus Imaginalis, Or the Imaginary and the Imaginal.* Dallas: Spring Publications.

Damrosch, L. 1980. *Symbol and Truth in Blake's Myth.* Princeton, N.J.: Princeton University Press.

Deri, S. 1978. Transitional phenomena: Vicissitudes of symbolization and creativity. In *Between Reality and Fantasy.* Simon Grolnik and Leonard Barkin, eds. New York: Jason Aronson.

Edinger, E. 1985. *Anatomy of the Psyche.* La Salle, Ill.: Open Court.

Eigen, M. 1981. The area of faith in Winnicott, Lacan and Bion. *International Journal of Psycho-Analysis* 62.

_____. 1983. Dual union or undifferentiation? A critique of Marion Milner's view of the sense of psychic creativeness. *International Review of Psycho-Analysis* 10.

_____. 1985. Toward Bion's starting point: Between catastrophe and faith. *International Journal of Psycho-Analysis* 66.

_____. 1986a. On human madness. *Pilgrimage* 12/4.

_____. 1986b. The personal and anonymous 'I'. *Voices* 21/3 and 4.

_____. 1987. *The Psychotic Core.* New York: Jason Aronson.

Eliade, M. Rencontre avec Jung. In *Combat: de la Resistance a la Revolution* (Paris). In *C. G. Jung Speaking,* 1977, W. McGuire and R. F. C. Hull, eds. Princeton, N. J.: Princeton University Press.

Elkin, H. 1972. On selfhood and the development of ego structures in infancy. *The Psychoanalytic Review* 59/3.

Epstein, L. and A. Feiner, eds. 1979. *Countertransference.* New York: Jason Aronson.

Fabricius, J. 1971. The individuation process as reflected by 'the rosary of the philosophers' (1550). *The Journal of Analytical Psychology* 16/1.

_____. 1976. *Alchemy.* Copenhagen: Rosenkilde and Bager.

Fairbairn, W. R. D. 1952. *An Object Relations Theory of Personality.* New York: Basic Books.

Federn, P. 1953. *Ego Psychology and the Psychoses.* London: Maresfield Reprints.

Ferguson, M. 1982. In *The Holographic Paradigm.* Ken Wilbur, ed. Boulder, Colo.: Shambala Press.

Fordham, M. 1976. *The Self and Autism.* London: William Heinemann Medical Books Ltd.

_____. 1986. Abandonment in infancy. *Chiron: A Review of Jungian Analysis.* Wilmette, Ill.: Chiron Publications.

Freud, S. 1923. The ego and the id. *Standard Edition of the Complete Psychological Works of Sigmund Freud.* Vol. 19. London: Hogarth Press, 1961.

Frosch, J. 1964. The psychotic character: Clinical psychiatric considerations. *Psychiatric Quarterly* 38:91–96.

Giovacchini, P. 1979. *Treatment of Primitive Mental States.* New York: Jason Aronson.

Goodheart, W. 1982. Successful and unsuccessful interventions in Jungian analysis: The construction and destruction of the spellbinding circle. *Chiron: A Review of Jungian Analysis.* Wilmette, Ill.: Chiron Publications.

Gordon, R. 1965. The concept of projective identification. *Journal of Analytical Psychology* 10/2.

_____. 1987. Masochism: The shadow side of the archetypal need to venerate and worship. *Journal of Analytical Psychology* 32/3.

Green, André. 1975. The analyst, symbolization and absence in the analytic setting (On changes in analytic practice and experience). *International Journal of Psycho-Analysis.* 56/1.

_____. 1977. The borderline concept. In *Borderline Personality Disorders.* P. Hartocollis, ed. New York: International Universities Press.

Green, Anita. 1984. Giving the body its due. *Quadrant* 17/2.

Grinberg, L. 1977. An approach to understanding borderline disorders. In *Borderline Personality Disorders.* P. Hartocollis, ed. New York: International Universities Press.

Grotstein, J. 1979. The psychoanalytic concept of the borderline organization. In *Advances in Psychotherapy of the Borderline Patient.* J. Le Boit and A. Capponi, eds. New York: Jason Aronson.

_____. 1981. *Splitting and Projective Identification.* New York: Jason Aronson.

Guntrip, H. 1969. *Schizoid Phenomena, Object Relations and the Self.* New York: International Universities Press.

Harding, M. Esther. 1934. *Women's Mysteries, Ancient and Modern.* New York: Harper and Row, 1976.

Hillman, J. 1972. *The Myth of Analysis.* New York: Harper and Row.

_____. 1979. The thought of the heart. *Eranos Yearbook* 48. Insel Verlag.

Hoch, P. H., and J. P. Cattell. 1959. The diagnosis of pseudoneurotic schizophrenia. *Psychiatric Quarterly* 33:17–43.

Hubback, J. 1983. Depressed patients and the coniunctio. *Journal of Analytical Psychology* 28/4.

Jacobsen, E. 1964. *The Self and the Object World.* New York: International Universities Press.

Jung, C. G. 1916. The transcendent function. In *Collected Works.* Vol. 8. Princeton, N. J.: Princeton University Press, 1960.

_____. 1918. *Studies in Word Association.* M. D. Eder, translator. New York: Russel and Russel.

_____. 1920. *Psychological Types.* In *Collected Works.* Vol. 6. Princeton, N. J.: Princeton University Press, 1971.

_____. 1934-39. *Psychological Analysis of Nietzsche's Zarathustra.* Unpublished seminar notes. Recorded and mimeographed by Mary Foote.

_____. 1934. The relation between the ego and the unconscious. In *Two Essays On Analytical Psychology.* In *Collected Works.* Vol. 7. Princeton, N. J.: Princeton University Press, 1966.

_____. 1937. Psychology and religion. In *Psychology and Religion: West and East.* In *Collected Works.* Vol. 14. Princeton, N.J.: Princeton University Press, 1958.

_____. 1942. A psychological approach to the Trinity. In *Collected Works.* Vol. 11. Princeton, N. J.: Princeton University Press, 1958.

_____. 1942a. On the psychology of the unconscious. In *Two Essays on Analytical Psychology.* In *Collected Works.* Vol. 7. Princeton, N. J.: Princeton University Press, 1953.

_____. 1946. Psychology of the transference. In *The Practice of Psychotherapy.* In *Collected Works.* Vol. 16. Princeton, N. J.: Princeton University Press, 1954.

_____. 1951. The psychology of the child archetype. In *Collected Works.* Vol. 9/1. Princeton, N. J.: Princeton University Press, 1959.

_____. 1952. Answer to Job. In *Collected Works.* Vol. 11. Princeton, N. J.: Princeton University Press, 1958.

_____. 1953a. *Psychology and Alchemy.* In *Collected Works.* Vol. 12. Princeton, N. J.: Princeton University Press, 1968.

_____. 1953b. The Spirit Mercurius. In *Collected Works.* Vol. 13. Princeton, N. J.: Princeton University Press, 1967.

_____. 1954. The visions of Zosimos. *Alchemical Studies.* In *Collected Works.* Vol. 13. Princeton, N. J.: Princeton University Press, 1967.

_____. 1955. *Mysterium Coniunctionis.* In *Collected Works.* Vol. 14. Princeton, N. J.: Princeton University Press, 1963.

_____. 1957. Commentary on "The Secret of the Golden Flower."

Alchemical Studies. In *Collected Works*. Vol. 13. Princeton, N. J.: Princeton University Press, 1967.

_____. 1959. *Aion.* In *Collected Works*. Vol. 9/2. Princeton, N. J.: Princeton University Press, 1968.

_____. 1975. *Letters*. Vol. 2. Princeton, N. J.: Princeton University Press.

Kahn, M. M. R. 1974. *The Privacy of the Self*. London: Hogarth.

Kerenyi, C. 1949. Kore. *Essays on a Science of Mythology*. C. G. Jung and C. Kerenyi, eds. R. F. C. Hull, translator. New York: Harper and Row.

Kernberg, O. 1975. *Borderline Conditions and Pathological Narcissism*. New York: Jason Aronson.

_____. 1984. *Severe Personality Disorders*. New Haven, Conn.: Yale University Press.

Klein, M. 1946. Notes on some schizoid mechanisms. *Envy and Gratitude*. London: Hogarth, 1975.

Knight, G. 1985. *The Rose Cross and the Goddess*. New York: Destiny Books.

Knight, R. P. 1953. Borderline states. In *Psychoanalytic Psychiatry and Psychology*. New York: International Universities Press.

Kohut, H. 1971. *The Analysis of the Self*. New York: International Universities Press.

Lacan, J. 1977. *Ecrits*. A. Sheridan, translator. New York: Norton.

Lévi-Strauss, C. 1967. *Structural Anthropology*. New York: Doubleday.

Mahler, M., et al. 1975. *The Psychological Birth of the Human Infant: Symbiosis and Individuation*. New York: Basic Books.

Mahler, M. 1980. Rapproachement subphase of the separation-individuation process. *Rapprochement*. Ruth Lax, et al., eds. New York: Jason Aronson.

Masterson, J. 1976. *Psychotherapy of the Borderline Adult*. New York: Brunner Mazel.

_____. 1981. *The Narcissistic and Borderline Disorders*. New York: Brunner Mazel.

Matoon, Mary Ann, ed. 1988. *The Archetype of Shadow in a Split World*. Tenth International Conference of Analytical Psychology, Berlin, 1986. Zürich: Daimon Verlag.

McLean, A., 1980. *The Rosary of the Philosophers.* Edinburgh: Magnum Opus Hermetic Sourceworks Number 6.

Mead, G. R. S. 1906. *Thrice Greatest Hermes.* London: Watkins, 1964.

————. 1919. *The Doctrine of the Subtle Body in Western Tradition.* London: Stuart and Watkins.

Meissner, W. 1984. *The Borderline Spectrum.* New York: Jason Aronson.

Meltzer, D. 1973. *Sexual States of Mind.* Perthshire, England: Clunie Press.

————. 1978. *The Clinical Significance of the Work of Bion.* In *The Kleinian Development.* Part III. Perthshire, England: Clunie Press.

Milner, M. 1957. *On Not Being Able to Paint.* New York: International Universities Press.

Mindell, A. 1982. *Dreambody.* Santa Monica, Calif.: Sigo.

Neumann, Erich. 1954. *The Origins and History of Consciousness.* New York: Pantheon Books.

————. 1956. *Amor and Psyche.* R. Manheim, translator. New York: Harper and Row.

Otto, R. 1926. *The Idea of the Holy.* J. Harvey, translator. London: Oxford University Press.

Ovid. 1916. *Metamorphoses.* Frank Justus Miller, translator. Cambridge, Mass.: Harvard University Press, 1984.

Perera, S. 1986. *The Scapegoat Complex: Toward a Mythology of Shadow and Guilt.* Toronto: Inner City Books.

Raine, K. 1982. *The Human Face of God.* London: Thames and Hudson.

Rinsley, D. 1982. *Borderline and Other Self Disorders.* New York: Jason Aronson.

Rosenfeld, H. 1979. Difficulties in the psychoanalytic treatment of borderline patients. In *Advances in Psychotherapy of the Borderline Patient.* J. Le Boit and A. Capponi, eds. New York: Jason Aronson.

Rundle Clark, R. T. 1959. *Myth and Symbol in Ancient Egypt.* London: Thames and Hudson.

Samuels, A. 1985. Countertransference, the mundus imaginalis, and a research project. *Journal of Analytical Psychology* 30/1.

Scholem, G. 1946. *Major Trends in Jewish Mysticism.* New York: Schocken.

Schwartz-Salant, N. 1982. *Narcissism and Character Transformation.* Toronto: Inner City Books.

_____. 1984. Archetypal factors underlying sexual acting-out in the transference/countertransference process. *Chiron: A Review of Jungian Analysis.* Wilmette, Ill.: Chiron Publications.

_____. 1986. On the subtle body concept in analytical practice. *Chiron: The Body in Analysis.* Wilmette, Ill.: Chiron Publications.

_____. 1987a. Patriarchy in transformation: Judaic, Christian and clinical perspectives. In *Jung's Challenge to Contemporary Religion.* M. Stein and R. Moore, eds. Wilmette, Ill.: Chiron Publications.

_____. 1987b. The dead self in borderline personality disorders. In *Pathologies of the Modern Self.* D. M. Levin, ed. New York: New York University Press.

_____. 1988. Archetypal foundations of projective identification. *Journal of Analytical Psychology* 33:39–64.

Searles, H. 1977. Dual- and multiple-identity processes in borderline ego-functioning. In *Borderline Personality Disorders.* P. Hartocollis, ed. New York: International Universities Press.

Segal, H. 1980. *Melanie Klein.* New York: Viking.

Stern, A. 1938. Psychoanalytic investigation of and therapy in the borderline group of neuroses. *Psychoanalytic Quarterly* 7:467–489.

Turner, V. 1974. *Dramas, Fields, and Metaphors.* Ithaca, N. Y.: Cornell University Press.

Ulman, R. and R. Stolorow. 1985. The transference-countertransference neurosis in psychoanalysis. *Bulletin of the Menninger Clinic* 49/1.

von Franz, M. L. 1974. *Number and Time.* Evanston, Ill.: Northwestern University Press.

_____. 1980. *A Psychological Interpretation of The Golden Ass of Apuleius.* Dallas: Spring Publications.

Whitmont, E. C. 1972. Body experience and psychological awareness. *Quadrant* 12:5–16.

Williams, R. 1980. *Christian Spirituality: A Theological History from the New Testament to Luther and St. John of the Cross.* Atlanta: John Knox Press. (British title: *The Wound of Knowledge.*)

Winnicott, D. W. 1971. *Playing and Reality.* London: Tavistock.

Woodman, M. 1984. Psyche/soma awareness. *Quadrant* 17/2.

Zilboorg, G. 1941. Ambulatory schizophrenias. *Psychiatry* 4:149–155.

Index

Abandonment fears, 3, 18, 22, 29,
32, 34, 36, 39, 48, 61, 68–69,
73–75, 80, 83, 86, 89, 125, 139,
142, 177–180, 184, 187, 189, 194,
206, 217–219.
Actualization, 93
Affective instability, 193
Agoraphobia, 80
Aggression, 62
Albedo, 46
Alchemical symbolism, 6–11, 46–47,
50–51, 77, 85–88, 97, 100–105,
108, 110, 113–115, 122, 135, 138,
143, 159–160, 163, 184–185, 191,
194–197, 201
"Ambulatory schizophrenia," 1
Anal fixation, 207–218, 211
Anger, 31, 193
Anxiety, 35–36, 47, 51, 67, 86, 134,
187, 189
Anubis, 210–211.
A priori state, 191, 197
Apuleius, 202, 205, 217
Aristomenes, 202, 206–208
"As-if" behavior, 28, 30–31, 69, 203
Assertiveness, 143
Autistic state, 89
Axiom of Maria, 138, 141
Aztec Indians, 2

"Background object," 197
Bamford, C., 90
Bardo, 84
Beebe, J., 28
Beginning of emotional object
constancy, 91
Bible (The), 22, 27, 77, 78, 194
Biology, 132
Binarius, 112
Bion, W. R., 26, 86, 103, 113, 143,
195–196
Blake, William, 27, 140, 143
"Blanking-out," 180
Bly, Robert, 125

Bohm, David, 84–85, 107
Book of Job, 22, 27
Borderline personality disorder,
affects of, 13, 19, 21–24, 31,
46, 74, 97, 184
attitudes toward change, 3
behavior of, 2, 25, 34, 36–38,
51, 54, 59, 62, 66–67, 76,
162, 174, 191–194, 213, 217
characteristics of, 2–4, 17–18,
21, 27–28, 34–37, 45–47,
50–52, 55–57, 59, 61,
69–70, 97, 112, 123, 131,
142, 161, 164, 177, 180, 184,
190–191, 198–199, 208–213,
217–218, 222
childhood problems of, 8,
147–151, 159, 164, 170–172,
177–179
definition of, 2, 218
development of, 8, 164
diagnostic criteria of, 193
dreams of, 20, 35–36, 43,
79–81, 145–146, 155,
157–158, 165, 171–172,
174, 220
fantasies of, 18, 54
feelings about self, 18, 50
parental influence on, 34–36,
55–58, 64, 82, 87–88, 134,
145–151, 153–155, 164,
168–174, 177–180, 184
sense of self in, 19, 46, 50,
52, 193
symbolic aspects of the
term, 9, 12
Brothers Karamazov (The)
(Dostoevsky), 159
Buber, Martin, 37
Byrhaena, 209, 212, 214

Catholic Church, 204
Cattell, J. P., 1
Charite, 221